LINKED COURSES FOR GENERAL EDUCATION AND INTEGRATIVE LEARNING

LINKED COURSES

LINKED COURSES FOR GENERAL EDUCATION AND INTEGRATIVE LEARNING

A Guide for Faculty and Administrators

EDITED BY

Margot Soven, Dolores Lehr,
Siskanna Naynaha, and Wendy Olson

Foreword by Betsy Barefoot

Sty/us

STERLING, VIRGINIA

COPYRIGHT © 2013 BY
STYLUS PUBLISHING, LLC.

Published by Stylus Publishing, LLC
22883 Quicksilver Drive
Sterling, Virginia 20166-2102

Library of Congress Cataloging-in-Publication Data
Linked courses for general education and integrative
learning : a guide for faculty and administrators / Edited By
Margot Soven, Dolores Lehr, Siskanna Naynaha, and
Wendy Olson.—First edition.
     pages   cm
Includes bibliographical references and index.
ISBN 978-1-57922-485-1 (cloth : alk. paper)
ISBN 978-1-57922-486-8 (pbk. : alk. paper)
ISBN 978-1-57922-878-1 (library networkable e-edition)
ISBN 978-1-57922-879-8 (consumer e-edition)
1. Interdisciplinary approach in education—United
States.   2. Professional learning communities—United
States.   3. General education—United States.
4. Education, Higher—United States.   I. Soven, Margot,
editor of compilation.
LB2361.5.L55   2012
371.3—dc23   2012012860

13-digit ISBN: 978-1-57922-485-1 (cloth)
13-digit ISBN: 978-1-57922-486-8 (paper)
13-digit ISBN: 978-1-57922-878-1(library networkable
e-edition)
13-digit ISBN: 978-1-57922-879-8 (consumer e-edition)

Printed in the United States of America

All first editions printed on acid free paper
that meets the American National Standards Institute
Z39-48 Standard.

Bulk Purchases

Quantity discounts are available for use in workshops
and for staff development.
Call 1-800-232-0223

First Edition, 2013

10   9   8   7   6   5   4   3   2

To our families and students.

CONTENTS

FOREWORD

The term *learning community* is a familiar one within the current higher education lexicon, but as most of us sooner or later discover, the term carries more than one precise meaning. To some educators the term means a single interdisciplinary course; to others a learning community is a cluster of courses with or without a residential component. The editors of this book wisely decided to focus on the most common variant of the learning community: two courses that are linked across the curriculum. Even within that more narrow definition, there are still a number of learning community differences that are described in this book's chapters. This work joins the growing amount of literature on learning communities but provides what many of them do not: a set of specific examples of best practice written by educators who are on the front lines of this innovation today.

In their descriptions of learning community differences, the contributors make one thing clear: In order for learning communities to have maximum impact on learning, faculty should collaborate and find ways to link course content. Interestingly, a number of learning communities have developed without this important linkage; and while students may derive some benefit from simply getting to know each other by being in the same set of classes, they can hardly be expected to discover connections between disciplines and content areas without help from instructors. Students, especially those in the first year, will often compartmentalize learning unless faculty intentionally help them see connections.

Why Learning Communities?

Why do institutions invest time, energy, and resources to create learning communities? Why are they almost exclusively placed in the first year? There is no single answer to either of these questions. However, the overriding motivation for the establishment of first-year learning communities at many institutions often has nothing to do with learning per se. Rather, it frequently relates to the desire to increase student retention from the first to the second year. And yes, learning communities have been correlated with higher rates of retention for participants. Thankfully, this book looks beyond retention research and includes examples of how learning communities actually enrich learning. I have often said that if retention is the only desired outcome of learning communities, there are probably easier ways to reach that goal.

In addition to the retention payoff, placement of learning communities in the first year relates to the greater ease of working within the curriculum when it is not controlled by courses in the major. As students advance through undergraduate education, it generally becomes far more difficult to escape the primary influence of the major in determining what courses can be taken and when. But as evidence builds for the effectiveness of learning communities to actually change what and how students learn, I hope that we in higher education can find ways to continue these powerful pedagogies beyond the first year.

The Scope of Learning Communities

In the fall of 2010, the Gardner Institute for Excellence in Undergraduate Education, where I serve as vice president, conducted a national survey of undergraduate student success initiatives in four-year institutions, a survey that can be accessed at the following link: www.jngi.org/wordpress/wp-con tent/uploads/2012/04/JNGInational_survey_web.pdf. The learning community was one of seven initiatives that were the subject of survey analysis. This national survey found that just over 56 percent of four-year colleges and universities in the United States offer some type of learning community, most often in the first year. But the more surprising finding was that, on average, these learning communities reach only 33 percent of eligible first-year students and much smaller percentages of students in subsequent years. While some colleges and universities intentionally offer learning communities only to certain student subgroups, this aggregate finding is disappointing and raises a number of questions about what seems to be the difficulty of bringing learning communities to scale. If only one-third of students, on average, are able to benefit from a learning community, we can surmise that this innovation has a great deal of untapped potential.

The Potential of Learning Communities

How do students learn in a learning community that is different from, and more powerful than, learning in freestanding courses? Almost 30 years ago, in 1985, Patrick Hill, Vice President for Academic Affairs at The Evergreen State College, in a speech before the inaugural National Learning Communities Conference offered the following rationale for learning communities—a rationale that continues to hold true today:

> . . . learning communities are responding [to] the growing complexity and interdependence of the problems we face with our disciplines—the problems we are trying to solve. . . . The unmanageability and incomprehensibility of contemporary events underline the need for an additional set of skills in the educated person. As John Kemeny, former president of Dartmouth said, "We desperately need individuals who can pull together knowledge from a wide variety of fields and integrate it in one mind. We are in an age where we are facing problems that no one discipline can solve. What we'd like our best students to be able to do is to walk in on a problem, a problem they know nothing at all about, and by working hard, in six months' time become fairly expert at it." He said "fairly expert," not "expert." My feeling is that unless we can do that, then democracy will fail. Unless we can train people to become fairly expert, at least expert enough to participate in decisions, then we are going to be relying on experts to make decisions for everybody.

I agree with Patrick Hill that what may be at stake in the way we structure collegiate learning experiences is the strength of the democracy. Unless we do a better job at introducing more students to the complexity and interrelationships inherent in fields of knowledge, they will not be prepared to make the best decisions for the future of our nation and our planet. And of all the curricular innovations available to us today, the learning community holds the greatest potential to make a positive difference toward the goal of a vital democratic way of life.

I am pleased to offer this foreword to a book that will help educators adopt and adapt the learning community model to their campus. I believe that this innovation is among the most powerful we have at our disposal. Read, learn, and enjoy!

Betsy Barefoot, EdD

INTRODUCTION
Why the Need for Learning Communities Now?

Higher education is "under the microscope," perhaps more than it has been in any previous decade. The debate about the value of a college education cannot be ignored. For the first time in the history of higher education in the United States, the public is asking, "Is a college education worth it?"

In the past, we took for granted that a college education would lead to a better life economically, socially, and intellectually. The reasons for this new ambivalence are many, with the increasing concern about where college will lead vocationally being just one important issue. However, what we find most striking in this debate is the "gut feeling" that many instructors have that students are simply not interested in our "product," partly for reasons beyond our control. Is the product (i.e., a college education) really less valuable than it was in the past, or are we simply paying more attention to students' lack of engagement in our courses and the research that suggests why this might be the case?

1. Much of the scholarship on this topic agrees that it's the social concerns of this age group that come first—especially in their first year at college. From *Coming of Age in New Jersey: College and American Culture* by Michael Moffatt (1989) to *The First Year Out: Understanding American Teens After High School* by Tim Clydesdale (2007), the message is the same: "Navigating relationships and managing gratifications are the primary foci of culturally mainstream American teens" (Clydesdale, 2007, p. ix).

2. Studies indicate that many students do not feel challenged by college, that many college courses seem like an extension of high school,

especially in the freshman year. Students discover that they can "get by" by studying for fewer hours than their teachers assume they will devote to their courses (Bok, 2006).

The decline in hours of study is shocking. The high point in study hours per week was achieved in the 1960s, and from then on, the number of hours of study has decreased. Derek Bok is not alone in suggesting that the first year of college is not sufficiently challenging. *Academically Adrift: Limited Learning on College Campuses* (Arum & Roksa, 2011) reinforces Bok's observations with up-to-date research.

But what about the faculty? Don't they care? Bok's research indicates that even at institutions where research may be the sine qua non for tenure and promotion, faculty care about their teaching. He says that although research tends to be rewarded more generously than instruction, teaching has intrinsic satisfactions that cause most professionals to work conscientiously at their classroom duties. Furthermore, according to faculty, on average, they spend more than half their time on matters related to teaching and less than 20 percent on research. Those who describe themselves as teachers and claim to care more about teaching than research greatly outnumber those who regard themselves primarily as researchers (Bok, 2006, p. 33).

No teacher likes looking out at a sea of bored, disinterested, perhaps yawning students. As one of Margot's colleagues at La Salle University lamented recently, "If only they would ask a question!"

However, instructional methods at college have remained "static" despite increasing concern about lack of student engagement for several reasons. The majority of the full-time faculty have completed PhD programs without much instruction in how to teach. Ironically, although 70 percent of most college instructors' time will be spent teaching, their graduate training does not prepare them for the most time-consuming part of their future profession. Furthermore, as Bok points out, "There is no compelling necessity to reexamine familiar forms of instruction and experiment with new pedagogic methods in an effort to help their students accomplish more" (p. 32). He contends that "the fundamental reason for the lack of such pressure is the difficulty in judging how successful colleges are in helping students learn" (p. 32).

Moreover, it is only since 2002, when the National Survey of Student Engagement (NSSE) was developed, that a survey has been available for measuring student engagement. Thanks to NSSE research, we now know which learning activities are more likely to engage students.

Some of the other activities identified by NSSE, such as travel aboard, service learning, and student faculty research, are structurally more difficult to arrange and often require special student abilities, additional individual expense by students, and a commitment to hours beyond classroom requirements. These activities may also be less available to students who commute rather than live on campus.

It would be naïve to expect that learning communities alone can solve the problem of student disengagement. However, because of their unique structure, learning communities offer the possibility of meeting students' social concerns with a course of study that clearly differentiates college from high school. At the same time, learning communities give faculty a strong incentive to improve instruction.

What Is a Learning Community?

Learning communities come in all sizes and shapes, but they have several characteristics in common. The most general definition of *learning communities* is Tinto's (1998): "Learning communities are supportive settings which require students to share the same learning experience with other students. Learning communities foster student relationships and are characterized by the features which define any community a responsibility towards other members of the community" (p. 387).

Some learning communities require students to live in the same dormitories and take the same courses at the same time, often in two or more different disciplines. Others, such as the La Salle Integrative Studies Program, require students to complete a similar group of courses, but not necessarily to take all of the courses in one year or one semester. These programs often include common out-of-class experiences as well, such as a service learning experience or a travel study component. "The pedagogical emphasis in learning communities often favors collaborative learning, increased attention to writing instruction, writing as a tool for learning, student self-reflection and self-evaluation, greater curricular coherence, and a shifting of faculty roles to emphasize facilitation and mentorship" (Williams, 2000, p. 2).

Instructors teaching in learning communities have a unique opportunity to think intentionally about how they are teaching their subject matter. According to Gabelnick, MacGregor, Matthews, and Smith, "It is virtually impossible to participate in a learning community without being transformed in some way" (1990, p. 54). They go on to say that, when trying to find a common thread to connect a course you typically teach with another course, you suddenly find yourself examining your discipline from a new perspective. For example, until she had the chance to teach a course in contemporary American literature linked with a course in political science during an election year, Margot had not included biography in the course. As a result of the linked course experience, the literature course became more interesting and current through the reading of biographies about the two presidential candidates: *The Prince of Tennessee* (Marananiss & Nakashima, 2000), a biography about Al Gore, and *Shrub* (Ivins, 2000), a biography about George W. Bush.

The five learning community models identified by Gabelnick et al. (1990) are still sufficiently comprehensive to describe most learning communities:

- Linked courses
- Clusters
- Federated learning communities
- Freshman interest groups (FIGs)
- Coordinated studies

The clustered course model usually includes three or four courses connected by a common theme. FIGs typically involve a group of students enrolled together in two or three courses, which are not necessarily based on a common theme, but these same students are also in a FIG seminar that serves as an introduction to campus life and methods of achieving academic success. The federated learning community model involves a faculty member who "travels" with students to several classes and helps them make connections between the courses. The coordinated studies model includes team teaching and "requires extensive faculty collaboration to assist students in connecting ideas and content across the whole curriculum" (Williams, 2000, pp. 2–3). This model, not as common as the other models, is exemplified by the New Century College at George Mason University.

This book focuses on the linked course model. As Tinto (1998) says, "The paired [linked course] model . . . is the simplest of Learning Community models in terms of curricular strategies; thus it is one of the most popular methods for creating learning communities" (388). Linked courses put together a cohort of students in two common courses. The faculty may teach independently or together and coordinate syllabi and assignments so that the classes complement each other (Kellog, 1999). These courses are often linked around a particular interdisciplinary theme (Laufgraben et al., 2004). "Paired [or linked] courses are two courses for which students co-register" (Washington Center, 1999, n.p.). The term *linked courses* is sometimes reserved for courses in which faculty may work to coordinate syllabi and assignments, but teach most of their courses separately. The term *paired course* is sometimes applied only to a team-taught course pair in which two or more courses are team taught in an integrated program with "faculty participating as learners as well as teachers" (Washington Center, 1999, n.p.). In this book the terms are used interchangeably because it appears that most programs cannot be categorized as purely one or the other.

Our book provides detailed information about the methods used by different institutions to design, implement, and evaluate linked (also called *clustered* or *paired*) courses in the freshman year. Each of the programs described in the book is unique, shaped by the structural features of its home institution. Several of the programs described are limited in scope and designed for specific populations, whereas some programs described are institutional requirements for all students. For example, at La Salle University all freshmen were required to enroll in a "Double" (two linked courses) as part of the general education requirement; scheduling and staffing linked courses for six hundred freshmen was indeed a challenge. How we managed to accomplish this aim with eighty courses is worth noting for schools interested in providing learning communities for all students.

This book also includes new insights related to the configuration of linked courses and the kinds of methods that work best to emphasize the connections between disciplines. For example, a business course and a literature course at La Salle were linked by giving students an opportunity to examine the "human cost" of business failure in relation to the financial cost. The Enron case was used specifically to explore these issues. In particular, this book highlights the ways in which general education programs might be supported and strengthened by linked course structures.

Several of the new insights we present on the subject of linked courses are embedded in the student evaluations of the courses at our respective schools. One of the clear signals we have from these evaluations is that the degree of student "buy in" to linked courses is heavily dependent on their view of faculty behaviors as indicated, for example, by degrees of collaboration or the lack of it. Assessment of the links pilot at Washington State University, for example, suggested that students were more committed to the linked learning experience when faculty collaboration was explicitly built into the semester schedule.

This book also includes descriptions of linked courses by the instructors who developed them. Each of these case studies demonstrates that the focus of a linked course varies, even when the general guidelines are similar, depending on the interests and strengths of the faculty in the pair. In these cases, the faculty worked together for several years before writing about their experiences.

Why Are Linked Courses the Most Popular Learning Community Model?

Perhaps the reason that the linked course model is the most popular learning community model is due to some combination of the following characteristics. The structural advantages of linked courses when compared with other learning community models are:

- Less complicated coordination than cluster courses: For the most part, instructors confer with one partner rather than a group of faculty, although occasionally all the instructors of linked courses may get together for faculty development workshops or informal meetings.
- Less complicated rostering than clusters: Linked courses require that the same group of students be scheduled in two courses rather than several courses.
- Less need for curriculum change than interdisciplinary courses: The general structure of each course in the link may remain "as is." Paired course learning communities are developed from individually taught and already established courses (Shapiro & Levine, 1994, p. 25). For example, Introduction to Psychology may include most of the content it included before being linked with Introduction to Religion.
- Less complicated to schedule than clusters: Linked courses are often scheduled back to back, which gives instructors the opportunity to schedule activities that may exceed the traditional classroom hour. Frequently, the instructors are not assigned to teach during both hours of the linked course, thereby allowing them to conduct team-taught lessons as often as they choose. The registrar is an important player in the success of any learning community. Two courses are easier to arrange for the same cohort of students than three or more.
- More freedom for faculty than team-taught interdisciplinary courses: Instructors have the option of linking only part of the course, rather

than "joining the courses at the hip." The interdisciplinary component may be emphasized in several assignments over a period of several weeks rather than throughout the entire semester.

The book includes twelve chapters in three sections: "Linked Course Pedagogies," "Linked Course Programs," and "Assessing Linked Courses." Part One, "Linked Course Pedagogies," includes several case studies of specific linked courses by the instructors who invented them. In Chapter 1, "Pairing Courses to Benefit Student Learning," Scott E. Gaier shares data from five years of pairing a study skills course with a worldview course. In doing so, he argues that such a linked model improves retention for at-risk students, demonstrating that students enrolled in these linked courses received a statistically significant higher grade point average compared with students enrolled in stand-alone study skills courses. In Chapter 2, "Linked Content Courses: A World Civilizations–World Religions Case Study," Jeffrey LaMonica reports on the development of linked courses at Delaware County Community College. He describes curricular and pedagogical strategies that allow for linked course structures that challenge students' compartmentalized thinking toward subject matter and that make them more attentive to connections between disciplines. Chapter 3, "Double Entry: Linking Introductory Financial Accounting and English Composition," describes how Bruce A. Leauby, an accounting instructor, and Mary C. Robertson, a composition instructor, constructed a unique linked course around a theme of communication and the methods each discipline uses to communicate with its audience. Results from this linked course model indicated that students learned the material in each course more effectively than students in stand-alone courses. In Chapter 4, "Multiple Majors, One Writing Class: Discovering Commonalities Through Problematization," Irene Clark discusses the administrative and theoretical issues that can arise in attempts to link courses. She suggests that some of these difficulties can be overcome by focusing on the generic concept of *problematization,* an approach that she suggests allows for finding commonalities across different disciplinary content.

Part Two, "Linked Course Programs," includes a description of several institutional programs representing a variety of linked course program models. Each chapter includes information about program implementation, staffing logistics and concerns, curriculum development, pedagogical strategies, and faculty development. In particular, contributors discuss the development and institutionalization of these campuswide linked course programs.

Chapter 5, "The Science of First-Year Learning Communities," by Brandi Kutil, describes the "Triads" and "Tetrads" at Texas A&M University-Corpus Christi. Kutil discusses how the program evolved to include several kinds of learning communities to meet the needs of a diverse student population. Furthermore, she describes how in-depth training of new instructors, coupled with ongoing faculty development, increased course integration. The chapter ends with a case study of science learning communities. In Chapter 6, "Implementing a Linked Course Requirement in the Core Curriculum," Margot Soven traces the development of La Salle's "Doubles," a linked course program in which two courses in different disciplines are linked thematically. She focuses on the benefits and limitations of the program, and on how La Salle University solved the organizational problems related to implementing linked courses for all freshmen.

The next two chapters address the benefits and challenges associated with the institutionalization of linked programs. In Chapter 7, "Academic Partnerships With Residential Learning Communities," Maggie C. Parker and Alex Kappus describe their institution's residential model, which attempts to provide an immersed learning environment, and which is supported through partnerships between academic and student affairs divisions. They discuss how connecting students to faculty with the resources they need remains a special challenge at a large, comprehensive flagship state university. In Chapter 8, "Learning Communities in the New University," Siskanna Naynaha and Wendy Olson explain the development of a pilot project designed as an alternative model to the university-wide, top-down linked course model. In doing so, they provide a number of recommendations for improving programs and pedagogies from the bottom up.

Part Three, "Assessing Linked Courses," highlights the role of assessment in supporting, maintaining, and improving linked course programs. Chapter 9, "The Nuts and Bolts of Evaluating Linked Courses," by Michael Roszkowski, includes a summary of a survey of linked course programs. The following additional chapters share assessment models and describe how faculty and administrators have used particular assessment practices to improve their linked course programs.

In Chapter 10, "Using Program Assessments and Faculty Development to Deepen Student Learning," Lynn Dunlap and Maureen Pettitt discuss how their college has used a variety of assessment models to improve curricular connections and to reflect on students' learning experiences. They describe how their college's most recent programmatic assessment has concluded that an analysis of integrative assignments and an online "Survey of

Students' Experiences of Learning in Learning Communities" are the most successful approaches for understanding program strengths. In Chapter 11, "Linked Course Assessment: The Problem With Quantitative Data," Bethany Blankenship discusses the cross-curricular and thematically linked program at University of Montana Western. In particular, she reports on how courses linked through blocked scheduling, a faculty-driven initiative to aid first-year experience, improved retention rates.

Chapter 12, "Constant Reconnaissance: Assessment for Validation and Change," addresses how both summative assessment information as well as formative assessment protocols are necessary for improving linked course programs. Authors Greg Smith and Geoffrey Mamerow describe how data on cumulative grade point averages and graduation rates of students in FIG communities in contrast with non-FIG students are collected to shape the direction of the program. In addition, they discuss the ways in which they use surveys and focus groups (formative assessment) to provide information and recommendations about the program, as well as to better understand faculty motivations for teaching in FIGs and how their participation may or may not have influenced their pedagogy and professional goals.

The Future of Learning Communities

Although the number of learning communities continued to increase during the 1990s and the last ten years (Laufgraben et al., 2004), the history of higher education tells us that, like all academic structures that are not confined within traditional department boundaries, learning communities such as linked courses are fragile. Their existence is often dependent on one or two individuals who promote the idea. Furthermore, linked courses are more subject to budget problems than traditional programs and are strongly dependent on the good will of the faculty. This book provides the information that administrators and faculty need to develop and sustain such programs. In an era in which faculty and administrators are being asked to do more, and often to do so in the face of diminishing resources, learning communities have an uncertain future despite the research that indicates their value.

References

Arum, R., & Roksa, J. (2011). *Academically adrift: Limited learning on college campuses.* Chicago: University of Chicago Press.

Bok, D. (2006). *Our underachieving colleges: A candid look at how much students learn and why they should be learning more.* Princeton: Princeton University Press.

Clydesdale, T. (2007). *The first year out: Understanding American teens after high school.* Chicago: Chicago University Press.

Gabelnick, F., MacGregor, J., Matthews, R., & Smith, B. (Eds.). (1990). Learning communities: Creating connections among students, faculty, and disciplines. *New Directions for Teaching and Learning,* 41–45.

Ivins, M. (2000). *Shrub: The short but happy political life of George W. Bush.* New York: Vintage House

Kellog, K. (1999). Learning communities. ERIC Digest ED430512.

Laufgraben, N. S., & Shapiro, N., et al. (2004). *Sustaining and improving learning communities.* San Francisco: Jossey-Bass.

Marananiss, D., & Nakashima, E. (2000). *The prince of Tennessee.* New York: Simon & Schuster.

Moffatt, M. (1989). *Coming of age in New Jersey.* New Brunswick, NJ: Rutgers University Press.

Tinto, V. (1998). Why learning communities? Why now? In J. Forest & K. Hunter (Eds.), *Higher education in the United States: An encyclopedia. Vol. 1.* (pp. 387–409). Santa Barbara, CA: ABC-CLIO.

Washington Center for Improving the Quality of Undergraduate Education. (1999). What Are Learning Communities? Retrieved January 15, 2012, from http://www.evergreen.edu/washcenter/lcfaq.htm

Williams, A. (2000). Learning communities: An overview. *inventio, 2*(2), 1–12.

Zhao, C., & Kuh, G. D. (2004). Adding value: Learning communities and student engagement. *Research in Higher Education, 45,* 115–138.

PART ONE

LINKED COURSE PEDAGOGIES

PAIRING COURSES TO BENEFIT STUDENT LEARNING

Scott E. Gaier

Sara was excited to start college. She had earned good grades in high school, having many Bs and an occasional A and C. Sara was a model student—consistently meeting teacher expectations, turning her work in on time, and doing her best to learn. She felt quite capable of her abilities to succeed academically. Unfortunately, unbeknownst to Sara, her high school experience had not equipped her to study effectively. Then there was John. John had squandered many opportunities in high school because there was always something more important to do than study. Not only did his grades reflect his lack of responsibility, but equally unfortunate was that he had never learned how to study. The likelihood that John would succeed in college was very low unless he got some help. For Katie it was different. Although she had a very strong work ethic and discipline, Katie had constantly struggled throughout high school. Regardless of her academic struggles, she had a deep desire to learn and succeed. Her dream was to graduate from college. Katie knew this would be a challenge, but she believed through hard work and good decision making she would earn her diploma.

Introduction to Paired Designs

Why a Paired Design? Helping Students Learn

What do Sara, John, and Katie have in common? They represent many students who struggle academically in college and consequently need extra support to ensure their success. Throughout higher education in the United

States, there is a growing concern that students are not as prepared as they need to be to succeed in college. For example, the ACT, in its national report, "The Condition of College and Career Readiness 2011," indicates "approximately 28% of all 2011 ACT-tested high school graduates did not meet any of the ACT College Readiness Benchmarks, meaning they were not prepared academically for first-year college courses in English Composition, College Algebra, Biology, and social sciences" (ACT, 2011, para. 1). There is also the reality that more students are going to college than ever before. The National Center for Education Statistics reports, "The traditional college-age population rose 14 percent between 1999 and 2009, and total college enrollment increased 38 percent during the same period" (U.S. Department of Education, 2011, para. 1). The increase is not expected to subside as "college enrollment is expected to continue setting new records from fall 2011 through fall 2019" (para. 1).

To meet this demand, colleges are now assuming a greater responsibility in equipping students with necessary fundamental learning skills to help students achieve their academic goals. The paired or linked course design, a form of a learning community (Boylan, 2002; Tinto, 2000), is an effective method for helping students, especially underprepared or academically at-risk students, to succeed in college (Boylan, 1999, 2002; Brittenham et al., 2003; Cargill & Kalikoff, 2007; Commander, Stratton, Callahan, & Smith, 1996; Gammill, Hansen, & Tinkler, 1992; Sills, 1991; Wilcox, del Mas, Stewart, Johnson, & Ghere, 1997). However, it should be noted that the research of Wilcox et al. (1997) demonstrates that academic benefits may be limited to only the period in which the students are enrolled in the courses and not long lasting. In addition to academic success, another benefit may be connected to reduced remediation. Boylan suggests that paired courses, among other alternatives, "would not only reduce the amount of time students spend in remediation, they [paired courses and other alternative techniques] might also reduce the number of students enrolled in remedial courses" (1999, p. 8). Research also indicates a possible connection between paired courses and increasing student retention (Brittenham et al., 2003; Cargill & Kalikoff, 2007; Commander et al., 1996). Overall, research suggests that students, especially those who are academically at risk, benefit from a paired course experience.

Types of Paired Designs

The paired course design consists of two courses that can positively enhance student learning outcomes through the sharing of content or learning experiences. Typically, there are two types of paired designs. One design method consists of a content course and paired course that supports or relies on the content course. Students in the paired course use the subject matter in the content course to help develop their learning in the paired course. For example, often in developmental education, the content course, such as a social science course, is paired with a study skills course (Boylan, 2002). In this design, the paired course utilizes the content in the sociology course to help students learn study skills.

The primary benefit for pairing a skills course with a content course is that it provides students the shared learning experiences of applying skills from the paired course to the material in the content course. In this design it is more likely that students will be able to master study skills and at the same time experience greater learning outcomes in the content course. For example, Cargill and Kalikoff (2007) found that "in taking the two courses together, students were able to master and retain the content from 'Abnormal Psychology' [the content course] and were perhaps simply more motivated and invested in their exam performance" (p. 90).

Another design method is to pair two content courses to function as complements. An example of this method is pairing a reading course with a writing course. In this design, learning is enhanced in each course through the sharing of content. The students in the writing course are utilizing the readings from the reading course to become better writers, while in the reading course the students are drawing on the content in the writing course to become better readers. When two content courses are paired, such as reading and writing, overall student learning likely increases in both courses because of the synergetic and complementary nature resulting from the pairing of courses.

Example of a Paired Design: A Study Skills Course Paired With a Worldview Course

Taylor University, a Christian liberal arts college located in Upland, Indiana, serves approximately 2,000 undergraduate students—98 percent are younger than 25 years old, and 56 percent are female and 44 percent are male. Taylor offers a study skills course for students who want to improve their academic skills. I am the faculty member responsible for teaching the study skills course. Each year Taylor accepts approximately 35 to 55 provisional students. The provisional status indicates that the university perceives the student has the ability to succeed academically yet requires additional and very intentional academic support to help establish the academic skills necessary to succeed in college. All provisionally accepted students are required to enroll in the study skills course.

The study skills course is a one-credit-hour, pass–fail course that meets twice per week for the entire fall semester. There are multiple sections of the study skills course. Typically, each section is limited to 18 students. The purpose of the course is to help students establish proficiency and eventually mastery in study skills. This skills course also functions as a primary intervention for helping students achieve their academic goals and remain at the University. One of the primary challenges for helping students learn study skills is to equip them to apply the skills. Thus they need to have actual—as opposed to hypothetical—opportunities to apply the skills they are learning. As previously mentioned, providing opportunities to apply the study skills is one of the primary benefits of pairing a study skills course with a content course.

As part of their general education, all new students at Taylor University are required to enroll in a worldview course. The worldview course is a three-credit-hour course, which meets twice per week for one-hour lectures and once per week for a one-hour discussion group. Lectures typically have approximately 120 students, whereas discussion groups average 15 students. The discussion group provides a venue for further discussing the worldviews, writing papers, and completing other projects. Four exams administered during lecture sessions account for two-thirds of the final grade while the remaining one-third of the final grade is based on the assignments from the discussion group.

In 2007, the study skills course was paired with the worldview course. This was a very fortuitous pairing since many of the skills necessary to succeed in college are also needed to succeed in the worldview course. Prior to using a paired design, students in the study skills course were required to apply the skills they were learning to a course or courses of their choice identified as a target course. Inevitably, in each section of the study skills course, there could be very many different target courses. This wide range created many challenges. For example, when students would learn about how best to prepare for exams, some students would have already taken exams, while others would not have exams for a few weeks.

The paired design remedied these challenges because all students who enrolled in the study skills course were also enrolled in the worldview course. The paired design provided the opportunity to have students apply the study skills they were learning to the content of the worldview course. Thus, as students in the study skills course learned how to best prepare for exams, they were actually preparing for the exams in the worldview course. This situation made for a very intentional and efficient delivery of instruction in the paired course because all students now had the shared experience of the same content course.

The Paired Design

Many factors should be considered when determining if a paired design should be used to deliver courses. The first consideration is deciding if the paired course design is an appropriate learning strategy. Courses should be designed to improve student learning. If the paired design will help generate student learning and achieve desired learning outcomes, then the paired design is a valid option and can be selected as the course design. Once the paired design is selected, the next consideration is to identify which courses would be best to pair—content with a support course or two content courses. The last thing to consider is the specific design of each paired course. Like all courses, the design of the course is very important for facilitating student learning.

Determining if the Paired Design Is an Appropriate Learning Strategy

Deciding if the paired design is an appropriate instructional method for your situation is very important for determining whether to implement paired courses. To help determine if the paired design is appropriate, it is necessary to evaluate student needs and course offerings, have the support of administration and faculty, and ensure collaboration between course instructors.

Student Learning Outcomes and Course Offerings

Not all courses lend themselves to a paired design. Given the content, schedule, and types of assignments, all courses cannot be included in a paired design. To determine if a course is a viable option for the paired design, the instructor needs to start with the objectives of the course and evaluate the feasibility of meeting these objectives through the linking of the course to another course. In the example of pairing a study skills course with a worldview course, it was easier to achieve the objectives of the study skills course and increase learning outcomes because the skills would be applied to the content course. If it is determined that the paired design will have a positive effect on learning objectives and outcomes, then the courses can be designed or redesigned to be efficiently paired—assignments, schedules, and learning experiences will then need to be established to complement each course.

The most important course to select is the content course because the paired course will need to be adapted to this course. Two things should be considered when determining the content course. First, the subject matter of the content course must be able to be used in the learning experiences of the other course because the learning outcomes of the paired course are dependent on the subject matter of the content course. Some content courses do not easily afford the opportunity to be part of a pairing.

Second, the structure of the content course must lend itself to a collaborative learning process. For the pairing to succeed, the instructor in the paired course must be able to (a) have access to the instructor of the content course, (b) attend the content course if beneficial, and (c) design the paired course to utilize subject matter from the content course. If the content course does not afford such opportunities, then it is best not to pair the courses.

It is important to remember that the selection of courses to be used in the paired design directly effects the success of the pairing. Courses that do not lend themselves to an effective pairing should not be considered. Forcing a pairing can negatively affect learning outcomes. Instructors should openly discuss the possibilities and challenges of the paired design to determine if their courses are a good fit for pairing.

Administration Support

Pairing courses needs the support of the administration (Commander et al., 1996). Paired courses should be in alignment with the educational goals and delivery methods of the university. Thus they need to have support, including long-range support (Gammill et al., 1992), from the department responsible for the courses and from Academic Affairs before implementing new course delivery methods. Pairing courses can also occur outside of departments and across division lines (Commander et al., 1996), which requires quality communication and university support. Because all students in the paired course are also in the content course, one must work closely with the registrar to ensure proper placement in paired courses. If the institution does not support cohort registration, then it will not be feasible to create paired courses.

Faculty Collegiality

The success of the paired design primarily falls on the faculty of the paired courses. Sills (1991) notes that pairing courses requires commitment from faculty and recommends pairing courses between two faculty members instead of a group of faculty because it is easier to meet balance and achieve goals. Faculty must be in favor of the paired design and need to be able to work together. If they are not in full support of the paired design and cannot work collaboratively, then it will be very difficult to create a successful pairing, meet course objectives, and optimize student learning.

Ultimately, if the paired design is going to work, then good collaboration and communication is a must. The first time a paired design is implemented, more frequent interaction between instructors is necessary. Subsequent offerings of the same pairing between the same instructors will not require the same amount of interaction as did the inaugural semester.

Because the essence of the paired course centers around the sharing of content, instructors from each course must collaborate with one another prior to the delivery of the courses. The instructors should interact to ensure a proper understanding of the objectives of the paired design, including the role of the paired design in achieving the learning objectives of both courses. Instructors should also determine any shared experiences and content—including exams, assignments, and learning activities. For example, at Taylor, my study skills course took on a major redesign in order to utilize the worldview content. However, it was not necessary to make any adjustments to the worldview course. Thus the worldview course remained unchanged. Even though the worldview course did not have any changes, pairing the courses would have been unsuccessful without support for the paired design from Academic Affairs and good collaboration between me and the worldview instructor.

Good communication and collaboration are also necessary throughout the semester. Because the worldview course at Taylor was unchanged, there was no need for the instructor of the worldview course to reference the paired study skills course to students enrolled in the worldview course. This was also appropriate because not everyone in the worldview course was also enrolled in my study skills course. However, I needed to have a good understanding of what was taking place in the worldview course to better leverage the worldview content to teach the study skills course. It also equipped me to provide accurate information from the worldview course if a student had a question because, as I learned, instructors from either course should not answer questions about the other course unless the instructor is very certain that the answer is correct.

Lastly, in my experience, regular communication is not only beneficial for the success of the paired objectives, but helps to generate collegiality and support between instructors. Being able to share struggles, express frustrations, and work through differences helps to make the courses better. Communicating successes, especially with student learning outcomes and the delivery of learning experiences, creates enthusiasm and good feelings about the courses and teaching.

Because there are many things that must come together for a paired design to be successful, faculty of the content and paired course and their respective departments need to be supportive of the pairing. If this design method is not fully supported, then it is best to not implement the paired courses.

Course Design

Once the objectives for the paired design are agreed on, then instructors can design their respective courses. The design of each course is straightforward. Instructors start with the objectives of the paired design, and they then design each course. Instructors need to follow good design practices that are used to create any course. Challenges can arise if a course needs to be redesigned, which may be very probable because the paired design typically utilizes existing courses. A helpful resource for the design and redesign of any course is *Blueprint for Learning: Constructing College Courses to Facilitate, Assess, and Document Learning* by Laurie Richlin (2006).

When I was designing my study skills course to be paired with the worldview course, it was appropriate to leave the design of the worldview course unchanged because of the objectives of the paired design and because a majority of the students in the worldview course were not enrolled in the study skills course. Even if all of the students in the worldview course were also enrolled in the paired study skills course, it is still likely that the course design of the worldview course would not have changed because it was a very effective stand-alone course. However, the design of the study skills course was significantly changed. The learning objectives remained the same, but the schedule and learning experiences were redesigned to account for the worldview content. Once the study skills course was redesigned, the pairing of the courses was complete.

Teaching Within a Paired Design

Teaching in a paired design can be very rewarding. Good paired design, support from the administration, and collaboration between instructors can create synergetic learning experiences and outcomes that would not be possible without a paired design. For a good teaching experience in any course, including courses that are paired, instructors need to be effective teachers.[1]

Clear Communication With Students

In addition to widely accepted practices for good teaching, when teaching paired courses both instructors need clear communication with students and collaboration between themselves. The syllabi from each course should communicate the learning objectives of the paired design. When explaining the syllabus and the course, both instructors need to explain to students the paired design and the objectives for pairing the courses. Helping students to understand why the courses have been paired will equip them to be more successful in the paired courses because they will understand the role that each course plays. For example, in my study skills course, until I explained the purpose of the design, students thought that the study skills course would provide additional instruction to the worldview course, which generated the false assumption that they did not need to go to the worldview course or be engaged during lectures in the worldview course because they could get the content in the study skills course. I did cover or reinforce content as I felt would benefit the students, but the primary learning objective of the course focused on the learning and mastery of study skills through the application of content.

Collaboration During the Semester

Once the courses are designed, the instructors can proceed as they would with any other type of course. As mentioned previously, communication and collaboration remain very important if the paired design is to be successful. If instructors do not communicate regularly and clearly, then it is very possible to generate confusion or mislead students. In a paired course design, it is not the responsibility of the instructor in the paired course to reteach or supplement the material from the content course. Yet because the primary purpose of the paired course is to enhance student learning through the content from the content course, it is helpful for the instructor of the paired course to understand what is taking place in the content course.

In my experience, the professor of the worldview course was extremely supportive of the paired design. He allowed me to attend all of the lectures in the worldview course so that I could better understand the content. I would also interact with him as necessary through e-mail or after lectures to ensure that I had a proper understanding of the worldview course. Understanding the worldview content was very beneficial, even necessary, given the study skills course learning objectives. Periodically, especially before exams, students would ask me to clarify content from the worldview course. I would do this only if I felt confident that my answer was congruent with what they were learning. I used extreme caution so that I would not give them inaccurate information. However, because they were all in the worldview course, it was easy to guide their questions to each other and generate collaborative learning among them. This situation provided opportunities for students to teach each other, which is a beneficial study skill.

The Learning Outcomes for a Paired Design

The ultimate reason for implementing any instructional method is to help students learn. Prior to implementing a paired design, it should be determined through quality research if redesigning a course to include a pairing is best. If a course is already effective in achieving learning objectives and generating student learning, then it may not be appropriate to redesign the course to accommodate a paired design. Also, even if all factors support the decision to implement a paired design, it is important that the pairing of courses help students learn. If students are not learning, then the paired design needs to be redesigned or no longer used. To help determine the effectiveness of the paired course, quality research and evaluation can help identify the benefit to student learning and teaching effectiveness.[2]

Results of Pairing a Study Skills Course With a Worldview Course: A Case Study

As stated earlier, we first paired the study skills course with the worldview course in the fall semester of 2007. Although the design was good, there were some initial issues within the study skills course that needed to be resolved. The issues primarily centered around which learning experiences were most beneficial for student learning using the content of the worldview course. Midway through the first semester, I checked exam scores in the worldview course as an attempt to determine the effect of the paired course. I compared the exam scores with the scores from students who were enrolled in the study skills course and worldview course the previous year, when the courses were not paired. This comparison revealed there was not much difference between the exam scores. This seemed to indicate that students were not benefiting from the paired design. Most likely, I had not equipped students to effectively apply their learning skills to the worldview course content. To help make their learning more meaningful, I then began attending the lectures of the worldview course and taking notes. By doing so, I was able to effectively understand how to apply study skills to what was being taught. The rest of the semester went much better. Unfortunately, at the end of the semester when I again compared worldview final grades of the students enrolled in the study skills course with previous study skills students, there was very little difference between the final grades. The means for the comparison of the final grade in the worldview course is reported in Table 1.1.

The following fall when I taught the paired study skills course again, I was much more prepared and aware of what needed to take place for the paired course to succeed. I made some major changes to the overall design of the study skills course (e.g., scheduling of assignments) and made sure from the beginning to attend the lectures in the worldview course and take thorough notes. I also made significant changes to many of my learning experiences to better incorporate active engagement and deep learning. Consequently, the second year of teaching the paired course went much better. I found pairing the courses to be beneficial because of the efficiency and success of being able to apply the study skills. However, final grades from the worldview course did not reflect much of a change (see Table 1.1).[3] Therefore, after the second year of teaching the paired course, I began placing more of an emphasis on the skills needed to succeed in the worldview course, such as spending more time on how to prepare for exams and also teaching how to learn content holistically.

Fall 2009 marked the third time I taught the paired course. Drawing on the experiences of the first two paired study skills courses, I totally redesigned

TABLE 1.1
Mean Grade of Students Enrolled in a Worldview Course

| Term | *Enrolled in a Paired Study Skills Course* | | | |
	Yes	*N*	*No*	*N*
Fall 2006[a]	1.89	36	3.05	454
Fall 2007	1.78	49	2.98	445
Fall 2008	1.82	36	3.13	425
Fall 2009	2.17	48	3.35	434
Fall 2010	2.20	48	3.16	373

Note: Grade Point Average Scale: A = 4.0, A− = 3.67, B+ = 3.33, B = 3.0, B− = 2.67, C+ = 2.33, C = 2.0, C− = 1.67, D+ = 1.33, D = 1.0, D− = .67, F = 0
[a] In fall 2006, students were enrolled in the study skills course and the worldview course, but these were not paired; pairing began in fall 2007.

the paired course in an attempt to enhance learning outcomes. The primary adjustment I made was with the study skills course schedule to ensure better connectedness to the worldview course schedule. For example, I allowed for more time to learn exam preparation skills and applying these skills to coincide better with the worldview course's exams. I also altered many learning experiences. In doing so, I placed greater emphasis on note taking and in turn equipped students to make their learning meaningful through the organization of the concepts from the worldview course. As shown in Table 1.1, eventually students enrolled in the study skills course showed detectable increases in final grades for the worldview course.

An analysis of variance was conducted between terms for those enrolled in the paired study skills course. The results ($F = 3.148, p = 0.015$) indicate a statistical significance difference in the final grades for the worldview course as measured in grade point average (GPA) between terms. Further analysis on data from the study skills course revealed a statistically significant increase in GPA between fall 2009 and fall 2008 ($F = 4.514, p = 0.037$). This increase indicates that students enrolled in the study skills course in 2009 had a statistically significant higher GPA compared with the students in 2008. Also, an analysis of variance was conducted between term fall 2010 and fall 2006—the most recent semester with the semester prior to pairing of the courses. Results indicate an almost statistically significant increase between fall 2010 and fall 2006 ($F = 3.141, p = 0.080$).

These outcomes indicate that the final worldview course grades for students also enrolled in the paired study skills course were improving. Specifically accounting for this change in grades between terms is difficult because data was not gathered to help determine causality. Anecdotally, there is good evidence to suggest that the change may be explained by adjustments in course design across terms (e.g., better schedule, more emphasis on note taking) and by emphasis on appropriate strategies for study skills in relationship to the content course—as suggested by McKeachie, Pintrich, and Lin (1985). However, a more thorough data analysis needs to be completed to determine if there were other factors contributing to the change in GPA (e.g., differences between student cohorts across respective years).

A Note on Benefit to Faculty

I have already noted some benefits that faculty will experience in teaching in a paired design—the ability to be more intentional in helping students learn, the opportunity to work with other faculty to generate student learning, and so forth. In addition, I need to be very explicit about evaluating the paired design based on the benefits to the instructors. If the paired design is helping students to succeed, then it is obvious and right to conclude that the paired course is effective and should be strongly considered to continue implementation. At the same time, it is easy to recognize that if the paired course design is negatively affecting learning outcomes, then the paired design should be abandoned. There is still a question, though, that needs to be answered: *Should a paired design continue to be implemented if student learning outcomes remain unchanged from before the paired design was implemented?*

I would answer "yes" if the design is beneficial to the instructor (e.g., helps to promote teaching and learning effectiveness). Also, I favor keeping the paired design because of the potential synergy it brings to the learning experience. I also continue to make sure to engage in a redesign process of the paired course to eventually see gains in learning outcomes. This seemed to be the case at Taylor.

Summary

The case study at Taylor supports much of the research—students in my study skills courses are better learners and have greater achievement because of the paired design. The beauty of the paired design is it provides a very synergetic partnership between courses that can have exponential results in student learning that may not have happened without the pairing of courses. For additional points to consider when pairing courses, see the Appendix to this chapter.

Notes

1. There are many good resources for teaching and learning effectiveness. Two books widely accepted for helping professors think through effective teaching are *What the Best College Teachers Do* by Ken Bain (2004) and *The Courage to Teach* by Parker Palmer (2007).

2. As mentioned previously, Richlin's (2006) book on course design is a very good resource for evaluating courses. Also, three resources that are very helpful for evaluating programs and courses designed for academically at-risk students are (a) *What Works: Research-Based Best Practices in Developmental Education* by Hunter R. Boylan (2002), (b) "Reading and Learning Strategies: Recommendations for the 21st Century" by Michele L. Simpson, Norman A. Stahl, and Michelle Anderson Francis (2004), and (c) "Principles for Effective Teaching in Developmental Education" by Patricia Smittle (2003).

3. This result was disappointing, but similar to what McKeachie, Pintrich, and Lin found in their study on teaching learning strategies in an introductory cognitive psychology course (1985). It seems from their research that there is a connection between the learning strategies being taught in a study skills course and those strategies necessary for achievement in a particular course. They suggest that "future research is needed to examine the relative effectiveness of different learning strategies for college courses that vary in content, format, and assessment procedures" (p. 158).

References

ACT. (2011). *The condition of college and career readiness 2011: National report.* Retrieved from http://www.act.org/research/policymakers/cccr11/pdf/Condition ofCollegeandCareerReadiness2011.pdf

Bain, K. (2004). *What the best college teachers do.* Cambridge, MA: Harvard University Press.

Boylan, H. R. (1999). Exploring alternatives to remediation. *Journal of Developmental Education, 22*(3), 2–10.

Boylan, H. R. (2002). *What works: Research-based best practices in developmental education.* Boone, NC: Continuous Quality Improvement Network with the National Center for Developmental Education.

Brittenham, R., Cook, R., Hall, J. B., Moore-Whitesell, P., Ruhl-Smith, C., Shafii-Mousavi, M., Showalter, J., Smith, K., & White, K. (2003). Connections: An integrated community of learners. *Journal of Developmental Education, 27*(1), 18–25.

Cargill, K., & Kalikoff, B. (2007). Linked psychology and writing courses across the curriculum. *The Journal of General Education, 56*(2), 83–92.

Commander, N. E., Stratton, C. B., Callahan, C. A., & Smith, B. D. (1996). A learning assistance model for expanding academic support. *Journal of Developmental Education, 20*(2), 8–16.

Gammill, L., Hansen, C., & Tinkler, S. (1992). Linked courses: A method to reinforce basic skills. *Journal of Education for Business, 67*, 358–360.

McKeachie, W. J., Pintrich, P. R., & Lin, Y. (1985). Teaching learning strategies. *Educational Psychologist, 20*(3), 153–160.

Palmer, P. J. (2007). *The courage to teach: Exploring the inner landscape of a teacher's life* (10th ed.). San Francisco: Jossey-Bass.

Richlin, L. (2006). *Blueprint for learning: Constructing college courses to facilitate, assess, and document learning.* Sterling, VA: Stylus.

Sills, C. K. (1991). Paired composition courses: Everything relates. *College Teaching, 39*, 61–64.

Simpson, M. L., Stahl, N. A., & Francis, M. A. (2004). Reading and learning strategies: Recommendations for the 21st century. *Journal of Developmental Education, 28*(2).

Smittle, P. (2003). Principles for effective teaching in developmental education. *Journal of Developmental Education, 26*(3), 10–16.

Tinto, V. (2000). What we have learned about the impact of learning communities on students? *Assessment Update: Progress, Trends, and Practices in Higher Education, 12*(2), 1–2, 12.

U.S. Department of Education, Institute of Education Sciences, National Center for Education Statistics. (2011). *Digest of education statistics* (NCES Publication No. 2011–015). Retrieved from http://nces.ed.gov/programs/digest/d10/

Wilcox, K. J., del Mas, R. C., Stewart, B., Johnson, A. B., & Ghere, D. (1997). The "package course" experience and developmental education. *Journal of Developmental Education, 20*(3), 18–26.

APPENDIX:
WHAT TO CONSIDER
WHEN PAIRING COURSES

Determine if a Paired Course Design Is Appropriate

- Do the academic needs of the students merit the paired design? The paired design is best for students who can benefit from the complementary nature of the courses.
- Will the administration support a paired design? The paired design will need to meet institutional expectations and policies that guide course design. Departmental support is necessary.
- Are the instructors of the paired courses able to support one another and work collaboratively? Because the essence of the paired design hinges on the sharing of information between two courses, it is of the utmost importance that instructors regularly meet, communicate effectively, and work collaboratively.

Designing the Paired Courses

- Prior to the start of the semester, instructors from each course need to meet to determine the relationship between the courses, the role each course will assume in the paired design, and desired learning outcomes. Often learning objectives will remain the same as if the courses were not paired. The difference is that the courses should be more effective in helping students meet the learning objectives because the complementary nature of the design and courses is leveraged.
- Once the overall paired design is established, instructors are now free to design their respective courses to meet the learning objectives. The role of each course in the paired design dictates the guidelines for the design of the respective course. It is possible that many of the content courses can stand alone without having much effect on the paired course, whereas the actual paired course will be tightly coupled to the content, schedule, and experiences in the content course.

Teaching in the Paired Design

- With any new course, the first few times that the course is taught there will be unique challenges. Therefore, the design phase is very important for successful teaching. Courses that are well designed are much more likely to generate student learning outcomes.

- Instructors need to regularly communicate and collaborate. More frequent communication will need to take place for the first couple of semesters during which the paired design is used. After initial iterations, it becomes a lot easier to be aware of what is taking place in both courses.
- There are two warnings: First, do not try to teach the same content in each course unless this is an intentional part of the design. This "reteaching" can generate misinformation and lead to confusion among students. Second, regularly teach and reinforce to students the unique benefits and practices of a paired design. This will equip them to make more meaningful connections in their learning. It will also clear up any misperceptions they may have.

Evaluating Learning Outcomes

- Students and instructors alike can benefit from the paired course design. However, if students are not learning, then the paired design needs to either be redesigned or brought to an end. Keep in mind that it might take some time, perhaps a few iterations of the course, to see significant benefits.

2

LINKED CONTENT COURSES
A World Civilizations–World Religions Case Study

Jeffrey LaMonica

Linked or "bundled" courses at Delaware County Community College (DCCC) in Media, Pennsylvania, consist of students enrolled in two separate back-to-back courses in which the instructors link their content throughout the semester using team teaching and shared assignments and activities. The purpose of this chapter is to present a case study for one possible rubric for linked courses and to discuss the process of initiating interdisciplinary education in a community college environment.

Introduction and Background

The presemester planning of linked courses involves constructing syllabi and creating assignments that meet the needs and objectives of both instructors and their disciplines through cooperation and compromise. This type of collaboration requires two instructors willing to improvise and deviate from their traditional approaches. In addition to connecting the curricular goals of both courses, linked courses meet several of the College's broader learning objectives, such as lifelong learning, problem solving, and global diversity. This semester-long interdisciplinary experience provides students with multisensory learning opportunities through team taught lectures and discussions, in-class group debates, related writing assignments, and online projects and presentations. These assignments and activities foster learning communities between the instructors, between the students, and between the instructors and students that may not naturally occur in stand-alone courses. Furthermore, linked courses challenge students' "compartmentalized" thinking toward subject matter and sensitize them to finding the connections between disciplines throughout their entire academic careers and beyond.

My experience with linked courses began in Philadelphia in 1999 as an assistant professor of history in La Salle University's Doubles Program. The University embedded the Doubles Program within its core curriculum. The program required that all first-year students take two linked courses. I taught Global History linked with the Christian Tradition for ten years. The two courses connected naturally in many ways, with Global History providing the historical context for the development of religious concepts covered in the Christian Tradition. My teaching partner, religion professor Sister Roseanne McDougall, and I made in-class group presentations a major point of contact for linking our courses. These presentations evolved over time, from groups of students summarizing primary sources and relating to both classes, into teams debating opposing viewpoints from McGraw Hill's *Taking Sides* series (2005) and Robert Van Voorst's *Readings in Christianity* (2000). The following is an excerpt from our linked syllabus describing this debate format:

DIFFERING VIEWS IN HISTORY AND RELIGION

Overview

Global History and the Christian Tradition linked courses explore critical issues in history and religion. In addition, they involve practice in the art and skills of rhetoric in a progressive manner in order to develop literacy in history and religion. The instructors provide an overview to each section of the courses. Debates on critical issues in history and religion serve as focus points for thought in this Double. Such debates serve to pinpoint issues in such a manner as to clarify their nature and importance. They also serve as springboards for reading, thinking, speaking in groups, speaking before a group, and writing.

Debates

Each debate team is composed of five students. Each student assumes a role on the debate team as indicated. The Antagonist summarizes the team's side of the issue. The Questioner raises questions based on specific passages in the text. The Conciliator offers a compromise position. The Point Author prepares a written summary (1–2 paragraphs) of the reading for the other group members to use. The Coordinator plans and organizes the team's presentation.

Textbooks

History Reader: *Taking Sides: Clashing Views on Controversial Issues in History, Volume 1.* Guilford, CT: McGraw Hill/Dushkin, 2005.
Religion Reader: Robert Van Voorst, *Readings in Christianity.* Belmont, CA: Wadsworth/Thomson Learning, 2001.

Debate Topics/Schedule

Teams 1 versus 2: Religion—Should women have an official role in the church?
Teams 3 versus 4: History—Did Christianity liberate women?
Teams 4 versus 1: Religion—Did God the Son have a beginning?
Teams 4 versus 2: History—Should Christians engage in warfare?
Teams 2 versus 3: Religion—Should kings have the divine right to appoint bishops?
Teams 1 versus 3: History—Could the Crusades be considered holy wars?
Teams 3 versus 4: Religion—Should Jesuits have fought with the Native Americans against the colonizers?
Teams 2 versus 1: History—Did Luther's reforms improve the lives of European Christians?

I began exploring the possibility of teaching linked courses at DCCC when I started there in 2009. DCCC faculty members frequently address interdisciplinary education through professional development. Thus far, faculty from history, religion, science, human services, sociology, and administration of justice meet regularly during faculty development workshops to discuss interdisciplinary education. Linked courses are just one part of these conversations. Other interdisciplinary initiatives at the College include collaborative seminars and a cross-disciplinary panel discussion that is part of the college's student orientation program. Collaborative seminars involve two or more classes coming together for a single lesson or presentation where a topic or theme is approached from different disciplines utilizing combined faculty, guest speakers, and student interaction. History, science, human services, sociology, and administration of justice classes combine each semester for single collaborative lessons and presentations on topics such as post-traumatic stress disorder, natural disasters, chemical warfare, imperialism, and terrorism. The interdisciplinary component to Campus Life's student orientation is a panel discussion where various faculty members address a common topic or theme from the perspectives of their disciplines. The College's goal is to expose incoming students to interdisciplinary ways of thinking during their initial visit to DCCC so that they may carry this mindset into their coursework over the next two years. A panel discussion involving faculty from history, religion, science, and human services was part of the College's spring 2011 and fall 2011 orientations.

DCCC faculty conversations regarding interdisciplinary education explore future aspirations as well. One idea is to embed interdisciplinary learning within an honors program. The College is currently piloting an honors program. The proposal is to require honors students to have at least one interdisciplinary learning experience, such as a project that links content from several courses or a service learning exercise that incorporates several disciplines. Another prospect is the implementation of technology as a tool for facilitating faculty collaboration. Students currently use blogs and wikis for interdisciplinary projects in linked courses at DCCC. A goal is to utilize wikis and blogs to initiate dialogue and collaboration among the College's faculty. This type of online presence increases awareness about interdisciplinary education at DCCC and helps establish consistency across the curriculum as the college expands its interdisciplinary initiatives.

Process and Method for Linked Content Courses

Linked courses existed prior to my arrival at DCCC in the form of "bundled" classes. This precedence made my appeal for linked courses less difficult. The deans and provost supported the revival of linked courses as a way to bring interdisciplinary education back into the College's curriculum. I proposed linking existing classes in the College's catalogue to avert the cumbersome task of writing new courses. Retaining each class's separate standalone status minimized the effect of linking courses on existing program requirements, transferability, and faculty teaching load policies. Furthermore, linking two separate courses avoided the complications of dividing the compensation for three credit hours between two faculty members. The College scheduled its first World Civilizations–World Religions linked courses for the spring 2010 semester. In the meantime, I found an enthusiastic teaching partner in religion professor Francesco Bellini.

Rather than having a general education core, DCCC is a competency-based institution. Broad learning objectives, or competencies, drive the curriculum. Each course has its own competencies corresponding to a degree program's competencies that ultimately correspond to the College's competencies. My partner and I worked to retain the competencies of both World Civilizations I and Introduction to World Religions as we planned our linked semester. It is important that students enrolled in our linked courses meet the same competencies as they would if taking both classes independently to satisfy their various degree programs and transfer requirements. Fortunately, the related content of the two courses and our similar delivery methods allow my partner and me to meet most of the competencies of both courses organically. The following is a list of the competencies, or learning objectives, for both courses:

Course Competencies for World Civilizations I

- To analyze the development and nature of separate world cultures created over several centuries
- To explain the creation of the political, economic, social, and religious foundations of civilization in the ancient period (3500 BC–500 AD)
- To view how societies devised different solutions to key difficulties in forging a durable civilization
- To examine the role of geography and environment in the development of diverse civilizations
- To gain a greater understanding of the roots of the modern world through the examination of the diversity, complexity, and individuality of major world civilizations
- To discuss the implications of early aspects of globalization in world history
- To utilize a variety of source material (documents, maps, Internet sources, etc.) to examine ancient and medieval world history

Course Competencies for Introduction to World Religions

- To explain the developmental stages of each of the five major religions
- To evaluate the principal tenets of each of these belief systems
- To describe the most important rituals of each of these religions
- To analyze the relationships that exists among these religions

Prior to the start of the semester, my partner and I agreed it was important to use the first day of class to explain to our students the meaning of interdisciplinary learning, as well as the purpose and nature of linked courses. We also adjusted our syllabi so that the courses dealt with corresponding topics and themes throughout the semester. For example, when the religion course examines the life and teachings of Jesus Christ during weeks three through five, the history course studies the expansion of Christianity in the Roman Empire. Students experience the connections between the courses as they read and discuss topics and themes from the perspectives of both disciplines simultaneously. My partner and I achieve these connections without deviating from what is normally covered by these courses and their competencies in their stand-alone format. The following is an example of the intersecting schedules of topics and themes for both courses:

World Civilizations I Schedule and Topics/Themes

Weeks One and Two: The Ancient Hebrews
Weeks Three through Five: The Roman Empire
Weeks Six through Eight: Medieval Europe
Weeks Nine and Ten: The Ancient Islamic World
Weeks Eleven and Twelve: Ancient India
Weeks Thirteen through Fifteen: Ancient China

Introduction to World Religions Schedule and Topics/Themes

Weeks One and Two: Judaism
Weeks Three through Five: Life and Teachings of Jesus Christ
Weeks Six through Eight: Central Beliefs of Christianity
Weeks Nine and Ten: Islam
Weeks Eleven and Twelve: Hinduism
Weeks Thirteen through Fifteen: Buddhism

Taking time to preplan each semester offers my partner and me regular opportunities to assess both our linked and independent teaching methods and to make adjustments. From one semester to the next, for example, we retained some traditional pedagogical forms, such as lecture and discussion, and added more innovative collaborative learning techniques, including group debates. After establishing the schedule of topics and themes for our linked semester, we decided that team-taught lectures and discussions would be the basic points of contact for our courses. We hold our team-taught classes during the religion course's fifty-five-minute period. My partner leads the discussion from a religious approach. I participate as an active member of the class, bringing a historical viewpoint to the conversation. We utilize some team-taught classes as a way to introduce a new topic or theme in both courses. For example, the class watches and discusses a short video on Jewish identity during week one as both classes begin exploring the ancient Hebrews and Judaism, respectively. My partner and I use other team-taught class periods to examine topics and themes especially conducive to linking our disciplines. For example, we hold a discussion on the life of the Prophet Muhammad (peace be upon him [PBUH]) and how his experiences living on the Arabian Peninsula in the AD 600s influenced his religious teachings. The following is a schedule of our team-taught class periods and their topics and themes:

Team-Taught Classes

Week One: Watch and discuss the video *The Tribe* and the history of the Jewish people.

Week Four: Discuss the life and teachings of Jesus Christ during the Roman Empire.

Week Ten: Discuss the life of the Prophet Muhammad (PBUH) on the Arabian Peninsula in the 600s.

Week Twelve: Discuss the *Bhagavad Gita* and ancient Indian society.

Week Thirteen: Watch parts of the movie *Little Buddha* and discuss the life of the Buddha in Ancient India.

In addition, my partner and I chose to use group debates as the more intense points of contact for our courses. Partnering during these student debates serves as another way to link the content of the two courses. Group debates also allow our students to learn collaboratively. Furthermore, we utilize these debates as graded assignments for our classes. We hold our debates during the fifty-five-minute history class period. Chapters from the *Taking Sides* reader (2005) dealing with issues relevant to both courses provide the foundation for these interdisciplinary debates. One group of five students presents the "yes" article while the other group is responsible for the "no" article. All five group members must assume a specific task and contribute to the presentation for at least five minutes each. The five assigned tasks include the following: to summarize the article and explain why the group supports the article's position, to link the arguments of the article to both courses, to rebut the points made by the opposing article, to suggest a compromise position between the two points of view, and to illustrate how the argument is related to current events and issues. The groups have one week to collaborate and prepare their presentations outside of class. Both instructors are present for these debates. For example, my partner and I are in the classroom together during week seven when the groups debate the role of religious differences as a cause for the Crusades. At this point in the semester, the history course is studying medieval Europe as the religion course explores the central beliefs of Christianity. Both instructors take time to relate the debate topic to their disciplines after both groups have presented their sides of the argument. The class period culminates in an interdisciplinary learning community, with interaction among and between the instructors and students. The following is a list of these interdisciplinary debate topics and themes:

Debate Topics and Themes

Week Five: Debate One, *Taking Sides,* Issue 5. Did Christianity Liberate Women?

Week Seven: Debate Two, *Taking Sides,* Issue 9. Could the Crusades Be Considered a Christian Holy War?

Week Fourteen: Debate Three, *Taking Sides,* Issue 13. Did China's Worldview Cause the Abrupt End of Its Voyages of Exploration?

For my World Civilizations I course, I added critical and analytical writing assignments based on these interdisciplinary debate topics and themes. After each classroom debate, I assign a short (two to three pages) essay to the entire class. The purpose of these exercises is to utilize critical and analytical writing skills to discuss the ways in which debating historical topics and themes makes studying the past relevant today. Each student is free to choose either the "yes" or "no" article from the recently debated *Taking Sides* issue. Roughly half of the assignment requires students to identify the article's thesis and summarize its argument points. The remainder of the assignment requires students to express why they either agree or disagree with the article's viewpoint. The assignment instructs the student to state their thesis in their introduction, provide specific examples from the article's argument in their summary, support their own viewpoint in the body of their essay, and restate their thesis in their conclusion. Students bring the insights they gained from the in-class debates to these writing assignments. Excerpts from two student papers addressing the subjects of Debate Two and Debate Three follow. The first writing sample reflects the student's grasp of the World Civilizations I course competency dealing with understanding the historical roots of modern conflicts and the Introduction to World Religions course competency pertaining to the analysis of relationships between different religions:

The Crusades as Holy War

Since the beginning of civilization, wars have been fought in the name of religion. The underlying force behind the Crusades was a difference of religion and what people feel was owed to their religion. Religion is supposed to be the most peaceful thing that is known to man, yet the place that Jesus walked has been fought over since that time. What some called a political war was actually a war of religion between the Muslims and the Christians, which still has remnants left to this day.

The modern day world is still seeing effects of the Crusades. Just the term alone gets some people in an uproar. When President Bush used that term, people got offended. It was a reminder of all the Crusades fought in the name of religion. People have taken lives and started wars in the name of religion. The most sacred place on earth is also the most violent place. The Crusades were fought in the name of religion and will be fought until the end of time. People just don't get that religion should be a symbol for peace and harmony.

The second writing sample illustrates the student's mastery of the World Civilizations I course competencies concerning students' understanding world cultures other than their own and utilizing source material to examine history:

China's Isolationism

When people think of great explorers, they usually think of Europeans like Christopher Columbus. However, unbeknownst to most, Asia had a great potential to be conquerors of perhaps the whole world. In his essay "1492: The Prequel," Nicholas D. Kristof described a China that many people never knew existed. Even though the Chinese were quite capable of achieving great things, China's worldview was the reason that they did not continue maritime exploration.

China's Confucian-influenced worldview caused the end of its maritime exploration. Nicholas D. Kristof presented interesting points in his essay "1492: The Prequel" regarding China's withdraw from naval expedition. According to Kristof, Europeans were concerned with making money and obtaining material goods. So they just took both from other nations. In contrast, the Chinese were quite content with themselves. They did not view the rest of the world very highly and thus did not mingle with them. Obtaining material goods was not a priority for them. The Chinese could have been the first ones to discover America. Who knows how many things would have been different if this happened.

After one year of collaborating, my partner and I developed an interdisciplinary final project for our linked courses. This assignment expands our employment of learning communities to include instructors acting as workshop leaders with a creative technological component. The project deals with an interdisciplinary topic or theme related to both courses, such as the concept of holy war. Two groups of five students approach the theme from a historical perspective, while two other groups of five students explore the issue from a religious standpoint. The groups have the entire semester to research the topic and prepare a presentation to be given at the end of the term. I work closely with the history groups, addressing their questions and suggesting source material. My partner provides the same guidance to the religion groups. Each group also creates an Internet page to complement their presentation. The groups use a free online interface, such as Wetpaint or Blogger .com, to construct a page that includes a description or outline of their perspective on the topic. This perspective is supported by images, videos, and links to other pertinent websites. The finished product is a student-created Internet page resembling a wiki or blog. Each group uses its page as an audiovisual supplement during its presentations. My partner and I use both fifty-five-minute class periods to accommodate all four group presentations during the last week of the semester. The project requires the groups to address questions pertaining to historical background, religious principles, current events, and speculation about the future. This variety of perspectives makes for lively interaction between the students and the instructors. The following is an example of the guidelines for this interdisciplinary final project:

Interdisciplinary Final Project: Twenty-First-Century Holy World War

Groups of students will create an online project with possible scenarios for a twenty-first-century holy war, considering the historical background and religious contexts of the conflict between Judeo-Christians and Muslims for world domination. An in-class tutorial will explain how to create the site. Groups will present their Internet sites to the rest of the class at the end of the semester. This is your final project for both classes, so it is expected to be high-quality work.

Requirements/Expectations

- Cutting and pasting information from other websites is not sufficient.
- Each page should include images, videos, and links to other websites.
- No two pages may include the same material.
- Pages will be graded on content and creativity.
- Each group member must contribute to the presentation for at least five minutes.
- The objectives are to summarize the topic, link the topic to both courses, and illustrate how the topic is related to current events/issues.

When preparing your project/site, consider and include the following:

Historical Aspects

- Past Christian/Muslim and Jewish/Muslim conflicts (Crusades, Arab/Israeli crisis, etc.)
- Present conflicts (Al-Quaeda, Arab/Israeli crisis, Iran, Iraq, Afghanistan, etc.)
- Future conflicts (How and where could they start? Who would be involved?)

It is also important to include clear diplomatic and military scenarios when describing past, present, and future conflicts.

Religious Aspects

- The roots of the three religions (i.e., the sons of Abraham)
- Theological/dogmatic grounds for dialogue in the three religions
- Theological/dogmatic grounds for conflict in the three religions

Other Things to Consider

- Where will it start? Who will start it? The first "provocation" or the last straw?
- How will it end? Who will win? (Crunch some numbers here.)
- What will the survivors do after the war? (A new Berlin Wall? A new NATO? A world without religions? One global religion?)
- Is this conflict inevitable and unavoidable?
- Is this conflict solely about religious differences, or are economic, political, and ethnic motives present?

Experimental collaboration has provided us opportunities to evaluate and improve our teaching and has changed the way we think about our disciplines. We incorporate innovative teaching methods into our linked courses, such as group debates and online projects, which are not part of our stand-alone courses. We continue to learn from each other during our team-teaching sessions as we witness our disciplines being examined from another perspective. Collaboration also adds dimension to how we assess and evaluate our students. We commonly compare our perspectives on a struggling student or share our views on the group dynamics of a particular class. Although my partner and I grade our students independently, we rarely encounter profound discrepancies in our assessments.

I expanded my linked course teaching load to include World Civilizations II paired with Experiences in Diversity during the fall 2011 semester.
The following is a list of the competencies for these courses:

Course Competencies for World Civilizations II

- Analyze the development and nature of separate world cultures created
  over several centuries.
- Understand the creation of a global community from 1500 through the
  nineteenth century.
- View how societies devised different responses to globalization.
- Examine the creation of the contemporary world through analysis of the
  major historical themes of the twentieth century.
- Gain a greater understanding of the diversity, complexity, and individual-
  ity of global societies since 1500.
- Utilize a variety of source material to examine modern world history.

Course Competencies for Experiences in Diversity

- Understand the etiology of racist, homophobic, ethnocentric, and sexist
  ideologies.
- Demonstrate critical thinking on issues of race and racism, ethnicity, sex
  and gender, and sexual orientation.
- Describe the impact of minority and majority status as it pertains to economic, psychological, and social experience.
- List contradictions between the idea that we all have certain inalienable
  rights and the reality that certain groups in our society continue to be
  denied many of those rights.
- List contributions of those outside of the "mainstream" and understand
  how those marginalized "others" started social movements that challenged
  the United States to become more democratic and inclusive.

Sociology professor Adriana Bohm and I plan to make the following
themes our points of contact for our linked courses: gender equality in modern revolutions, racism and imperialism, ethnic hatred and genocide, and
religious tolerance and Islam. We adapted the interdisciplinary final project
from my previous linked course to suit our linked courses with the role of
racism in imperialism as a theme. The following is an example of the tentative guidelines for our interdisciplinary final project:

Interdisciplinary Final Project: Imperialism and Race

Groups of students will create an online project to explain how attitudes
about race factored into the New Imperialism from the mid-1800s until

1945, how these racial stereotypes still resonate today, and how they will look in the future. An in-class tutorial will explain how to create the site. Groups will present their Internet sites to the rest of the class at the end of the semester. This is your final project for both classes, so it is expected to be high-quality work.

Requirements/Expectations

- Cutting and pasting information from other websites is not sufficient.
- Each page should include images, videos, and links to other websites.
- No two pages may include the same material.
- Pages will be graded on content and creativity.
- Each group member must contribute to the presentation for at least five minutes.
- The objectives are to summarize the topic, link the topic to both courses, and illustrate how the topic is related to current events/issues.

When preparing your project/site, consider and include the following:

Historical Aspect

- Consider Social Darwinism, "The White Man's Burden," and the Civilization Mission as racial motives for the New Imperialism from the mid-1800s until 1945.
- Choose a historical case study as an example, such as the British in India, Americans in the Philippines, Italians in Ethiopia, Japanese in Korea, etc.
- Consider the ways in which race impacted other causes of imperialism, such as economic gain, Christian missionary work, military/strategic motives, etc.
- Consider the racial attitudes of the native population forced to operate within the imperialist system.

Sociological Aspect

- Consider the impetus behind and ramifications of the creation of racial categories following European Global Expansion starting in the late 1400s.
  - Who created racial categories?
  - Why were they created?
  - How were they used socially, economically, religiously, scientifically, politically, etc. to create and shape the "new" world [order]?
  - How were bi- and multi-racial children categorized and treated in the United States from the 1500s–2011? (Make sure to pay special attention to the laws the government created regarding race.)

- o How was interracial sex and rape—on the part of the dominant group—explained, not only in the South but the North as well? What purpose did exploitive sex serve for the dominant class? How were true interracial "love" and "romantic" relationships treated?
- o How did race and ethnicity impact the assimilation process of all new arrivals in America?
- o What were the outcomes of racial categorization both historically and contemporarily?
- What individuals and groups challenged American racial categorizations? For instance, how did Black Americans respond to slavery? What was the abolitionist movement? Who was John Brown? What are contemporary examples of antiracist coalition building? Why did some Americans come together across racial lines to object to and fight against racial categories?
- What happened when the racial system was challenged in the United States by interracial groups and movements? How did the state respond? How was the state forced to incorporate some of the racial challenges into the post–civil rights era of American history?

Other Things to Consider

- How did race factor into decolonization after 1945?
- How do the racial attitudes of the past still resonate in the post-imperial or neo-imperial world we live in today?
- Does contemporary globalization represent more progressive attitudes toward race or a step backward?

Conclusion

The interdisciplinary nature of our linked courses generates a level of student interest and enthusiasm not often found in required survey courses in a stand-alone format. This energy is best reflected in the high level of student participation and interaction during our debates and presentations. This engagement aids in retention, as dropouts are a rarity in our linked courses. Furthermore, the diverse assignments and activities offered by our multisensory pedagogy increase opportunities for students to succeed. In addition to achieving the goals of both courses, students enrolled in the linked World Civilizations–World Religions courses meet several of DCCC's college-wide competencies. The following is a sample of some of the competencies met by our linked courses:

Delaware County Community College Competencies

- Competency 4—Graduates of DCCC should have the skills to pursue lifelong learning. Demonstrate that learning is a lifelong process. Explore beyond discipline/career boundaries to envision a broader awareness of self. Select learning experiences that complement and enrich previously learned information.
- Competency 5—Graduates of DCCC should be able to use decision-making processes to solve problems.
- Competency 7—Graduates of DCCC should have the skills necessary to analyze social, political, business, and economic systems in order to function effectively within them. Identify those activities and institutions which constitute the social aspects of a culture (e.g., geographic factors; governmental; business and economic systems; religious, marital and familial institutions; employment and civic, volunteer and recreational organizations). Integrate the developments of history into current social and economic processes and institutions.
- Competency 10—Graduates of DCCC should have a concept of diversity that enables them to appreciate individual and group differences and to recognize that appreciating these differences benefits everyone. Use the tools of civil discourse to live comfortably in a world of diverse cultures and ideas.

In the absence of an institutional survey for students enrolled in linked courses at DCCC, my partner and I canvass our classes at the end of each semester to gauge their appreciation for interdisciplinary education. Our evaluation form asks students to choose their most valuable learning activity from a list of all assignments and activities performed throughout the semester in both courses. Forty-two percent of our students identified linked exercises, particularly team-taught lectures and discussions, as their most valuable experiences in spring 2010. Eighty-three percent indicated either team-taught lectures and discussions or debates as activities from which they gained the most in fall 2010. Seventy percent noted either team-taught lectures and discussions or debates in spring 2011. Students sometimes offer feedback on these surveys. The following is a sampling of student comments:

> "I personally felt that I learned a lot from the joint discussions and group debates. They helped enhance my critical thinking skills."
> "In-class debates and combo lessons helped me the most."
> "I learned a lot by having both teachers share their knowledge and perspectives of the material."

My partner and I hope the College will assist us in developing and administering a more sophisticated survey for students taking linked courses in the future. As DCCC's linked courses grow in number, it will be necessary to create and administer a standardized survey to collect data from students enrolled in these courses over an extended period to measure their success and quantify the value of interdisciplinary learning for today's community college student. The statistical and anecdotal data collected from a standard ongoing survey of students exposed to interdisciplinary education will assist instructors in identifying "best practices" in linked courses. Furthermore, the College will be able to use this evidence for institutional assessment and establishing curricular goals.

The fact that DCCC's linked courses are neither part of a general education core nor required by a program presents some challenges. Retaining each linked course's stand-alone status minimizes the effect on existing program and transferability requirements as well as faculty teaching load policies. Unfortunately, this attempt to avoid collateral disruption contributes to a lack of clarity about linked courses and creates logistical difficulties. The College lists linked courses as separate stand-alone three-credit courses in its catalogue without a description or special notation explaining their interdisciplinary nature and purpose. Most students do not know why their World Civilizations I and Introduction to World Religions courses are linked until my partner and I explain our interdisciplinary objectives on the first day of class. DCCC's online registration interface presents students who enroll in a linked course with a message directing them to register for its corresponding course. Academic advisors and councilors have the ability to override this directive. This practice interferes with the cohesion of our linked courses when my partner and I have to accommodate students enrolled in one class but not the other. A clearer explanation of linked courses in the College's catalogue and on its online registration interface would increase enrollment in linked courses and eliminate registration overrides.

The College lists linked classes as separate stand-alone courses on student transcripts as well. DCCC has not yet adopted a procedure for recognizing students who complete linked courses. It is our hope the College will create a notation on student transcripts signifying their successful completion of linked courses. Granting recognition on transcripts for students who complete linked courses will provide an added incentive for students to enroll in linked courses.

After successfully teaching linked history–religion courses at DCCC for several consecutive semesters, a goal is to now encourage the expansion of the College's "bundled" course offerings and other interdisciplinary initiatives by inviting more interested faculty across more disciplines and possibly other institutions to participate in meetings, workshops, and brainstorming sessions about collaborative education. These faculty conversations will continue to explore new interdisciplinary possibilities, such as the implementation of digital technology as a tool for facilitating instructor collaboration. Although the College does not offer monetary incentives for the interdisciplinary teaching and professional development, the opportunity to refresh their methods of instruction by gaining new perspectives on their disciplines is a prime factor in drawing faculty to get involved with interdisciplinary education. Increasing awareness about the College's interdisciplinary activities is a way to attract faculty volunteers from both on and off campus. With this in mind, faculty from history, human services, and science obtained a grant through DCCC's Center to Promote Excellence in Teaching and Learning to coauthor a resource guide for DCCC faculty interested in learning about and implementing interdisciplinary pedagogy. Human services professor Kathleen Schank, science professor Debra Metz, and I are writing the booklet. The guide will include several sections, each providing a possible modality for delivering interdisciplinary pedagogy. This in-house publication will promote awareness about interdisciplinary education at DCCC and be on hand as a tool for all faculty involved in collaborative teaching.

This chapter presents one possible model for linking courses, a model that challenges students to think critically and analytically about history and religion through interdisciplinary education and multisensory learning. A variety of assignments and activities, including team-taught lectures and discussions, shared readings, classroom presentations and debates with both professors presiding, writing assignments, and online projects, allow all types of learners to master the content of both courses collaboratively and independently. Students form learning communities with their peers and instructors through team-taught discussions, presentations and debates, and online projects. At the same time, writing assignments provide students with opportunities for individual analysis and reflection. These assignments complement and reinforce each other by exposing students to the topics and themes of both courses through different modalities, creating a learning process with repetition and variety.

References

Mitchell, J. R., & Mitchell, H. B. (2005). *Taking Sides: Clashing Views on Controversial Issues in History, Volume 1*. Guilford, CT: McGraw-Hill/Dushkin.

Van Voorst, R. E. (2000). *Readings in Christianity* (2nd ed.). Belmont, CA: Wadsworth.

3

DOUBLE ENTRY

Linking Introductory Financial Accounting and English Composition

Bruce A. Leauby and Mary C. Robertson

The Washington Center for Improving the Quality of Undergraduate Education at Evergreen State College, a nationally known institute, advocates the benefits of learning communities emphasizing multi-disciplinary perspectives (Washington Center, n.d.). The Washington Center offers overall guidance in structuring learning communities and references more than 300 different applications of community learning in colleges and universities. However, no specific program mentioned by the Washington Center included introductory accounting.

In 1999, La Salle University piloted its version of a learning community, called the *Doubles* program, with "linked" courses in the freshman year. In 2000, the Accounting Department was invited to participate in the program because Introductory Financial Accounting is both a core requirement for business students and is taught to all incoming freshman business students.[1]

To enhance accounting students' awareness of "conceptions of understanding in academic disciplines" (Langer, 1992, p. 69), we took a creative approach to curriculum integration by linking freshman English composition and introductory financial accounting through our Doubles program.[2] The students attended both courses as a cohort; thus, the same students met together to take three credit hours of accounting and three credit hours of English each week.

The linkage between accounting and freshman composition fits in with Writing Across the Curriculum programs, which advocate integration of writing projects into every discipline because writing plays an essential part in developing students' thinking skills and helping students gain a better understanding of the subject (Emig, 1997; Langer, 1992). Although many accounting courses have writing components in place, this Doubles took the unique step of combining two totally different courses into an integrated pair.

The main theme of "communication" and the methods each discipline uses to communicate with its intended audience connected the courses. Through readings, experiential trips, the creation of financial information and segments of business plans, and the sequencing of material, students learned to interpret and understand similar information from different academic and real-life perspectives and to integrate material across related disciplines.

There is little argument about how beneficial writing assignments are for students. Combining English and accounting created a unique synergy whereby the accounting instructor continued to concentrate on normal course content but gained the advantage of writing skill intervention while having accounting content also concurrently reinforced in English class assignments. When experiential learning was added, as in this case, the experience became more meaningful because the students had the opportunity to engage to a certain extent in the writing they will do as professionals (Zawacki & Taliaferro, 2001). The curricular coherence with reinforcement and integration of ideas across disciplines improved the overall education process resulting in "connected knowing" (Washington Center, n.d.).

This chapter describes the development process and details of our linked accounting and English course. Based on our experience, a linked introductory financial accounting–English course was a viable option for meeting the challenge to provide more integrative and value-added undergraduate accounting education, which more concretely illustrates to students how important communication skills affect all facets of life, both within and outside a business context. This was especially useful because, as Hirsch and Collins (1988) lament, "Students often do not realize that accounting is an information system and that written and oral skills are necessary to allow an accurate and efficient exchange of accounting information" (p. 16). Moreover, because integrative approaches have previously occurred only in business courses or beyond the freshman year, it made sense to consider implementing this approach in the freshman year to align academic programs with the goal of emphasizing the communication skills needed professionally.

Linked Financial Accounting–English Course

Initial Planning Platform

The initial pairing of introductory financial accounting with English composition required making a connection so students could internally validate the linked courses; thus our expressed link was the theme of communication. This prompted students to consider the ways through which each discipline communicates, and pushed students to understand the format by which information is conveyed (e.g., through set-up, organization, and style) and the rationale behind both the differences and the similarities in approach. Students sharpened their sense of audience, so in the process of developing competencies in each discipline, they developed a macroscopic understanding of each discipline as well. Figure 3.1 shows the linkages between each course, stressing the various components of communicating to others.

Our colleagues perceived our Doubles as a "funky" pairing because, in contrast to linkages such as economics with sociology, ours created dissonance for faculty and students. They questioned how a word-focused discipline could be paired with a numbers-focused discipline, a situation unlike those mentioned in articles by English, Bonanno, Ihnatki, Webb, and Jones (1999), Hirsch and Collins (1988), and McIsaac and Sepe (1996) in which English "liaison" instructors worked within the context of an accounting class. This dissonance worked to our advantage. Students used the theme of communication to deal with the dissonance, and this theme helped them to see bridges between the two disciplines. At the very outset and throughout the semester, each professor purposefully asked students to consider discipline commonalities and differences. This tactic acknowledged the dissonance and prompted students to confront it as they dealt with both classes. In the course of doing so, the students achieved some of the goals that Albrecht and Sack (2000) argue that accounting programs need to accomplish, such as learning to focus on the uses and users of accounting information rather than just on the preparation of the information.

Accounting is part of a structured curriculum in the School of Business, so major revisions from the established course content are limited because subsequent courses rely and build on assumed coverage of selected topics. Thus the agreement between the Doubles faculty resulted in minor changes in the accounting coverage and major changes to the composition course as it was adapted to create business and accounting as its core theme.

FIGURE 3.1
Communications: Linking accounting and English composition

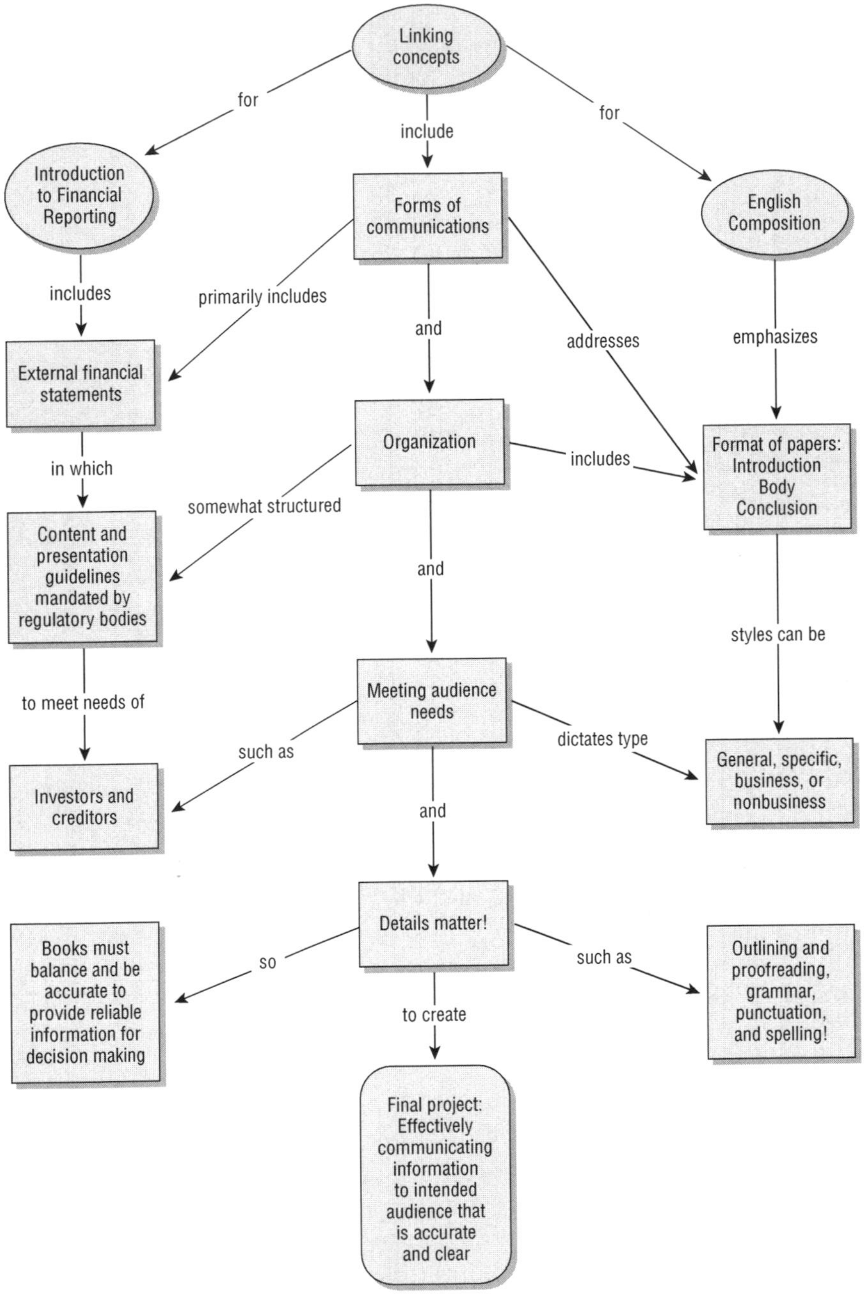

Planning Connections

An early and major task was selecting and using readings that could make connections between both courses. One book selected, Daniel Gross's *Forbes Greatest Business Stories of All Time* (1996), contains stories of entrepreneurs who revolutionized the business world and helped shape contemporary society. In Gross's book, short chapters describe the lives of business people such as Robert Morris, John D. Rockefeller, Henry Ford, Walt Disney, John H. Johnson, Ray Kroc, Mary Kay Ash, Sam Walton, and Bill Gates, among others, as well as the trajectories of companies such as Harley-Davidson and American Express. In a later semester, when we decided to tweak the Double, we chose as the reading in the writing class Jon Krakauer's *Into Thin Air* (1997) because in the process of recounting the disastrous effort to summit Mount Everest in 1996 by two commercially guided expeditions, the book provides some financial insight into this somewhat unusual commercial venture. The following sections of this chapter provide examples of how we used *Into Thin Air* and selections from *Forbes* to synergistically weave composition and accounting together.

Another early concern was making certain that we met together with the class and that each instructor stressed the importance of the "communication" theme between the two courses. In the first week of class we jointly met with our students during a class and devoted the class to getting acquainted. Having us both together helped to reinforce a bond between the two classes. We also had multiple opportunities during the semester to get together to emphasize the connections between the classes and the bonding of the professors.

Financial Statement Emphasis—Income Statement Perspective

After reading Jon Krakauer's *Into Thin Air* (1997), the students were asked in a writing assignment to analyze and argue whether a commercial guide business on Everest made sense. As part of the overall assignment, students worked in groups to prepare a logical income statement based in large part on the financial information provided by Jon Krakauer in his book. Students were amazed that adventurers willingly paid $65,000 or more for the opportunity to tackle Mount Everest and thus perceived such a business venture as a very highly profitable one. To help students put this business venture into a more realistic perspective, we team-taught a class offering guidance on the preparation of an income statement related to a climbing expedition as shown in Figure 3.2. This assignment occurred in the last third of the semester so students had already studied the income statement and its components.

Prior to this class dedicated to the income statement, students did online research on similar types of companies to gain an understanding of the financial profile of travel and adventure types of businesses.[3] The goal of our team-taught class was to reinforce the connections between the two disciplines (communication of information) while allowing students to give

FIGURE 3.2
Income statement and balance sheet perspective

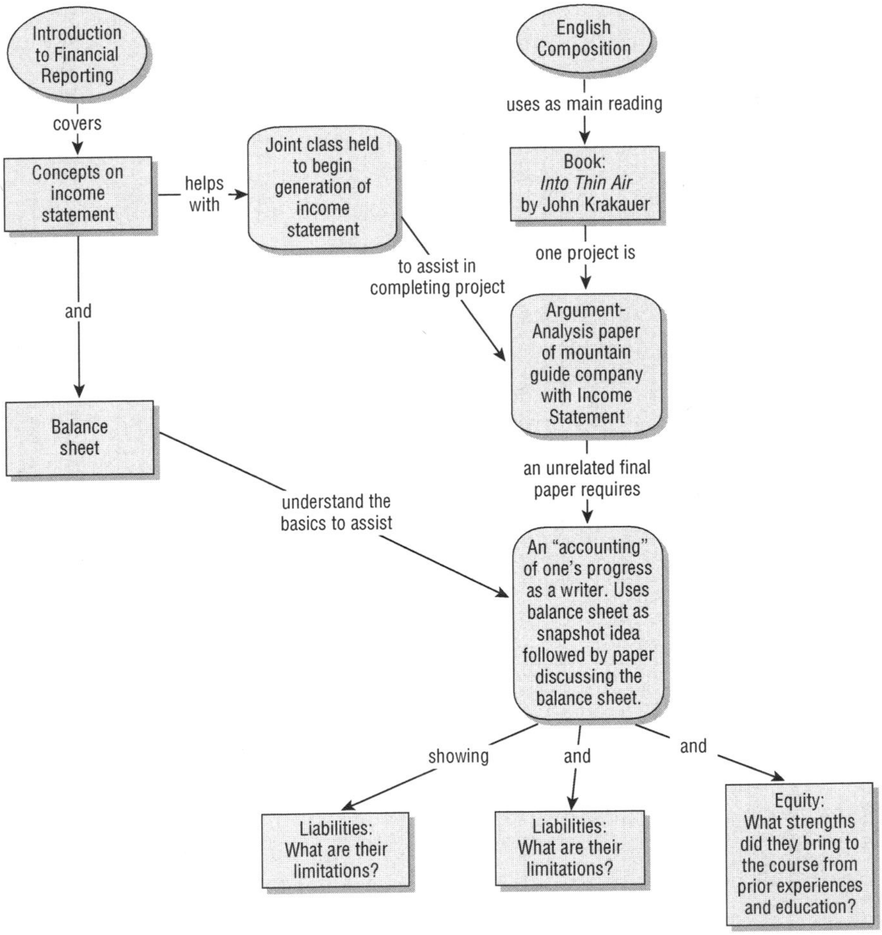

suggestions and receive feedback on types of expenses they thought might be incurred with a mountain climbing business. Very often, the students overlooked many obvious expenses such as salaries and items like tents, but with some prodding, they began to contribute ideas with confidence.[4] Moreover, having the students work in groups allowed them to brainstorm ideas together and to assign each other online research tasks such as determining what kinds of equipment are needed for this business and the cost of such equipment. This had the effect of reinforcing accounting concepts for one another. Looking at how an owner-operator of such a business would plan a trip and coordinate resources created a paradigm for students to consider when starting a business. This assignment and related class work helped students organize their thoughts when constructing a comprehensive income statement.

This income statement exercise part of the assignment connected course content with the realities and uncertainty of planning a business. The income statement, evaluated by both of us, served as a key component in the students' analysis and argument because a commercially guided mountain climbing business might or might not make sense for reasons other than solely financial ones.[5] The financial viability of such a business had to be considered as a part of the total analysis and argument just as it would be in real life.

Creating a Financial Statement Emphasis—Balance Sheet Perspective Connection

Near the end of the semester, students in the English course were required to evaluate their writing progress using a balance sheet format as shown in Figure 3.2. Their assets consisted of what they learned or what improvements they made to their writing as a result of this Doubles, their liabilities were their limitations, and their equity consisted of what they brought to the course upon entering college augmented by their new learning (profits). After presenting the balance sheet overview, students wrote a paper more fully exploring their strengths and weaknesses as writers.

Students easily related to a balance sheet consisting of their personal attributes. They realized over time that their writing improved and understood that the balance sheet was merely a snapshot of their abilities at one point in time. This carryover from accounting helped students appreciate the purposes and potential uses of balance sheet information for users of financial statements. Besides the self-reflection this assignment prompted, it also reinforced how financial instruments such as income statements and balance sheets offer a financial picture while the accompanying text in documents such as annual reports explains business decisions and future opportunities and threats to create a larger context for evaluating the financial profile.

Business Plan Formation—Joint Visit to Italian Market

One special aspect of our university's Doubles program was the requirement to use Philadelphia as an educational resource. Faculty were provided resources for trips into the city for experiential learning. Our favorite and most popular trip was a walking tour of the Italian Market during which we used a professional tour guide to learn the history and cultural significance of this section of South Philadelphia.[6] Students learned the history of the first fire insurance company in the United States begun by Benjamin Franklin, visited multiple stores and vendors, and at various sites were offered food samples. In the process they gained insights into the history of the family-owned stores and the products offered. Some of the businesses included a pasta-making store, cheese shop, spice shop, chocolate store, cooking utensils and hardware store, bread bakery, pastry bakery, and pizza shop, among others.

This half-day experience allowed both of us as faculty to interact with the students outside of the classroom and enjoy lunch at one of Philadelphia's famous cheese steak vendors with students where they had the opportunity to reflect on and discuss the morning's events. In this discussion, students commented on the free samples they received and on the shops— some of which were quite small but very lively—not really aware yet that they were commenting on and evaluating marketing techniques. Later, in the classroom, we built on this experience through an assignment that asked students to create a marketing plan for a retail business they hypothetically planned to open in the Italian Market.

Here the accounting instructor presented an overview of an entire business plan and provided examples of marketing sections for students' consideration.[7] We purposely used only the marketing section of the business plan because it was manageable to prepare and represented one of the more interesting aspects of a complete business plan. This assignment offered students the opportunity to be creative, which they enjoyed, and achieved the accounting instructor's goal of having students apply their limited business knowledge to creating the start of a formal business plan and the English instructor's goal of having students meet a business audience's needs through written text, bullet points, and formatting, a combination often new for them. The assignment also invited students into the world of "risk and uncertainty," two elements that Albrecht and Sack (2000) argue accounting programs should stress more to prepare students for their roles in a global economy.

Furthermore, this assignment built on the students' earlier experiences in the Italian Market, and we assisted the students in creating realistic marketing strategies. Students needed such assistance because, based on our experience in prior years, they initially suggested advertising on television and in major newspapers; however, both Philadelphia venues are much too expensive for any retail establishment the students would be proposing. Therefore, we asked them to consider the kinds of marketing they encountered in the Italian Market and elsewhere in local retail shops, and the students' plans then became much more realistic and creative. We also spent time discussing pricing and cost models so students could gain an appreciation that delivering high-quality products while underselling their competitors is not always feasible.[8]

As noted in Figure 3.3, the marketing business plan was separately evaluated by each of us, and then we compared our initial assessments with each other before finalizing grades. We often adjusted our initial grades based on input from each other because we each approached the business plan from a different perspective.[9]

The combination of the visit to the Italian Market and the business plan achieved multiple objectives. Students bonded socially with other students and with us to create a viable learning community, they gained an appreciation of the historical significance of the city where they attended college, and they were able to relate an out-of-classroom experience to an academic assignment.

Business Benefits Beyond Accounting

Any instructor teaching introductory financial accounting will attest that the course coverage goes beyond accounting. Students entering this introductory course often get their first exposure to business concepts, terminology, and procedures; consequently, the course must transcend accounting and become a combined accounting and introduction to business class. This broad business perspective fitted nicely with the pieces assigned from *Forbes Greatest Business Stories of All Time* that emphasize selected business practices and sensitized students to the influence of business on society.

FIGURE 3.3
Italian Market trip and marketing business plan

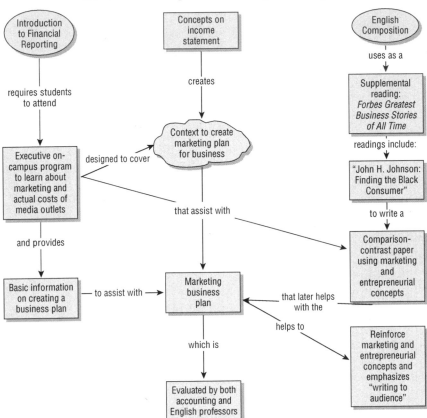

In the process of learning summarization skills and how to write a summary, the students in the English instructor's class used one of two chapters in *Forbes Greatest Business Stories of All Time,* "The Turnaround at Harley-Davidson" or "American Express and the Charge Card" (Gross, 1996). When they summarized the Harley-Davidson chapter, the students learned not only about identifying key concepts and distinguishing them from supporting information, but also about a popular company that almost went out of business because of an economic recession, competition from foreign motorcycle manufacturers, and a lack of quality controls in its own manufacturing process. Concurrently, the accounting class covered intangible assets, specifically addressing trademarks, which tied into the branding issues that confronted Harley-Davidson. Students also saw both managerial concepts (e.g., just-in-time inventory and statistical controls systems) and financial concepts in this assignment. Students could appreciate the value of controlling costs and monitoring quality from a managerial perspective while many financial concepts were also interwoven into the story of the company's recovery. The financial performance was on display in the discussion of a leveraged buyout by management, debt written off by banks as Harley-Davidson struggled, and the key role improved inventory turnover played in the recovery process. As students worked with this chapter, they were also introduced to the risk-return tradeoff when investors received a tenfold increase in return on investment.

"American Express and the Charge Card" describes the company's beginnings, the invention of the traveler's check,[10] and American Express's bumpy foray into the credit card business (Gross, 1996). Reading it, students in the English class were therefore introduced to the problem of extending credit and the potential consequence of delinquent accounts. For the related English assignment, the class was asked to summarize American Express's experience with launching and marketing a credit card business, research its recent research marketing techniques, and then draw a connection between what they found out about credit and their own or other college students' experience with credit cards. When the American Express story was used for this summary assignment, students had already learned about cash, accounts receivable, and bad debts. Purchasing with credit is a standard practice in business, and this story placed special emphasis on the fees charged to firms accepting credit cards. Because buying on credit is commonplace and students often carry several cards, the story was easily digested by the students.

Figure 3.4 shows the connections between the materials taught in accounting and the chapters that student read and wrote about in their English course.

Assessment

An overriding concern with any new educational approach is its effectiveness. To determine whether our Doubles experience was meeting its goals, we made an outcomes assessment. Our outcomes were more objective concerning student performance in the accounting portion of the Doubles and student response to the Doubles, while student performance in the English portion of the Doubles was more subjective.

FIGURE 3.4
Connections between selected readings

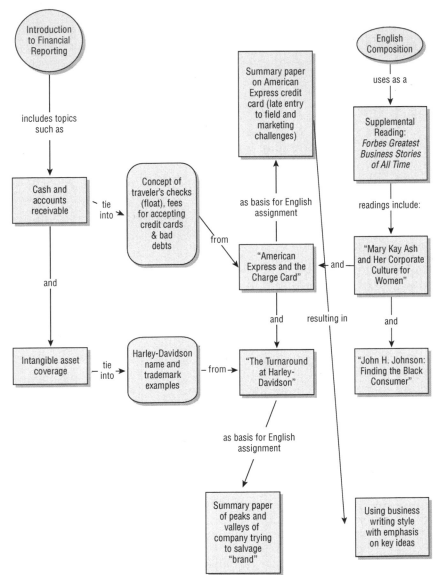

Student Outcomes in Accounting

Student performance outcomes included intellectual development as measured by Doubles test scores compared with test scores of a control group. Student perceptions and reactions to the Doubles experience were measured by what they wrote on the surveys.

Because the accounting instructor taught a stand-alone accounting course, a core curriculum requirement, during the same semester as we taught the composition-accounting Doubles, both control and experimental accounting groups existed for comparison purposes. The teaching approach in both courses included lectures, group work (including group exams), problem solving, and basic financial statement analyses. Students in both accounting courses participated in an almost identical environment using the same accounting text and exams, and having the same instructor. The difference in the learning environment for the Doubles accounting class was the inclusion of the additional activities and a smaller class size. While the Doubles class was limited to twenty freshman students, the traditional class was capped at thirty students and allowed students of any class level to register. Because these were traditionally freshman-based courses, and because our university registration office assigned freshmen to course sections, a random sample was assumed.

To determine if freshmen had equal ability entering college, their SAT scores for both English and math were compared between the control and experimental groups. No significant differences existed, so we assumed students in each group were equivalent in terms of prior achievement. These results are not presented. Test scores were gathered from three years (fall 2004–2006) and excluded any student not classified as a freshman in the traditional group, limiting the test score comparisons to freshmen. The accounting instructor gave three individual exams each semester, and the exam scores served as a way of showing whether differences in learning were associated with different learning environments. The first and second exams lasted 75 minutes and covered four chapters each. The final exam was cumulative, covering 13 chapters, and always included the preparation of financial statements from an adjusted trial balance. Comparisons of Doubles (nontraditional course) and non-Doubles students (traditional course) showed no statistical evidence of a difference in any exam score, which indicated the Doubles learning community provided no advantage over a traditional learning environment (Table 3.1).[11]

However, an investigation of the change in score from one exam to another showed statistically significant differences. Initially, no significant

TABLE 3.1
Summary Statistics and Tests of Difference Between Learning Environments
With Respect to Student Performance

| | Mean (SD) | | Test of Equality | |
| | Traditional | Doubles | Test Statistic | |
Variable	($n = 59$)	($n = 56$)		p Value
Final Exam	65.5 (15.70)	68.4 (12.62)	1.10	0.276
Exam 2 (E2)	75.1 (16.64)	70.6 (15.54)	-1.50	0.136
Exam 1(E1)	75.9 (16.63)	71.7 (13.09)	-1.51	0.135
Final-E2	-9.6 (14.91)	-2.2 (12.70)	2.87	0.005
Final-E1	-10.4 (14.77)	-3.3 (12.63)	2.79	0.006
E2-E1	-0.8 (14.60)	-1.1 (15.11)	-0.11	0.916

findings appeared from Exam 1 to Exam 2 ($t = -0.11$, $p = 0.916$). However, significant results occurred when we compared scores on Exam 1 with the final exam ($t = 2.79$, $p = 0.006$) and Exam 2 to the final exam ($t = 2.87$, $p = 0.005$).

Student Performance in English

The accounting Doubles course not only covered the same accounting information as the non-Doubles accounting course, but also evaluated students' mastery of the material in the same way through quantifiable tests, the results of which could be easily compared. In contrast, the English composition Doubles described herein differed from the non-Doubles composition courses both in theme and in the majority of the written assignments. However, regardless of the theme of the course, organization and attention to audience were strongly stressed in each offering.

The English instructor always stressed organization and audience in writing courses, so we found that students in the English courses—both Doubles and non-Doubles—improved in organizational skills and in developing a sense of audience. However, we believe that the Doubles English composition students completed the course with a stronger sense of audience and organization than did the instructor's non-Doubles students. Certainly, the Doubles students' self-assessments in the "Balance Sheet" assignment attested to a clear awareness and emphasis on organization. In papers from 2002–2005, the majority of students noted that their organizational skills had improved over the semester even if they felt they had come into the course with reasonable skills in this area. This assessment is noteworthy because the students designated what they considered to be assets and liabilities based on their review of their writing done over the semester. The assets that students listed ranged from improved grammar and sentence structure to a better drafting process to improved topic development. However, of all the elements that students could list as an asset, organization appeared on the list most consistently.

Even if the Doubles students did not specify "improved organization" on their balance sheets, we believe that the Doubles students' organizational skills were stronger overall than the non-Doubles students because the accounting half of the Doubles reinforced organization through the preparation of income statements and balance sheets and thus led students to very consciously address organization in their writing as well. Some students who in fact had good organizational skills, as well as those who knew they were weak in this area, listed organization as a liability on their balance sheets for the final English composition, which meant they recognized the need to strengthen or maintain this skill.

Another way the students benefitted in the English portion of the Doubles was their heightened sense of audience compared with that of students in non-Doubles courses. As we both stressed the importance of audience in writing and accounting, the Doubles students encountered the need to be attentive to audience more frequently in one semester than they might have been otherwise. In fact, even if they were to learn this concept in two separate classes, they were probably less likely to recognize the importance of the concept in this context than in a context in which they were explicitly asked to see connections between two disciplines. Moreover, the two disciplines conjured different images of audiences—a more abstract one for English (e.g., writing for "another faculty member" or "an intelligent reader") and a more concrete one for accounting, such as potential investors or creditors for the marketing paper—which strengthened the students' understanding and appreciation of writing to meet different audience expectations.

Survey Information

At the end of each semester, our Office of Institutional Research surveyed students about their experience with the Doubles program. The first part of the survey specifically gathered information relating to the Doubles. The second part compared the Doubles experience with other courses taken during the semester. Both sections of the survey were based on a five-point scale. (See the survey on p. 133.)

Table 3.2 gives the survey questions and shows the responses from three years (fall 2004 to fall 2006) from all students in the Doubles program split between our group and all other participants. Overall, students tended to like the Doubles experience. The average responses of our students were higher than other Doubles on seven out of eight questions (lower on question 3). The three questions with the greatest difference were question 2: "Professors seemed to work well together" (4.57 versus 3.81), question 5:

TABLE 3.2
Survey Questions Related to Doubles Course—Responses Fall 2004–2006
(five-point scale)

Question	Average Response of All Students (Excluding Ours) (n = 1,133)	Average Response of Our Students (n = 51)	Difference
1. Doubles were a good learning experience.	3.78	3.98	0.20
2. Professors seemed to work well together.	3.81	4.57	0.76
3. Doubles are a good idea.	3.60	3.57	−0.03
4. Would recommend Doubles to incoming freshman.	3.51	3.64	0.13
5. Got to see relationships that I would not see if I took courses separately.	3.42	3.72	0.30
6. Doubles helped me understand connections between subjects.	3.52	3.59	0.07
7. Activities outside of the class helped to achieve goals of the Doubles.	3.17	3.24	0.07
8. Doubles are useful.	3.43	3.71	0.28

"Got to see relationships that I would not see if I took courses separately" (3.72 versus 3.42), and question 8: "Doubles are useful" (3.71 versus 3.43).

Table 3.3 gives the survey questions that asked students to compare the Doubles with other courses and addresses how our Doubles course related to other courses the freshman students were taking. The responses were generally in the same range between our group and all other students in a Doubles. Students tended to value the Doubles experience as a worthwhile academic program. However, one caveat related to the results is that the participants were first-semester students who had no choice in their courses, class time, or professors. Nonetheless, the four questions for which our students ranked us higher (based on differences in average response) are question 12: "Helping you work with other students" (4.08 versus 3.85), question 4: "Teaching you how to solve problems" (3.53 versus 3.31), question 13: "Helping you work more closely with the instructor" (3.74 versus 3.54), and question 9: "Helping you to evaluate ideas" (3.78 versus 3.59).

Discussion and Limitations

Too often, accounting instructors superficially cover accounting material, hoping applications and connections will be made later or become clearer in more advanced courses. The advantage of this Doubles was that students, very early in their educational experience, were applying and integrating material learned from accounting into English writing assignments. This direct reinforcement of accounting content helped students improve their learning of basic accounting and connected some of their writing to a specific discipline of academic discourse.

The empirical data statistically showed that students in this Doubles, compared with students in a traditional instruction setting, were able to consistently perform better. The Doubles group remained fairly consistent in exam scores throughout each of the three exams. In contrast, the traditional group dropped a full grade in the final exam. The nonsignificant result on each individual exam was viewed as positive. Although there was no evidence of a significant increase in student performance after being part of the Doubles learning community, there was also no evidence of a decrease. But what stood out was the relatively small change in scores by the Doubles group between all exams. Students in the Doubles tended to score more consistently throughout the entire semester when compared with the traditional group. The traditional group consistently averaged in the midseventies and then fell almost a full grade (9.6 points) in the final exam.

TABLE 3.3
**Survey Questions Comparing Doubles With Other Courses Taken—Responses
Fall 2004–2006 (five-point scale)**

Question	Average Response of All Students (Excluding Ours) ($n = 1133$)	Average Response of Our Students ($n = 51$)	Difference
1. Allowing you to think critically	3.62	3.66	0.04
2. Made learning a pleasant experience	3.64	3.73	0.09
3. Allowing you to interpret ideas	3.69	3.66	−0.03
4. Teaching you how to solve problems	3.31	3.53	0.22
5. Helping you retain what you learned	3.57	3.59	0.02
6. Challenging your thinking	3.69	3.77	0.08
7. Capturing your interests	3.47	3.56	0.09
8. Helping you integrate ideas	3.63	3.63	0.00
9. Helping you evaluate ideas	3.59	3.78	0.19
10. Allowing you to appreciate different perspectives	3.75	3.71	−0.04
11. Engaging you in the learning process	3.63	3.63	0.00
12. Helping you work with other students	3.85	4.08	0.23
13. Helping you work more closely with the instructor	3.54	3.74	0.20

TABLE 3.3 (continued)

Question	Average Response of All Students (Excluding Ours) (*n* = 1133)	Average Response of Our Students (*n* = 51)	Difference
14. Fostering student interactions	3.71	3.75	0.04
15. Making the material relevant to your everyday concerns	3.41	3.43	0.02
16. Deepening your interest in the subject	3.5	3.47	−0.03

Conversely, the Doubles group tended to stay in the low seventies and only dropped a small amount (2.2 points) in the final. Something happened to make the Doubles group better prepared for the final exam. Thus, although the Doubles group tended to lag during the first and second exam (although not statistically significantly), they did better on the final exam. We concluded that the semester-long Doubles emphasis on learning accounting and business topics through both accounting and English assignments helped to reinforce accounting concepts that surfaced when students were challenged by the more difficult final exam. Perhaps the initial dissonance of connecting each course contributed to students' lower scores on the first two exams.

We believe the consistent performance resulted in part not only from the integrated course content, but also from the fact that Doubles students knew each other better in Doubles courses than did students in non-Doubles courses. The learning community effect was at times dramatic. One semester, the Doubles class members would occasionally telephone a tardy classmate to wake her up. Apparently, her mother had always woken her, so she had difficulty adjusting to an alarm to wake up and the class members knew this. This communal effort testified not only to how well students knew one another as a result of the Doubles, but also the degree to which students felt it important to help one another academically. Although students in non-Doubles classes bonded to a certain extent as a result of group work, we observed that the sense of a learning community was stronger among students in Doubles courses.

Our emphasis in making connections between the two different courses was also supported by the survey results. We strongly stressed student collaboration. Students in the accounting course had group exams that they completed in a group setting of three to four students before taking an individual exam in the next scheduled class. These same groups were created for various assignments in the composition course. The objectives of group assignments were to help build community, help students learn subject matter from each other, and help in the social bonding among students and between students and instructors required for successful transition to a college environment.

We both became very involved with our students because individual contact with the professors was built into our Doubles design. We purposely and continuously stressed the importance of our theme of "communication" between the two courses and also made sure students saw us together so the connections were reinforced visually. As noted earlier, we began our courses by meeting the students jointly, we attended experiential trips together, and we team-taught a class together and constantly referred to one other in our separate classes.[12] Students had individual conferences after the writing class to discuss their writing, and often met with the accounting professor for informal advising. As a consequence, students became better acquainted with us and thus had a further link to the university community. The students also received the message that communication mattered in both disciplines even though their approaches might vary. These results came from a concerted effort because we were located in different campus buildings. The intention of our entire program was to show the interrelationships between distinct disciplines, and our efforts worked.

As we found in survey results, helping students solve problems and evaluate ideas might have been directly related to two separate assignments. First, preparing the students to analyze the expedition business and the related income statement involved a team-teaching approach in which we actually guided the students through their planning process. This joint class was devoted to getting them started in the right direction and worked much better than when we did not hold a joint session. When student groups worked on the income statements only in the English class, the income statements were less substantial than those developed as a result of joint classes. Because the English class income statement discussion matched that of the joint class, we theorize that the joint class helped students bridge the two disciplines more easily. Second, our visit to the Italian Market subsequently involved creating the marketing segment of a business plan and students received pre- and postsubmission feedback on the positive and negative aspects of their creation. The ideas students created were discussed in class, and students came to appreciate that "great ideas" need critical evaluation to determine feasibility. This attention to their ideas and help in developing a realistic model that could work in a true business situation had an entrepreneurial and team-oriented spirit that boosted students' business confidence as well as sharpened their focus on presentation.

For the accounting class, the English assignments helped build a strong foundation of basic concepts and fundamental financial statements that allowed students to learn the more difficult material presented later in the accounting course. Consequently, the linkage between accounting and English was a viable instructional strategy to positively expand learning outcomes in accounting. Obviously, tradeoffs required structuring the Doubles accounting course somewhat differently than traditional courses by using more class time to integrate and help build the skills needed for the related Doubles material. However, this change in pedagogy supports the vision of the American Institute of Certified Public Accountants *Core Competency Framework* (2000), suggesting further efforts be directed toward creating a skills-based curriculum and reducing the current emphasis on a knowledge-based curriculum.

Survey results suggest students perceived the Doubles as a valuable learning experience, saw connections they might not have seen if each course were presented as a stand-alone course, and bonded with other students and at least two faculty members. These accomplishments alone made the Doubles experience a worthwhile endeavor. Although the results in this study were limited to freshmen and cannot be generalized, they add further evidence to previous research findings that building learning communities via linked courses is a viable approach in the learning process and helping first-year students adjust to college.

Although the benefits seem evident, they did not come without cost or constraints. Accounting educators already feel the pressure to cover more accounting material as well as other skills each semester in a limited number of class periods. The single largest impediment of doing a linked course can be the amount of time that instructors are willing to set aside for planning meaningful course connections. Obviously, instructors must plan linked courses so that they allow for increased time to be spent with students and reinforce the "communication" link between both courses. The faculty must coordinate between the timing of material and the joint reading and discussion of English assignments to stay connected. After the linkage is established, it must be refined to reflect student feedback and to eliminate what does not work. Although this process is a normal part of teaching, a Doubles involves extra time because two courses, not one, need to be adjusted and brought into alignment. A Doubles linkage of accounting and English composition is not the same as a business writing course or an accounting course that has an English-liaison instructor. The consequence for the accounting course inevitably means less accounting textbook material coverage. We have found the constraints to be worthwhile tradeoffs and suggest that they are a small price to pay to focus on improving how students learn and enabling them to learn because, importantly, this learning occurred at the freshman level, which meant students when reaching upper-level courses could invest their energies building on a strong foundation rather than on creating a foundation.

Although our results suggest increased learning outcomes, as measured by how students performed on the final accounting exam test scores, we encourage others to experiment with linked courses to help generalize the results to the entire accounting field and to add an enriching approach to educate future accountants.

Notes

1. Students majoring in disciplines outside of business may take Introductory Financial Accounting in their freshman year, but the percentage is normally small. Although our School of Business is accredited by the Association of Advance Collegiate Schools of Business, we are somewhat unusual because we offer our first accounting course during the freshman year.

2. Not every introductory accounting course participated in the Doubles program. Normally ten or more sections are offered each fall, but only one to three sections typically participated in the Doubles program. The Doubles described in this paper had been in existence since the first year (2000) of our University's linked course program.

3. Students were provided guidelines on researching various online sites to establish a foundation for future course work both within and outside of the School of Business. Students were instructed to find relationships between sales and expenses and to generally understand the margins associated with these types of businesses. These research demands were consistent with the abilities of first-year students.

4. In the course of describing the 1996 disaster on Mount Everest, Krakauer mentions a number of the business expenses incurred by a commercially guided expedition and details the kinds of equipment, transportation, and personnel (with salaries) required as well. This information gave the students a good starting place for their income statements.

5. As part of the preparation for the assignment, students viewed a PBS *NOVA* program, *Everest: The Death Zone* (Breashers & Clark, 1999), in which researchers evaluate the effect of high altitude on Mount Everest climbers of varying physical abilities. The program highlights conditions such as high-altitude cerebral edema and high-altitude pulmonary edema.

6. The Italian Market is the oldest and largest working outdoor market in the United States. Italian immigrants came in significant numbers to this area around 1884 and merchants began catering to this Italian community. The site gained worldwide recognition when the movie *Rocky* featured the Italian Market.

7. Second-semester freshmen are required to take Business Perspectives, which provides a basic introduction to all functional areas of business. As such, the course is taught by faculty from a variety of business disciplines (i.e., accounting, management, finance, and marketing) with cooperation of executives from Johnson and Johnson (J&J). During the term, students work in teams to develop a business plan for a product or service within the consumer health-care industry and then later introduce their idea to J&J executives in a formal presentation. Thus our introduction to the marketing segment of a business plan helped students get ready for a complete business plan in their next semester.

8. Our Executive on Campus program has professional working alumni share their experience about starting businesses during class visits, and the executives are told to focus on this class project when practical.

9. The English instructor completed several MBA courses; thus, her background included exposure to business practices. This also helped when she conducted her classes or evaluated assignments because she knew the content of the accounting course very well.

10. Students also had a lesson on "float" and came to appreciate the enormous interest income American Express is able to generate on uncashed traveler's checks.

11. To determine if freshmen had equal ability entering college, their SAT scores for both English and math were compared between the control and experimental groups. No significant differences existed, and so we assumed students in each group were equivalent in terms of prior achievement. These results are not presented.

12. The accounting class met on Tuesdays and Thursdays, and the English composition class met Mondays, Wednesdays, and Fridays, in contrast to many Doubles classes that were scheduled back to back to facilitate instructors' ability to conduct joint classes. The survey results here indicated that the value of the connections we created mattered.

References

Albrecht, W. S., & Sack, R. J. (2000). *Accounting education: Charting the course through a perilous future. American education series* (Vol. 16). Sarasota, FL: American Accounting Association.

American Institute of Certified Public Accountants. (2000). *AICPA core competency framework for entry into the accounting profession*. Retrieved April 15, 2012, from

http://www.aicpa.org/interestareas/accountingeducation/resources/ pages/core
com petency.aspx

Breashers, D., & Clark, L. (Directors) & Clark, L. (Episode producer). (1999). Everest: The death zone. [Television series episode]. In B. Hoppe (Series producer),
NOVA. Boston, MA: WGBH Video.

English, L., Bonanno, H., Ihnatki, T., Webb, C., & Jones, J. (1999). Learning
through writing in a first-year accounting course. *Journal of Accounting Education, 17,* 221–254.

Emig, J. (1997). Writing as a mode of learning. *College Composition and Communication, 28,* 122–128.

Gross, D. (1996). *Forbes greatest business stories of all time.* New York: John Wiley &
Sons, Inc.

Hirsch, M. L., & Collins, J. D. (1988). An integrated approach to communication
skills in an accounting curriculum. *Journal of Accounting Education, 6,* 15–31.

Krakauer, J. (1997). *Into thin air.* New York: Anchor Books.

Langer, J. A. (1992). Speaking of knowing: Conceptions of understanding in academic disciplines. In A. Herrington & C. Horna (Eds.), *Writing, teaching, and
learning in the disciplines* (pp. 69–85). New York: Modern Language Association.

McIsaac, C. M., & Sepe, J. F. (1996). Improving the writing of accounting students:
A cooperative venture. *Journal of Accounting Education, 14,* 515–533.

Washington Center for Improving the Quality of Undergraduate Education. (n.d.).
Learning Communities National Resource Center. Retrieved August 31, 2007, from
http://www.evergreen.edu/washcenter/project.asp?pid = 73

Zawacki, T. M., & Taliaferro, W. A. (2001). Is it still WAC? Writing within interdisciplinary communities. In S. H. McLeod, E. Miraglia, M. Soven, & C. Ihaiss
(Eds.). *WAC for the new millennium: Strategies for continuing Writing-Across-the-
Curriculum programs* (pp. 109–140). Urbana, IL: National Council of Teachers
of English.

4

MULTIPLE MAJORS, ONE WRITING CLASS

Discovering Commonalities Through Problematization

Irene Clark

Recent concern about fostering academic success in underprepared college students has generated interest in the concept of learning communities in which students enroll in linked or "paired" courses. Often, as Boylan (2002) notes, a typical model consists of a discipline-based course that is paired with a skill-based course, such as a writing class, the idea being that students will be able to use disciplinary content material as a subject for writing, and that the act of writing about that material will enhance student learning. However, although there are many benefits to such a design, administrative issues may sometimes interfere, particularly at large public institutions, which many underprepared students attend. Moreover, the concept of "disciplinary" writing raises a number of theoretical issues that are important to address when considering community-based learning. This chapter discusses the administrative and theoretical issues that can arise in attempts to link or pair courses and suggest that some of these difficulties can be overcome by focusing on the generic concept of *problematization*.

The Complicated Nature of Disciplinarity

When courses are successfully linked or paired, there is little doubt that students will benefit. However, given the burgeoning of new disciplines and sub-disciplines in every field, the meaning of the term *discipline* must also be considered. In their discussion of the term *discipline,* Thaiss and Zawacki (2006) cited Toulmin's definition of *discipline* as "a collective human enterprise" in which "men's shared commitment to a sufficiently agreed set of ideals leads to the development of an isolable and self-defining repertory of procedures" (p. 14). However, Toulmin also noted the variation in the relative stability among disciplines. Some disciplines, he maintained, are "compact," meaning that there is a high level of agreement about the processes of intellectual inquiry. Other disciplines are diffuse, meaning that concepts are still evolving, whereas others are "quasi," with unity and coherence preserved across ever-changing techniques (Thaiss & Zwacki, 2006, p. 14). Moreover, disciplinarity does not necessarily correspond to traditional departmental designations or majors, which are themselves being redefined, another factor that complicates decisions about the first-year writing course and about what it means to teach students to write.

The difficulty of defining writing exclusively in a disciplinary context was highlighted for me several years ago, when I was involved in the development of a set of upper-division writing courses that were being offered through a stand-alone writing program. Our problem was that if we adhered strictly to the idea that writing is situated in a particular discipline or major, our task would be monumental, because we would have had to develop several hundred writing courses to correspond with the many majors available at the university. Because this was impossible, we finally decided to develop seven courses: "Writing in the Humanities," "Writing in the Social Sciences," "Writing for Law," "Writing for Business," "Writing in the Sciences," "Writing for Engineering," and "Writing for Health Professionals." Law, business, and engineering seemed reasonably straightforward. But some of the other categories were more problematic. For example, the category "Writing in the Health Sciences" included potential doctors, nurses, and public health professionals. Was it likely that these three professions all used writing in the same way? Then the course titled "Writing in the Social Sciences" included sociology, anthropology, economics, political science, and geography, categories that reflected departmental categories and that certainly involve different types of writing. I, myself, am somewhat familiar with the discipline of geography, and I am aware that physical geographers utilize a very different type of writing than do cultural geographers. If it is difficult to decide what sort of writing a geography student should be taught, would a course titled "Writing in the Social Sciences" be able to address the writing needs of students in all the social sciences?

The Problem of Transferability

Another important issue to consider in attempting to implement linked or paired courses is the extent to which "academic" writing, which is often the focus in stand-alone writing courses, pertains across disciplinary contexts. The extensive literature on transferability has yet to present a consistent perspective on this issue, with some scholars maintaining that at least some features of academic writing can transfer to other disciplines, and others arguing that they cannot, because all writing is situated (Beaufort, 2007; Downs & Wardle, 2007; Petraglia, 1995; Russell, 1995; Thaiss & Zawacki, 2006; Wardle, 2009). Most teachers and scholars have argued that at least some features transfer to other disciplinary and professional writing tasks. However, these same teachers and scholars would also agree that writing in different fields means privileging different formats, genres, and styles. And then there are those that have maintained that the general writing skills learned in composition courses do not transfer at all to writing in upper-division writing courses or in professional settings.

Administrative Difficulties and the Role of Problematization

Even if one assumes that transfer is likely and even when a curriculum has been developed that utilizes paired or linked courses, unforeseen circumstances may interfere, which is what occurred at my institution a few years ago when I attempted to implement a linked course model, working with a professor of geography to link an intermediate writing class with a course titled "Introduction to Geographic Research." When the project was developed, the intention was to focus on improving students' writing skills by incorporating content associated with geography into the writing course, a usual "Writing in the Disciplines" approach. The geography professor and I had planned carefully, the writing assignments were in place, and the curriculum was structured. However, when I met my class, I discovered that for a variety of administrative reasons, only five students in the class were actually majoring in geography. More than half of the students were liberal studies majors, a focus selected by prospective elementary school teachers. The other students were majoring in business. What emerged from this initially perplexing situation was a strategy that can be useful in all linked or paired classes, even when students are not from the same discipline—a focus on the generic concept of *problematization*.

This concept of problematization enabled the students from these three different disciplines to find commonalities—that is, for two of the assignments, students chose a problem in their respective disciplines about which there was some debate, an emphasis that corresponds to the perspectives of a number of scholars (e.g., Flower & Hayes, 1980; Graff, 2003; MacDonald, 1987). This focus on a *problem* helped students understand the connection between rhetoric and academic argument—that is, that an important goal of academic argument is to address a problem deemed worth writing about in order to influence an audience in some way. Discussions about how to achieve credibility with an intended audience gave relevance to rhetorical concepts such as ethos, logos, pathos, and exigence, and the effectiveness of students' work was considered in terms of their ability to convey information persuasively to an audience—that is, to convince an intended audience that what they had to say was worth considering. In fact, the question, "Is your idea worth considering?" became a mantra in the classroom.

The final assignment required students to write a grant proposal for $10,000 to GEBCO, a giant, fictional publicly held corporation I created for the class. The primary concern of this "corporation" was to foster public awareness of ethical issues in the fields of geography, education, and business with a particular interest in projects that are relevant for undergraduate students. The grant proposal genre enabled students to reexamine the "problem" they had been writing about in terms of "real-world" concerns, and to consider ways of fostering awareness of this problem.

The course that resulted focused on four concepts associated with writing: rhetoric, genre, identity, and values. An additional emphasis was on students' attitudes toward writing, in particular on helping students develop a sense of comfort with the writing process and with the various activities that enable writers to improve beyond a particular course. At the end of the semester, surveys and reflective comments indicated that students were pleased that the class had included three different majors. They felt it had been enlightening and interesting to learn about writing and thinking in different disciplines and to meet people who intended to follow different career paths than those within their own majors. My own impression was that the focus on problem-based assignments had enabled us to find commonalities among different disciplines, an insight worth exploring in the context of linked classes.

Rhetoric, Problematization, and Exigence

Although rhetoric plays an important role in any writing scene, most students are not consciously aware of that role nor of the connection between a rhetorical situation and an underlying "exigence," which may be the source of a textual response or may be called into existence because someone—a rhetor—decides that a textual response is necessary and possible. This interconnection between exigence and a rhetorical situation is addressed in the Bitzer–Vatz debate, which highlights differences between realist and social-constructionist views of exigence. Bitzer (1968) maintained that a rhetorical response responds to an exigence or problematic situation ("The Rhetorical Situation") and that any rhetorical discourse requires an exigence, defined as a "problem" existing in the world that can be changed by human interaction. That exigence becomes a rhetorical situation when it can be modified through persuasion, and an example of such an exigence would be a president's speech in favor of health care or the need for military action in a crisis.

Vatz (1973), however, challenged Bitzer's concept of the rhetorical situation, maintaining that an exigence is socially constructed and that rhetoric itself generates an exigence or rhetorical situation ("The Myth of the Rhetorical Situation"). Quoting from Chaim Perelman, Vatz argued that when rhetors or persuaders choose particular issues or events to write about, they create *presence* or *salience* (Perelman's terms)—in essence, it is the choice to focus on the situation that creates the exigence. Thus a president who chooses to focus on health care or military action, according to Vatz, has constructed the exigence toward which the rhetoric is addressed.

Both Bitzer's realistic and Vatz's social constructionist approaches were relevant in the forging of problem-based assignments in the class, with initial discussions focusing on what constitutes an exigence in the context of each discipline, exigence being equated with issues that had generated disagreement and were considered problematic. Following that discussion, the first assignment required students to select a "problem" in their discipline about which there was some debate and write an academic essay or argument that took a thoughtful position about that problem (see assignments in Appendix A at the end of this chapter). This emphasis on a disciplinary problem corresponds to the perspectives of a number of scholars who define *academic argument* in terms of problematization. A number of years ago, Susan Peck MacDonald (1987) argued for the pervasiveness of "problem definition" in multiple academic venues, noting that "the subject of academic writing either already is or is soon turned into a problem before the writer proceeds. No matter how tentative the solutions are, it is problem-solving that generates all academic writing" (p. 316). The idea of "problem" is also featured in the more recent work of Gerald Graff (2003) who, in *Clueless in Academe*, referred to "the problem problem and other oddities of academic discourse"

(p. 43). Graff asserted that "nothing better exemplifies the apparently counterintuitive nature of intellectual practices than their preoccupation with what often appears to be bogus 'problems.' Academic assignments ask students . . . to cultivate problems to an extent that seems perverse or bizarre" (p. 45), which is why he refers to this phenomenon as the "problem problem." However, the difficulty Graff noted of finding or constructing a "problem" seems to be more difficult in the humanities, perhaps most particularly in literary studies, which may require students to construct problems about the meaning of words (the meaning of *love* in different eras, for example, which students may not think matters much) or to discover new meanings in literary texts that seem straightforward to them.

The students in geography, education, and business, however, seemed to have little difficulty in locating a problem within their own discipline, although narrowing the topic sufficiently was an issue for them, as it is for many writers, both novice and expert. The geography students tended to focus on environmental issues such as "Let's not be hasty about immediately embracing nuclear energy as a source of power because we haven't figured out what we should do with nuclear waste" or on the effects of global warming. The education students focused on issues such as sex education in the schools, the grouping of students in classes according to ability, and the limits of No Child Left Behind; the business students chose topics such as what can be done about false advertising, the privatization of prisons, and the neglected business opportunities resulting from the U.S. policy toward Cuba. Most students had no difficulty in finding problems that they cared about and which they considered were actual, real-world problems that were important in their respective disciplines. To help students focus on the exigence inherent in their chosen problem, they were asked to respond in writing to the following questions:

1. What is the problem you plan to address?
2. Why is this problem important?
3. What do most people think about this problem?
4. What ethical controversies are associated with this problem?
5. What direction are you inclined to write about in addressing this problem?

This focus on a problem helped students understand how rhetoric informs academic argument—that is, that academic argument addresses a problem deemed worth writing about with the goal of influencing an audience in some way. It is an approach that was addressed some years ago by

Wayne Booth in *Modern Dogma and the Rhetoric of Assent* (1974), who posed the question, "How should [people] work when they try to change each other's minds?" (p. 12), a question that contributed significantly to the focus of the class, and generated a rhetorical approach that directly affected all writing assignments.

Another concept that informed the class was the term *genre,* which was used not in the context of literary form, but rather as it has been redefined more recently as a typified social action that responds to a recurring situation—that is, "that people use genres to do things in the world (social action and purpose) and that these ways of acting become typified through occurring under what is perceived as recurring circumstances" (Devitt, 2000, p. 698). This perspective on genre was particularly important for the second assignment, which asked students to write about the problem they had selected and to address their writing to a specific audience using a text genre they felt would be most appropriate. The other requirement for this second assignment was for students to include a graphic component, such as a chart or graph, and a number of students created fliers and brochures that incorporated visual components.

In terms of audience, to complete the second assignment, some students chose students who were entering their field. Others chose policy makers or administrators in their particular discipline, urging them to take action on the problem—parents, teachers, and potential investors. Different possibilities were discussed, and students were asked to prepare for the assignment by responding to the following questions:

1. Who is your audience?
2. Why did you choose this audience?
3. What values does this audience think are most important? How will you use these values in persuading your audience to accept what you have to say?
4. What genre will you choose? Why? How does this genre differ from the academic essay you wrote for Assignment 1?
5. What is the purpose of your writing? What do you hope to accomplish by writing to this audience in this genre?
6. What visual materials will be useful for your purpose?

They were also asked to complete the following statement:

I am writing a (which genre?)_____ about (problem) _____ because I want to convince my audience that _____.

Identity and Values

The focus on rhetoric and genre also led to discussions of how genres affect the identity of the writer and the idea that when students write in a disciplinary context, they begin to take on a new identity and a corresponding set of values and behaviors. Thus when students completed the second assignment, it was important for them to view themselves not as generic students enrolled in a junior-level writing course, but rather as geographers, educators, and business majors.

Identity is a key term in rhetorical genre theory. Devitt, Reiff, and Bawarshi's book, *Scenes of Writing* (2004), began with a discussion of the concept of "role" and scene and of the importance of reading a scene appropriately. Defining *scene* as "a place in which communication happens among groups of people with some shared objectives" (p. 7), the book emphasized connections between writing, scene, and the assumption of a role. Extending this metaphor, writing assignments contain implicit directions that determine the constructed identity of the players and contain implicit assumptions about what constitutes an acceptable performance within a scene. As a performer, a student who is new to a field may not be able to interpret the scene as insightfully as an insider can and, understandably, will be unsure about how to identify with the role.

This was an underlying assumption in Bartholomae's much-anthologized essay, "Inventing the University" (1985), which referred to the importance of beginning college students having "to learn to speak our language, to speak as we do, to try on the peculiar ways of knowing, selecting, evaluating, reporting, concluding and arguing that define the discourse of the academic community" (p. 134). However, what was not discussed in that article is that in order to write within a particular genre, a student must assume a particular identity or role that to some extent, at least initially, may be quite different from the "identity" he or she believes is most authentic. In some instances, this new identity is a type of performance, perhaps an uncomfortable or unconvincing one at first. However, I maintain that when a writer "performs" an identity long enough, that identity then becomes so interwoven into one's habits and modes of thinking that it no longer seems like, and in fact no longer is, a role. As James Gee (1990) argued, disciplinary writing is not simply a matter of a particular form; it also encompasses a way of thinking, an attitude toward life, a set of values, beliefs, ideologies, and behaviors that can be viewed as a type of "identity kit" (p. 142). Bazerman (2002) similarly affirmed the interconnections between genre and identity, affecting who we become, a perspective similar to that of Richard Coe (1994), who noted that particular genres require writers and speakers not only to assume particular attitudes and values, but also to adopt particular rhetorical stances, to write or speak from particular subject positions.

The study of genre thus emphasizes that *identity*, whether we conceive of it in the context of a postmodern perspective or as some sort of psychological construct, is not a fixed, unalterable entity. Rather, it is an evolving role, constructed by genre, for which players must rehearse to enact an acceptable performance. The suitability of the "performance" is determined through an awareness of genre—and in the context of preparing students for their professional roles, particularly in classes oriented toward particular professions—recent understandings of genre provide the context for generating the appropriate role or identity that student writers must assume. The assumption of a role thus enables a novice to function with increasing competence within a community of practice.

These concepts of identity and role are intricately connected to the idea of values, which became the focus of a number of class discussions, and a fundamental question was, "Are the values of students majoring in geography similar to or different from those majoring in education and business?" Another question was, "How does the notion of ethics inform these values?" For example, one student, who was a business major, chose as his problem the issue of how to deal with the burgeoning prison population, his solution being to privatize prisons and run them as successful businesses. His initial draft of essay 2, which was addressed to a group of potential investors, focused solely on the monetary advantages of such a venture, a perspective that the geography and education students found abhorrent. "Shouldn't part of the argument focus on the possibility of improving the quality of prisons?" they wanted to know, a question that generated considerable discussion and led the business student to acknowledge that even in business, a writer should be aware of ethical issues and convey a concern with ethics in the identity constructed in the text. In writing about a problem, shouldn't business writers construct themselves as concerned human beings who care about their fellow human beings? Is a statement such as, "We all know that business is about making money and here is a good opportunity to do so" considered appropriate in the business world? One business student thought it was. "Let's be honest," he said. "Business is about making money." However, other business students and all the students in the other disciplines did not agree. Certainly, this was a question worth discussing.

The Third Assignment: The Grant Proposal

The grant proposal assignment enabled students to reexamine the "problem" they had been writing about in the previous two assignments and to consider ways of fostering awareness of this problem. Target audiences included other students (e.g., a poster contest intended for students about the problem of disposing of nuclear waste or a workshop on helping students understand the dangers of credit card debt) or parents in the community (e.g., a workshop on teaching parents strategies for monitoring their children's access to the Internet). To prepare students for writing the grant proposal, students responded to questions that incorporated the concepts of rhetoric, genre, identity, and values that had informed the previous assignments. Preparatory questions included the following:

1. What is the issue or need?
2. Can you suggest a project that will address this issue or need?
3. How will this project address this issue or need?
4. What questions might an opponent have about this project?
5. What audience are you writing for?
6. What are the values of that audience?
7. How can you use the values of that audience to convince your readers that your proposed project is worthwhile?
8. How is a grant proposal similar to and different from an academic argument?

The grant proposal generated considerable enthusiasm among the students, who felt they were learning something they might really be able to use in their professional lives. One young woman, whose "problem" was the illusion that social security would cover living expenses after retirement, said that she was planning to apply for a real grant to discuss retirement issues in a community organization to which she belonged.

Decreasing Writing Anxiety

The focus on rhetoric, genre, identity, and values constituted a direction for the class that I think is appropriate for linked classes or classes in which there are students from different disciplines. However, an additional and equally important goal of the class was to help students feel more comfortable about writing, and about the activities that enable writing to improve. To assess the extent to which this occurred, I distributed a survey gauging attitudes toward writing both at the beginning and the end of the semester. The survey included 26 questions, but the ones that are particularly relevant are those that addressed students' comfort level with writing.

Responses to the survey ranged from 1—*disagree strongly*, 2—*disagree*, 3—*agree somewhat*, 4—*agree*, and 5—*agree strongly*, and I was gratified to note that for the questions that addressed comfort with writing, a comparison between the responses at the beginning of the semester with those at the end suggests that more students felt comfortable at the end of the semester than they did at the beginning (see Appendix B). For example, on question 4, "I am fearful of writing when I know my work will be judged," at the beginning of the semester, fourteen out of twenty-three students agreed somewhat, agreed, or agreed strongly. However, at the end of the semester, only eight students out of eighteen agreed, suggesting that the fear level had gone down (or perhaps the really fearful students had dropped the course). For question 5, "Being enrolled in a writing class makes me frightened," at the beginning of the semester, fourteen students out of twenty-three agreed, whereas at the end, only five out of eighteen agreed.

For question 7, "I cannot think when I try to work on a writing assignment," fourteen out of twenty-three students agreed. But at the end, only seven out of eighteen agreed. For question 13, "I'm anxious about writing," fourteen out of twenty-three agreed, whereas at the end, only seven out of eighteen agreed. Finally, for question 20, "I enjoy sharing my work with others," fourteen out of twenty-three students agreed with this statement at the beginning of the semester, with nine disagreeing, whereas sixteen out of eighteen agreed with this statement at the end. I felt that this change was particularly important, because it suggests that the group work that characterized many of the classes was perceived as enjoyable by the students and perhaps constitutes a perspective that students might be able to use in other classes.

The focus on problematization constitutes an important direction for linked or paired courses, one that can be used to foster community-based learning. The focus on problematization for all three assignments and an underlying emphasis on rhetoric, genre, identity, values, and comfort helped students from three different disciplines gain insight into what was involved in learning to write and seemed to help them gain confidence in their writing ability. As one student wrote on a "thank you" card at the end of the semester, "When I first enrolled in this class, I was frightened to death. Now, I am so proud of myself. I know I have a long way to go. But now I know how to get there." This insight is a crucial factor in preparing students for academic success.

References

Bartholomae, D. (1985). Inventing the university. In M. Rose (Ed.), *When a writer can't write: Studies in writer's block and other composing-process problems*. New York: Guilford.

Bazerman, C. (2002). Genre and identity: Citizenship in the age of the Internet and the age of global capitalism. In R. Coe, L. Lingard, & T. Teslenko (Eds.), *The rhetoric and ideology of genre: Strategies for stability and change* (pp. 13–38). Cresskill, NJ: Hampton.

Beaufort, A. (2007). *College writing and beyond*. Logan, UT: Utah State University Press.

Bitzer, L. (1968). The rhetorical situation. *Philosophy & Rhetoric, 1*(1), 1–14.

Booth, W. C. (1974). *Modern dogma and the rhetoric of assent*. Chicago: University of Chicago Press.

Boylan, H. R. (2002). *What works: Research-based best practices in developmental education*. Boone, NC: Continuous Quality Improvement Network with the National Center for Developmental Education.

Coe, R. M. (1994). Teaching genre as process. In A. Freedman & P. Medway (Eds.), *Learning and teaching genre* (pp. 151–169).Portsmouth, NH: Boynton–Cook.

Devitt, A. J. (2000). Integrating rhetorical and literary theories of genre. *College English, 62*(6), 696–718.

Devitt, A. J., Reiff, M. J., & Bawarshi, A. (2004). *Scenes of writing: Strategies for composition with genres*. New York: Longman.

Downs, D., & Wardle, E. (2007). Teaching about writing, righting misconceptions: (Re)envisioning "first-year composition" as "introduction to writing studies." *College Composition and Communication 58*(4), 552–584.

Flower, L., & Hayes, J. R. (1980). The cognition of discovery: Defining a rhetorical problem. *College Composition and Communication, 31*(1), 21–43.

Gee, J. (1990). *Social linguistics and literacies: Ideology in discourses, critical perspectives on literacy and education*. New York: Routledge.

Graff, G. (2003). *Clueless in academe: How schooling obscures the life of the mind*. New Haven, CT: Yale University Press.

MacDonald, S. P. (1987). Problem definition in academic writing. *College English, 49*(3), 315–331.

Petraglia, J. (1995). *Reconceiving Writing, Rethinking Writing Instruction*. Hillsdale, NJ: Erlbaum.

Russell, D. R. (1995). Activity theory and its implications for writing instruction (pp. 51–78). In J. Petraglia (Ed), *Reconceiving writing, rethinking writing instruction*. Hillsdale, NJ: Erlbaum.

Thaiss, C., & Zawacki, T. M. (2006). *Engaged writers, dynamic disciplines*. Portsmouth, NH: Boynton–Cook.

Vatz, R. E. (1973). The myth of the rhetorical situation. *Philosophy & Rhetoric, 6*(3), 154–161.

Wardle, E. (2009). Mutt genres and the goal of FYC: Can we help students write the genres of the university? *College Composition and Communication, 60*(4), 765–789.

Assignment 1 (with implications for Assignment 2 and Assignment 3)

Assignment 1 is concerned with a problem, issue, question, or controversy that you will select for yourself within three subject areas: geography, education, or business, depending on your major or disciplinary focus. The problem you choose should be one in which you have a genuine interest, one that you feel is important and is sufficiently complex, so that it requires research and reflection. It should be a problem or issue that has generated significant controversy, perhaps one that is currently being debated. However, please do not choose an issue that is related to a religious belief.

As a way of engaging with your topic, please respond to the following questions:

1. What is the problem you plan to address?
2. Why is this topic important?
3. What do most people think about this topic?
4. What ethical controversies are associated with this topic?
5. What direction are you inclined to write about in addressing this topic?

Assignment 2

Assignment 1 required you to write a generic academic argument about a problem, question, or controversy in your field, and Assignment 2 builds on the research you did for that assignment. For this assignment, however, you will be addressing a specific audience, which you will choose yourself. For example, you might wish to refocus your essay toward an audience of students entering your field because you think this is an important issue for them to know about. Or you might wish to orient your writing toward an audience of policy makers or administrators in your field, urging them to take action on the issue you have chosen. As an educator, you might want to address teachers or parents. The choice of audience and purpose will, of course, have an effect on the genre you choose. For example, if you are writing to an administrator or policy maker, you may wish to refocus your essay as a report, rather than as an essay.

The other requirement for this assignment is to include a visual element—a chart, graph, or picture that contributes to your purpose and to which you refer in your essay or report.

Please come to class having answered these questions in writing (typed, and included in your journal):

1. Who is your audience?
2. Why did you choose this audience?
3. What values does this audience think are most important? How will you use these values in persuading your audience to accept what you have to say?
4. What genre will you choose? Why? How does this genre differ from the academic essay you wrote for Assignment 1?
5. What is the purpose of your writing? What do you hope to accomplish by writing to this audience in this genre?
6. What visual materials will be useful for your purpose?
7. Please fill in the following statement:

I am writing a (which genre?) _____ about (topic) _____ because I want to convince my audience that _____
_____.

Assignment 3

Welcome to GEBCO, Inc!

The third assignment in English 305 is to write a grant proposal for $10,000 to GEBCO, a giant, *fictional* publicly held corporation, with headquarters in Los Angeles and branch offices in several major U.S. cities. The specifics of the proposal are listed here.

About GEBCO:

GEBCO is concerned with fostering public awareness of ethical issues in the fields of geography, education, and business, and has sponsored a number of outreach and education programs concerned with these fields. GEBCO is interested in helping institutions of higher education improve the teaching of business, education, and geography and its emphasis is on fostering students' understanding of ethical issues associated with these fields, particularly those that have policy or curricular implications.

Obtaining a GEBCO Grant:

GEBCO grants of $10,000 are intended to support innovative projects in the fields of geography, education, and business that will be useful for undergraduate students. Priority will be given to projects that promote understanding of ethical issues associated with these fields. Other possibilities that interest the company are projects that utilize distance learning and the use of technology in fostering student learning.

Applying for a GEBCO Grant:

Please complete all sections of the proposal form. Proposals that are incomplete will not be considered.

Title of the Proposal _____

PROPOSAL NARRATIVE: (3 pages)

Definition of the issue or need

This section should explain the issue or need in terms of the goals of GEBCO.

Description of a project or curricular plan that will address this issue or need.

Explanation of how the proposed project or plan will address the issue or need.

Conclusion.

This section should sum up the proposal and reiterate its importance.

BUDGET

To Prepare for Writing Your Proposal:

Provisional Title:

Define the issue or need:

Suggest a project that will address this issue or need. How will this project address this issue or need?

What questions might an opponent have about this project?

What audience are you writing for?

What are the values of that audience?

How can you use the values of that audience to convince your readers that your proposed project is worthwhile?

How is a grant proposal similar to and different from an academic argument?

QUESTIONS CONCERNING COMFORT LEVEL

		Beginning		End	
Question		Disagree	Agree	Disagree	Agree
4	I am fearful of writing when I know my work will be judged.	9	14	10	8
5	Being enrolled in a writing class makes me frightened.	9	14	13	5
7	I cannot think when I try to work on a writing assignment.	9	14	11	7
13	I'm anxious about writing.	9	14	11	7
20	I enjoy sharing my work with others.	9	14	2	16

PART TWO

LINKED COURSE PROGRAMS

THE SCIENCE OF FIRST-YEAR
LEARNING COMMUNITIES

Brandi Kutil

T his chapter discusses the evolution of the learning communities program at Texas A&M University-Corpus Christi (TAMU-CC). This innovative and nationally recognized program serves the entire class of incoming first-year students and has been used as a model for other learning community programs in Texas and across the nation. After a brief historical background and an overview of the basic structure of the learning communities program, examples of successful learning community arrangements are provided. As part of this discussion, the first-year seminar course is fully detailed, as it is the one course that all learning communities have in common. The topics of integration, co-enrollment, and consistency are addressed in relation to one of our most established learning communities—the science learning community.

The discussion then shifts to faculty recruitment, training, and development. One of the most unique and challenging aspects of the learning communities program at TAMU-CC is its reliance on instructors at various levels: graduate teaching assistants (GTAs), adjuncts, and full-time instructors as well as associate, assistant, and full professors. To provide a quality experience for students, effective planning and cooperation between learning community team members are vital, and our efforts to promote successful teaching teams are outlined in detail.

The last section of the chapter focuses on program assessment. Over the past 17 years, the program has undergone various internal and external assessments to improve the quality of instruction and overall experience for first-year students. Whenever changes to the program are made, they have always been supported by a combination of serious reflection, student and instructor feedback, and assessment data. In this way, the learning communities program at TAMU-CC has evolved dramatically over the years, but always with the goal of constant improvement at the forefront of any decision.

Background

In 1994, the faculty of TAMU-CC set out a lofty ambition to enroll all incoming freshmen in a supportive learning community program. Prior to this time, TAMU-CC had served only upper-level undergraduate students and master's degree students. As the university set out to expand "downward," it was vital to create a learning environment specifically designed to help first-year students succeed. Learning communities were seen as an intervention to not only increase student success and retention, but also help establish a strong sense of identity among the first incoming class.

By the fall of 2010, TAMU-CC had a total enrollment of 10,000 students, including nearly 1,600 students in first-year learning communities. Despite the challenges of serving this rapidly expanding population on increasingly strained budgets, the faculty and administration remain committed to the mandatory participation of all full-time students in first-year learning communities. The First-Year Learning Communities Program (FYLCP) at TAMU-CC has evolved greatly over the past 17 years to adapt to changing student populations and economic climates, but it continues nonetheless to be committed to the success of all incoming first-year students.

Learning Community Structure

Learning communities at different universities vary greatly in the level of integration between linked courses. At TAMU-CC the learning communities emphasize interdisciplinary connections, but each course still maintains its discipline identity and primary content. The learning communities at TAMU-CC are built around an integrated core curriculum. Participation in a learning community requires co-enrollment in at least two linked courses, though it may include up to seven linked courses.

Many of the first-year students at TAMU-CC are enrolled in general education learning communities that include students of various majors.

Most co-enrollment sections include 25 students in a first-year seminar course and composition course linked to a large lecture core class (such as history, political science, or psychology) of 200 to 250 students. However, several discipline-specific learning communities have also been created to better meet the needs of certain majors.

For example, all education majors are enrolled into the same reserved sections of a history learning community. There are no education courses in the core curriculum, and students majoring in education would not usually take any courses specific to their major during their first two semesters. However, this co-enrollment allows faculty and advisors from the College of Education early access to their students. Although the first-year seminar leaders focus primarily on development of ideas related to a linked history lecture course, they also facilitate discussions of particular ideas as they relate to education and provide a forum for the education advisors to interact directly with their first-year students.

The most comprehensive, discipline-specific learning community is the science learning community that enrolls more than 300 biology, chemistry, and biomedical sciences majors into linked sections of biology, chemistry, composition, and first-year seminar, along with the required laboratory courses. Each section of twenty-four students (limited by lab space) is co-enrolled in first-year seminar, biology lab, chemistry lab, and usually a composition class. Multiple sections of twenty-four students are combined into each biology and chemistry large lecture course. Some sections linked to individual math courses including algebra, pre-calculus, or calculus, and of course sections without the composition course are offered for students who have previously earned college-level composition credits.

This conglomeration of course offerings requires very careful scheduling and flexibility during course registration, but allows each student to choose the learning community that best suits his or her needs. Because enrollment in learning communities is mandatory, and the science learning communities have established a good reputation for helping students to be more successful in the rigorous courses required during their first year, recruitment is not an issue. In fact, the support available that learning communities provide is used as a recruitment tool for the university.

One of the most successful learning communities at TAMU-CC has been the honors science learning community. This learning community is offered to a maximum of twenty-four honors science students during the spring of their freshmen year. All students must be enrolled in the linked first-year seminar course as well as biology II, chemistry II, and both labs.

Students who need composition are placed in a linked composition course as well. The learning community follows the same basic structure as the non-honors science learning communities; however, in the honors learning community, students have the opportunity to design, conduct, and present original research projects. Students are encouraged to self-select groups based on shared research interests. Through first-year seminar and composition they conduct background research to produce a written research proposal, including an experimental design, budget (usually less than $100), justification of research questions, and a timeline that will allow them to present their findings in approximately six weeks. The lab instructors assist in conducting the actual experiment while the large lecture professors and other faculty serve as mentors throughout the research process. The assignment rubric created by Frances Johnson is included as an appendix at the end of this chapter for reference.

First-Year Seminar

The first-year seminar is mandatory for all learning communities and fosters the interdisciplinary connections between the other linked courses. The primary focus of the first-year seminar is to help students to succeed in their other courses and throughout their collegiate experience. Utilizing mostly discussion and student-centered active learning formats, the first-year seminar uses content from the other courses to help students develop the critical thinking and study skills necessary for success.

The following syllabus excerpts are taken from a first-year seminar course in the science learning communities. They help establish the framework for integration that enables integrated assignments to successfully meet the program goals. The course description establishes the purpose for the course and conveys what will be expected from the students.

Course Description

First-year seminar is a discovery of the skills necessary for your success as a university student in science and technology and as a future professional. Acquisition of these skills is integrated into an exploration of the concepts encountered in your large lecture courses, BIOL 1406, CHEM 1311, and in ENGL 1301 composition course. First-year seminar is a one-credit-hour discussion course in which you learn to communicate verbally and work collaboratively on complex science topics and relate them to your role as a developing scientist.

Course Objectives and Learning Outcomes

The following are the primary objectives of the first-year seminar for students.

- Explore the interconnections among the Triad/Tetrad courses.
- Develop critical thinking skills *and* significant learning.
- Clarify personal values, goals, and strengths.
- Develop the ability to learn through study, discussion, writing, cooperation, and collaboration.

The first-year seminar has two learning outcomes.

- Students will apply interdisciplinary knowledge to address and analyze real-world issues.
- Students will interpret and evaluate various research materials and perspectives.

The course objectives and learning outcomes are consistent across all first-year seminar courses at the University. They are established by the administration of the FYLCP with extensive contribution and feedback from the instructors teaching the first-year seminar courses.

Because first-year seminar does not have a standard curriculum, each instructor is charged with ensuring that every class meeting is working toward one or more of the course objectives. These course objectives provide guidance for instructors and consistency across the program. Although the content in each first-year seminar course may vary greatly, all students should achieve the same objectives and learning outcomes. Although the learning outcomes do not necessarily represent each of the specific course objectives, they were designed to be measurable and applicable across disciplines while still encompassing the objectives in general.

Integrating Learning Outcomes

In addition to the program-wide objectives and learning outcomes, the instructors within each learning community work together to establish a common set of learning outcomes that apply to many (if not all) of the courses in that learning community. These learning outcomes are listed separately on the syllabus for each course in that learning community. Individual course instructors may choose to leave out any specific outcomes that do not apply specifically to their course, but most find that including the list in its entirety helps students to understand how the courses complement each other. For instance, specific learning outcomes of the science learning community are as follows:

- Take personal responsibility and become a self-directed college learner.
- Effectively read and comprehend scientific articles, reports, and books.
- Evaluate the scientific accuracy of claims made in literature relating to science.
- Apply scientific principles to make decisions.
- Understand the scientific method.
- Understand the assumptions and limitations of science.
- Collaborate effectively as both an effective leader and follower.
- Communicate on controversial topics related to science.
- Relate science to other ways of knowing.
- Understand the nature of scientific research.
- Apply concepts of biology and chemistry to new situations.
- Understand the role and purpose of different forms of science literature.
- Effectively use library research tools to research on science topics.
- Communicate about science topics verbally, in writing, and via multimedia presentation.
- Understand and apply the conventions of science discourse.
- Get along with others.
- Develop awareness of one's present and future role in the science community.
- Understand the role of science in greater sociopolitical world context.
- Understand the role of mathematics in science.
- Be able to use mathematics such as graphs and basic statistics to support scientific hypotheses.
- Develop interpersonal communication skills.
- Use online learning technology effectively.
- Be successful.

The FYLCP provides students with the framework to achieve these critical goals by combining the science gateway courses of biology and chemistry with the introductory composition writing course and first-year seminar discussion course in an integrated first-year experience. Of course, although these learning outcomes are specific to a small subset of the TAMU-CC learning communities, they are representative of the types of learning outcomes that occur in all of the learning communities. Individual assignments vary based on the goals of each instructor, but the shared learning outcomes provide more opportunities for connections across courses. They also help students to recognize the positive effects made by the learning community, particularly when working in more abstract areas are not directly related to content knowledge. Students need to know that their time is valued. For the most part, any assignment perceived as busy-work will be given less effort and result in increased student dissatisfaction. One of the most effective ways to help students understand the importance of a particular assignment is to reference specific learning outcomes or objectives in the assignment description.

Integration Across Disciplines

The first-year seminar is not solely responsible for integration in the learning community. The instructor for each linked course is expected to integrate concepts with the other linked courses whenever possible. This is facilitated via multiple meetings prior to the start of each semester and weekly or biweekly meetings throughout the semester. The team of instructors for all linked courses establishes a set of common objectives and learning outcomes as well as a theme for the semester. For example, a triad including political science, composition, and first-year seminar during the fall 2010 semester chose a theme of water because our university is on an island and many students are interested in the health of the Gulf of Mexico in light of the recent BP oil spill. The content in each course was largely unchanged, but assigned readings dealt with various political issues related to water pollution, coastal management, and water rights, and students were encouraged to research related topics in first-year seminar and write about these in composition.

Composition instructors are also encouraged to allow students to write about topics related to the large lecture material. For example, students enrolled in the science learning community, which links biology, chemistry, composition, and first-year seminar, generally prefer to research and write about scientific topics. These topics may be outside the comfort zone for some writing professors; therefore, first-year seminar instructors (FYSIs) who have strong science backgrounds are expected to collaborate with the composition instructors to help students develop scientific content. The composition course also assists students with writing assignments for other courses, such as biology lab reports. At the same time, the professors of large biology and chemistry lectures occasionally emphasize the importance of specific composition assignments (such as a formal poster presentation) in their own disciplines. These types of interdisciplinary connections are particularly effective at helping students to transfer knowledge between courses and create significant learning experiences.

The science learning communities were not intentionally designed to be major-specific, but because few nonscience majors would choose to take both biology and chemistry during their first semester, almost all students enrolled are science majors. Initially, these learning communities were treated much like the other learning communities but because few of the adjuncts had any significant science background, they were unable to support the biology and chemistry content even after attending both large lectures. The first-year seminar was linked with composition, but the students reported that it was disconnected from the science lectures and these learning communities were widely unpopular. In 2005, the first full-time FYSIs were hired specifically to teach in the science learning communities. These instructors had advanced science degrees and extensive experience in their disciplines. For the first time, these instructors were dedicated to communicating effectively with both the science professors and the composition instructors and revamped first-year seminar into a discipline-specific course tailored to meet the needs of freshmen science majors. In this first-year seminar course, student-led facilitations and exam reviews reinforce major concepts from biology and chemistry, and particular emphasis is placed on application of content knowledge to real-world situations. The first-year seminar leaders also work closely with composition instructors to ensure that students develop the research and writing skills they will need throughout their science courses. Throughout the semester, the students conduct a collaborative research project that integrates knowledge from all of the learning community courses and results in a grade in each of their classes. With the theme of helping students to develop their science identity, the science learning communities have seen dramatic increases in student and faculty satisfaction and have become a model for developing other discipline-specific learning communities within the program.

Although considerable time and energy is spent integrating material, it should be noted that each course maintains its distinct identity. Most assignments in each course are independent of all other learning community courses. For example, the large biology and chemistry lecture courses linked to the learning communities are nearly identical to the unlinked courses taught by the same professors. One major difference is the integrated assignment, which counts for approximately 10 percent of the final grade in each of the courses linked in the learning community.

Co-Enrollment

In the science learning communities, we have found that students are more successful, both socially and academically, when they are co-enrolled with peers taking as many of the same courses as possible. Co-enrollment facilitates the formation of study groups and tends to result in increased success in each linked course. Students with "broken" links—for example, a different composition course because of scheduling requirements—have lower success rates in the unlinked course.

Consistency Among Instructors

One of the factors that has helped the science learning communities to be successful is longevity. Without the rapid turnover of graduate teaching assistants (GTAs) and adjuncts, the instructors are able to build on the successes of previous semesters. Because all instructors are familiar with each other's courses, it is much easier to integrate content and create new exercises that fit well into the existing learning community framework. Of course, longevity of instructors is not always a factor that can be controlled. As new instructors are brought into established learning communities, the expectation that they will initially follow the guidance of experienced instructors has helped to improve the overall consistency of student experiences. New ideas are welcomed, but expecting that initially they will be worked into the existing framework reduces the potential for inconsistency.

Faculty Recruitment and Training

First-Year Seminar Instructors

Recruitment for GTAs and Adjuncts

The FYLCP hires new GTAs and adjuncts annually for the upcoming academic year during the months of March and April. An application is posted on the FYLCP website and sent out to graduate program coordinators all over campus to distribute to students who meet the credit hour (at least 18 hours of graduate-level course in the lecture discipline) and grade point average (GPS—here 3.0) requirements. Applicants must have completed a master-level degree to be considered for adjunct positions. Applicants are asked to submit a brief information form as well as a statement of purpose, transcripts from all undergraduate and graduate work, and recommendation forms that attest to the applicant's abilities to communicate and collaborate effectively. The applications are read by the FYLCP director and first-year seminar coordinator and ranked accordingly. All applicants who meet the minimum requirements are interviewed by a panel that may include the FYLCP director, first-year seminar coordinator, first-year writing program coordinator, large lecture faculty, and current FYSIs. Successful interviews lead to job offers for the upcoming academic year.

Recruitment for Full-Time Seminar Instructors

The FYLCP has made a concerted effort to increase the number of full-time instructors teaching for the program over the past six years. In 2005, two full-time instructors were hired to teach first-year seminar in the science learning communities. In 2009, four additional full-time instructor positions were created to teach first-year seminar in the liberal arts learning communities. Most recently, a new full-time instructor position was filled in May 2011 to begin teaching in the 2011–2012 academic year, resulting in at least one full-time instructor in each learning community; roughly two thirds of all first-year seminar classes are taught by professional instructors.

To recruit for full-time instructor positions, job advertisements are posted to the campus human resources page, as well as in local newspapers and on appropriate listservs. Applicants for full-time FYSI positions submit curricula vitae, transcripts, letters of reference, and an educational philosophy statement. For each hiring cycle, a search committee is created. This committee includes the FYLCP director, the first-year seminar coordinator, the first-year writing program coordinator, and at least two large lecture faculty members. The committee meets to review and rank the applicants. Phone interviews may precede face-to-face interviews when there are a large number of quality applications. The face-to-face interview includes a session with the search committee, as well as a session open to the campus community to meet with the applicant. The search committee follows campus hiring protocol for making job offers to the most highly qualified candidates.

First-Year Seminar Instructor Training

All incoming FYSIs (GTAs, adjuncts, and full-time instructors) are required to attend a training workshop during the summer leading up to the academic year for which they were hired. This training workshop is led by the first-year seminar coordinator and consists of twenty-four hours, divided between either eight days (three hours a day) or four days (six hours a day), depending on the schedule for the workshop participants. The first-year seminar coordinator collaborates with the newly hired FYSIs to determine the workshop schedule that will work best for everyone involved. The incoming FYSIs are not paid for this training, but participation in the workshop is a condition of employment outlined in the job offer letter.

The workshop is specifically designed to train incoming instructors to teach first-year seminar in the FYLCP. As part of this workshop, incoming instructors learn about the FYLCP and the role of the first-year seminar course and instructor. New instructors examine the theory behind the course (significant and active learning, critical thinking) and discuss the use of learning portfolios, a major form of assessment in the program. Participants also analyze the characteristics of good discussion; explore the vital relationship between various learning community members; discuss, create, and implement lesson plans; and set up a personal wiki page on which to post course information. The workshop is modeled after the types of activities and lesson designs that are directly applicable to the first-year seminar classroom.

The workshop uses McGlynn's *Successful Beginnings for College Teaching* (2001) as a framework, focusing in order on semester planning, first-day activities and icebreakers, creating a welcoming environment for students, encouraging participation in class discussions, managing the classroom, and maintaining momentum all the way through the mid-semester "blahs" to the end. Bean's *Engaging Ideas* (2001) and Brookfield and Preskill's *Discussion as a Way of Teaching* (2005) are used as supplements to these discussions, because both include theoretical foundations for writing, discussion, and collaboration as well as practical suggestions for how to implement these strategies in the classroom. Most recently, the training literature has grown to include excerpts from Conley's *Redefining College Readiness* (2007) and Dweck's *Self-Theories* (2000) to address issues that incoming freshmen face today. In addition, significant time in the workshop is focused on understanding the Millennial generation, so participants are asked to read and discuss reports like *Millennials Go to College* (Eubanks, 2003).

In addition to the content of the training, a major goal of the workshop is to demonstrate practical strategies for implementation in the classroom. Thus participants are asked to engage in the types of writing, group work, critical thinking activities, and discussion that they themselves can turn around and use with their students in the upcoming year. As much as possible, this training is meant to simulate for new instructors how to conduct a successful first-year seminar class. In fact, the final assignment for the new

FYSIs in the workshop is to create and then implement a 20–25 minute lesson plan using the other new instructors as their proxy students.

Composition Instructors

Recruiting Graduate Teaching Assistants

Current English graduate students apply to teach first-year composition (ENGL 1301 and 1302) during the spring semester for the upcoming academic year. Minimum qualifications to teach in the first-year writing program include an overall GPA of 3.5 in eighteen graduate hours of English coursework that includes such courses as Bibliography and Research, Composition Theory and Pedagogy, and at least one elective in Rhetoric and Composition. The English graduate faculty read all of the applications and offer positions to qualified candidates for the upcoming academic year.

Composition Practicum

All incoming GTAs must complete ENGL 5392, Practicum for Composition Instructors, which is offered during a 5-week summer semester every year and taught by the first-year writing program coordinator. Successful completion of this course is a requirement for employment in the upcoming academic year.

The practicum continues the work that GTAs have done in their composition theory and pedagogy coursework as graduate students. The goal is to prepare new GTAs for their multifaceted role in the first-year writing program, as a teacher in a particular learning community, and as a teacher of writing at the college level. The texts that inform the coursework include Lindemann's *A Rhetoric for Writing Teachers* (1995) and Beaufort's *College Writing and Beyond* (2007). Much of the focus of the practicum is on the study of writing as process and the study of academic writing as a form of discourse. A considerable amount of time in the course is also devoted to discussions about multilingual learners, as well as the various literacies of incoming college students. In addition, the final week of the semester focuses on the evaluation and assessment of student writing using portfolios.

Because many of the composition practicum topics overlap with those in the first-year seminar training workshop, the first-year writing program coordinator and first-year seminar coordinator are sometimes able to combine the groups for shared discussions about millennials, portfolio evaluation, and international students. In the past, the schedule for these workshops has also allowed for various team-building activities like luncheons or icebreaker sessions between the two new groups of instructors.

Adjuncts and Full-Time Composition Instructors

The FYLCP is committed to supporting the English graduate program at TAMU-CC by training and hiring GTAs to teach the ENGL 1301 and 1302 courses. However, there are several adjuncts who teach in the FYLCP, many of whom are recent graduates of the English program. Most of these adjuncts are nontransitory and teach in the same learning communities from year to year. Some adjuncts, though, are hired from outside the university to fill in teachings positions as needed.

The English department has also hired three full-time composition instructors recently. These instructors are all graduates from the English MA program at TAMU-CC and have taught for many years in the program as adjuncts. Whether hiring composition instructors over adjuncts is effective remains an empirical question; anecdotal evidence appears to indicate that full time composition instructors increase consistency within the program and serve as an invaluable resource for the incoming class of new GTAs each year.

Large Lecture Faculty

All of the large lecture faculty members who teach in the FYLCP are experts holding terminal degrees in their respective fields. Each semester, department chairs for each course decide who will teach in the FYLCP during the upcoming semester. This decision is based on past records of success and the department chairs' executive decisions about who would work best in a collaborative teaching environment.

The incentive to teach a large lecture class within a learning community has typically been release time of one course for the semester to allow time to meet and plan with learning community team members. However, because of budget constraints, this has not always been possible. Most large lecture faculty members who have taught in the learning community once are eager to teach in one again. They speak to the nonremunerative benefits involved in team teaching that include more student interaction, an increased opportunity for the implementation of new teaching strategies with subsequent feedback, and the availability of a support system for handling student issues.

Large lecture faculty members who have never taught in a learning community before are required to complete a half-day workshop aptly entitled *Learning Community 101*. This training is led by the director of the FYLCP and begins with an introduction to the program as a whole, specifically focusing on the role of each course within the learning community.

In addition to a discussion of the theoretical foundations and known benefits of learning communities, large lecture faculty members learn what is expected of them as team members. First, all large lecture faculty are required to relate assignments and activities to course content to make an integrated learning community. In other words, the faculty member needs to create connections across the courses in the learning community. Second, faculty members must ensure that their learning communities have at least one integrated experience that integrates material from all of the courses and counts for credit in all of the courses. Finally, large lecture faculty members must provide opportunities for active learning in the large lecture course. Fortunately, many of the faculty members who teach large lecture in the FYLCP are already well aware of the pedagogy on active learning and have already adapted their teaching styles to meet student needs.

Faculty Development

Over the past few years, the first-year writing program coordinator and first-year seminar coordinator have made an effort to increase the number of faculty development opportunities for instructors in the FYLCP. During the past year, the programs offered combined professional development sessions on building partnerships with the library and on academic dishonesty. The most ambitious faculty development venture was a workshop in May 2011 bringing together all instructors who teach first-year students. At this faculty development day, Dr. Steve Seidel, a TAMU-CC psychology professor and learning community faculty member, spoke on the psychology of student failure. Breakout sessions were arranged for large lecture faculty, FYSIs, and composition instructors to meet about various topics specific to their respective roles within the learning communities.

Best Practices Workshop

The first-year writing program coordinator and first-year seminar coordinator hold a workshop the day before classes begin called *Best Practices.* All instructors, adjuncts, and GTAs teaching first-year seminar or composition in the FYLCP are required to attend, and often this is the only point in the semester when all of the instructors are in the same room. Best Practices often begins with announcements and reminders for the upcoming semester, but then transitions into faculty development sessions for the instructors. Sometimes the groups are kept together for shared discussions; other times, the first-year seminar and composition instructors break out into different groups to share successful strategies and provide advice to the incoming instructors. Even returning instructors appreciate the opportunity to share successful lesson plans, which they often choose to adapt for their own learning communities.

Faculty Development Committee

In fall 2010, four of the full-time FYSIs created the FYLCP Faculty Development Committee. Members of the Faculty Development Committee worked with incoming seminar GTAs and adjuncts individually to conduct formative evaluations of their teaching. The Faculty Development Committee also arranged a mid-semester Best Practices session in the fall, another session in the spring to discuss the creation of an expectations document for FYSIs, and out-of-office gatherings to encourage team building within the learning communities and across the program as a whole. This committee has been particularly effective because their ideas are generated by the instructors themselves and when issues are identified, solutions have been implemented in a timely manner.

Learning Community Planning

The learning communities are determined each semester based on which large lecture faculty members have been selected to teach for the program by their department chairs. After the faculty decisions are made, the courses are built and scheduled. Although it is usually not possible at that point to determine all of the first-year seminar and composition teaching assignments, mostly because of the often unpredictable numbers of incoming and returning GTAs and adjuncts, the first-year seminar coordinator and first-year writing program coordinator typically try to assign at least one full-time seminar instructor and one full-time (or returning adjunct) composition instructor to each learning community to begin planning with the large lecture faculty member for the upcoming semester. This usually happens in late November for the fall and late April for the spring.

Planning Retreats

Prior to each semester, the instructors for each learning community meet for planning retreats and the director, first-year writing program coordinator, and first-year seminar coordinator lead the teams through a series of activities based on a heuristic developed by Gillies Malnarich and Emily Lardner (2003) of the Washington Center for Improving the Quality of Undergraduate Education at Evergreen State College. The goal of the planning retreat is to help each team determine the theme or focus for the learning community. These themes may stem from a current event (such as a presidential election or the BP oil spill) or may be entirely discipline-specific (developing a science identity), but they are always a result of a collaboration between the large lecture, first-year seminar, and composition faculty members. These retreats are also the first opportunity that the instructors have to begin working out a schedule for assignments and exams within the learning community.

Because many of the large lecture faculty return to teach in the program each year, often with at least one returning composition and FYSI, the planning retreats also provide the opportunity to reflect on the previous iteration of the learning community. This reflection allows the team to discuss the successes and struggles of past semesters and informs the creation or modification of assignments and activities to better help students achieve the goals of the learning community.

Making teaching assignments for composition and FYSIs in each learning community is a task that takes considerable time and collaboration. Once the learning community schedule is created, composition and FYSIs complete teaching request forms that identify desired learning communities and teaching hours. The first-year writing program coordinator and first-year seminar coordinator meet to determine teaching partners, making every effort possible to create partnerships that will be successful. Often, this situation is not unlike an "arranged marriage" because many of the instructors are new GTAs or adjuncts and their ability to work in a collaborative teaching team is yet unknown.

Once the teams are set—which usually is not until late July for the fall semester and late December for the spring—large lecture faculty members are asked to arrange at least one follow-up meeting for their teams in the weeks leading up to the first class day. This meeting hopefully includes all of the first-year seminar and composition instructors who have been assigned to teach in the learning community. At this meeting, the results of the planning retreat are shared and often adjusted, and decisions about due dates and other learning community policies are made. Teams also must decide on a time to meet regularly during the course of the semester.

Continued communication among all instructors of a learning community is a key component to satisfaction among students and instructors. Without ample communication, the learning community becomes disjointed, resulting in a frustrating experience for everyone involved. Instructor teams for each learning community are expected to meet in person at least once every two weeks, and new instructors are encouraged to meet with their more experienced counterparts at least weekly. Instructors share lesson plans and discuss areas of concern. This helps to identify possible areas for connecting content knowledge between courses in a timely manner throughout the semester. It also helps to form a safety net for students who may be experiencing difficulties in one or more classes.

Program Evolution and Assessment

Evolution of First-Year Seminar

Perhaps the aspect of the FYLCP that has evolved the most over the past seventeen years has been the first-year seminar course. In 1994, when the FYLCP began, the first-year seminar course was linked to large lectures and composition, but the content of the course was not integrated in any way. First-year seminar was strictly a study skills and career exploration class that even included a 12-hour community service requirement. All seminar students had to complete a learning log each week to track their academic progress and all sections of first-year seminar used the same textbook.

In 1997, first-year seminar saw a bit of a change when FYSIs started attending the large lecture course. First-year seminar was transformed into a course that was half about the large lecture content and half about study skills and career exploration. FYSIs in the liberal arts learning communities were also hired as graders for the large lecture courses, making the linkage between first-year seminar and lecture even more deliberate. The course was transformed yet again when new leadership joined the program in 2000. Their first step was to eliminate the shared textbook, eliminating the need for first-year seminar courses to cover a mandatory, independent content. Because of their efforts, first-year seminar was made into much of what it is today: a discussion-based course centered on the content of large lecture and making connections with composition.

Since 2000, the first-year seminar course has continued to evolve into the focal point of a deeply integrated learning community experience. FYSIs are charged with helping their students make connections between the other courses in the learning community as well as coaching students with academic skills like reading and note taking. Because the needs of each learning community are different, there is not a standard curriculum for the first-year seminar course. This flexibility allows our instructors to offer support as needed to the students, but always in the context of the other courses within the learning community.

Assessment

In the first decade after its inception, the FYLCP relied mostly on student course evaluations and teacher feedback for assessment purposes. Internal reports indicated that the learning communities were effective in the formulation of student communities and that they led to increased student-faculty interaction. Sterba-Boatwright (2000) conducted a study of the program from 1997–1999 and found that freshmen who took history and political science courses within a learning community out-performed freshmen who took nonlearning community sections of the same courses.

As the FYLCP evolved, so did its aptitude for assessment. Araiza (2006) conducted the first qualitative study of the program by meeting with focus groups of students who had just completed their first year at TAMU-CC. The results from this study revealed two weaknesses of the program: a perceived lack of integration between the classes and inconsistent experiences between courses taught by different FYSIs. The FYLCP set out to address these concerns almost immediately.

Increasing Integration

First, to address the perceived lack of integration, the FYLCP sought out the expert guidance of Malnarich and Lardner from the Washington Center for Improving the Quality of Undergraduate Education. Malnarich and Lardner's (2003) heuristic for the development of integrated courses led to the implementation of integrated assignments as not only a tool for making connections between the disciplines, but also a means for program assessment.

Since 2008, every learning community in the FYLCP has implemented at least one integrated assignment constructed so that success on this assignment indicates successful mastery of the program goals and learning outcomes. The results from these integrated assignments have been used as a direct measure of student learning for program-wide assessment (Huerta & Sperry, 2010). The success rates of this intervention across the program for the 2008–2009 and 2009–2010 academic years can be found in Table 5.1.

Although student success on the integrated assignment appears to decrease over this period, we believe that this is most likely because of increased expectations for integrative work within the learning communities. Each learning community is responsible for defining what "success" on the integrated assignment means for their students. As teams gain expertise in facilitating and evaluating integrative work, they have acknowledged raising

TABLE 5.1
Integrated Assignment Aggregate Data, 2008–2010

Semester	Students Successful	Students Not Successful	Success Rate
Fall 2008	1040	157	86.9%
Spring 2009	870	160	84.5%
Fall 2009	1099	223	83.1%
Spring 2010	809	262	75.5%

the standards for students to demonstrate mastery of program goals. In fall 2008, for example, many learning community teams set their standard for "success" rather low but decided to raise the standard substantially in fall 2009 and even higher during spring 2010.

Most recently, FYLCP administrators explored the relationship between the successful completion of integrated assignments within the learning communities and first-semester GPA. The findings indicated that the successful completion of an integrated assignment shared a significant positive relationship with first-semester GPA, contributing to 7.9 percent of the explained variance when controlling for high school performance, standardized test scores, ethnicity, and parent education levels. In fact, successfully completing the integrated assignment was shown to contribute 0.72 points to first-semester GPA. This study generates significant implications for our program and its commitment to integration. Further investigation will be necessary to determine the underlying motivations and student-teacher interactions that affect integrative assignment success.

Increasing Consistency

The second concern for the FYLCP outlined in Araiza's (2006) study was the noticeable discrepancy between student experiences based on the FYSI. When the FYLCP was established in 1994, the vision included faculty in each discipline serving as first-year seminar leaders, but this quickly became impractical. After years of graduate students serving as first-year seminar leaders, program reviews and student evaluations consistently linked ineffectual learning communities to inexperienced first-year seminar leaders. In fact, Hartlaub and Jozwiak (2010b) analyzed student evaluation data and found that all three full-time FYSIs at the time ranked higher than their nonprofessional (GTA and adjunct) counterparts on student satisfaction survey responses, most noticeably in their ability to clearly present material.

Also, first-year students were more likely to recommend full-time instructors to other students. Student responses also indicated that students would prefer more experienced instructors who could "handle the students" (p. 32).

Courses taught by professional FYSIs also have significantly higher student success rates compared with first-year seminar courses taught by GTAs and adjuncts, with half as many students earning a D or F or withdrawing (14.2 percent versus 28.7 percent) in their classes (Hartlaub & Jozwiak, 2010a). In fall 2009, in part because of the work of Hartlaub and Jozwiak, four additional full-time instructors were hired to teach the first-year seminar in the liberal arts learning communities, significantly decreasing the program's reliance on GTAs and adjuncts to teach this seminar. Most learning communities now include at least one full-time instructor with a master's or doctoral degree in the large lecture discipline as the lead FYSI for that learning community. GTAs and adjuncts are assigned to teach the remaining sections in each learning community under the guidance of the full-time FYSI. In addition to having successfully completed at least eighteen hours of graduate level coursework in the discipline they will be teaching, all new instructors, adjuncts, and GTAs are also expected to complete an extensive training program during the summer prior to their first semester teaching.

The FYLCP has also conducted internal assessment through the use of an online survey for the past five years. All learning community instructors encourage students to take the survey, but participation is voluntary. This survey asks students about their satisfaction and experience in first-year seminar, composition, and large lecture as well as the FYLCP as a whole. The survey prompts were originally based on best practices for successful learning communities (Taylor, Moore, MacGregor, & Lindblad, 2003) and now address additional factors shown by Kuh (2008) and Conley (2007) to improve engagement and increase student success in college. The results from the Fall 2010 FYLCP Survey can be found in Tables 5.2 and 5.3.

Overall, these results indicate that students believe their learning communities have positively affected their first-year experience and helped them to make successful academic and social transitions. Results can also be divided among different learning communities, which have proven to be an effective mechanisms for collecting feedback and continuous improvement of learning community practice.

Conclusion

The FYLCP at TAMU-CC has evolved considerably since its inception in 1994. Although the program's structure has remained relatively constant over

TABLE 5.2
First-Year Learning Communities Program Survey:
Fall 2010 Student Satisfaction

n = 596	*Very Dissatisfied*	*Dissatisfied*	*Satisfied*	*Very Satisfied*
Large lecture course(s)	2.1%	8.7%	59.9%	29.3%
First-year seminar class	4.6%	6.9%	45.4%	43.1%
English composition class	3.1%	10.2%	47.2%	39.5%
Entire FYLCP	1.9%	7.6%	52.5%	38.2%

TABLE 5.3
First-Year Learning Communities Program Survey:
Fall 2010 FYLCP Experiences

n = 596	*Strongly Agree or Agree*
The FYLCP helped me succeed in my first year of college.	76.1%
The FYLCP improved my writing skills.	76.9%
Because of the FYLCP, I am able to integrate knowledge and skills. . . .	80.7%
The FYLCP improved my critical thinking skills.	80.8%
The FYLCP helped me succeed in my triad/tetrad courses.	81.9%
Because of the FYLCP, I developed the academic skills to succeed in college.	82.5%
The FYLCP helped me make new friends.	85.4%
Because of the FYLCP, I recognized that . . . we have different viewpoints about issues facing our society.	86.4%

the years, the increased connections between the learning community courses have created a more integrated experience for first-year students. Nowhere is this integration more apparent than in the science learning community, a coordinated set of courses that introduces first-year science majors to the realities of working in the sciences. When assessment data indicated a need for the professionalization of the first-year seminar, full-time instructors were hired to bring consistency and expertise to the program. Student satisfaction surveys indicate that students are benefitting from participating in the learning communities, and recent research supports the program's commitment to integrated work. The FYLCP at TAMU-CC has consistently made empirically-based decisions when making changes to the program, thus demonstrating that learning community work is not just an art, but a science as well.

References

Araiza, I. (2006). An assessment of the First-Year Learning Community Program: A report on three focus groups with Texas A&M University–Corpus Christi students enrolled in the First-Year Learning Communities Program. Unpublished manuscript, First-Year Experience Council, Texas A&M University–Corpus Christi, Corpus Christi, TX.

Bean, J. C. (2001). *Engaging ideas: The professor's guide to integrating writing, critical thinking, and active learning in the classroom.* San Francisco, CA: Jossey-Bass.

Beaufort, A. (2007). *College writing and beyond.* Logan, UT: Utah State University Press.

Brookfield, S. D., & Preskill, S. (2005). *Discussion as a way of teaching: Tools and techniques for democratic classrooms* (2nd ed.). San Francisco, CA: Jossey-Bass.

Conley, D. T. (2007). *Redefining college readiness.* Eugene, OR: Educational Policy Improvement Center.

Dweck, C. S. (2000). *Self-theories: Their role in motivation, personality, and development.* Philadelphia, PA: Psychology Press.

Eubanks, S. (2003). *Millennials go to college* (Executive summary). Retrieved from http://eubie.com/millennials.pdf

Hartlaub, M. G., & Jozwiak, J. (2010a, November). *Seminar leaders: Professionalization and student performance.* Presented at the 15th Annual National Learning Communities Conference, Bay City, MI.

Hartlaub, M. G., & Jozwiak, J. (2010b). Strengthening the lynchpins: The professionalization of Texas A&M University Corpus Christi's First-Year Seminar leaders. *Journal of Learning Community Research, 5*(1), 25–38.

Huerta, J. C., & Sperry, R. A. (2010). Pulling it together: Using integrative assignments as empirical direct measures of student learning for learning community program assessment. *Journal of Learning Communities Research, 5*(1), 85–92.

Kuh, G. (2008). *High-impact educational practices: What they are, who has access to them, and why they matter.* Washington, DC: Association of American Colleges and Universities.

Lindemann, E. (1995). *A rhetoric for writing teachers* (4th ed.). New York: Oxford University Press.

Malnarich, G., & Lardner, E. D. (2003). Designing integrated learning for students: A heuristic for teaching, assessment, and curriculum design. Olympia, WA: Washington Center for Improving the Quality of Undergraduate Education.

McGlynn, A. P. (2001). *Successful beginnings for college teaching: Engaging your students from the first day.* Madison, WI: Atwood Publishing.

Sterba-Boatwright, B. (2000). The effects of mandatory freshman learning communities: A statistical report. *Assessment Update, 12*(2), 4–5.

Taylor, K., Moore, W. S., MacGregor, J., & Lindblad, J. (2003). *Learning community research and assessment: What we know now.* National Learning Communities Project Monograph Series. Olympia, WA: The Evergreen State College, Washington Center for Improving the Quality of Undergraduate Education, in cooperation with the American Association for Higher Education.

APPENDIX

Section Number: _____ / Research Topic:

Presenters:

Category	5-Excellent	4-Good	3-Fair	2-Poor	1-Grim	0-Missed	Total
Audio Visual							
Presentation is formatted using discourse conventions of science using logic-based arguments to present a convincing argument.							5
Slides emphasize important information using appropriately sized font with a reasonable amount of text per slide.							5
Slides are free of mistakes, spelling and mechanical errors, using proper scientific terminology, italicized scientific names.							5
Use appropriate in-text citations in APA format for information not considered common knowledge are used.							5
Appropriate figures and statistics are included with at least **one original graph** created by the group to convey essential data or evidence.							5
Total AV							**25**

Organization

Category	5-Excellent	4-Good	3-Fair	2-Poor	1-Grim	0-Missed	Total
Logical presentation of ideas should follow scientific conventions including a descriptive title using correct terminology.							5
Introduction clearly states objectives and provides relevant background information.							5
Body describes how information was gathered (if applicable), compares current hypothesis to current literature on topic, and provides sound reasoning for necessity of proposed research.							5
Conclusion summarizes ideas and discusses implications and applications to daily life.							5
Include a correctly formatted literature cited section with a *minimum* of 10 peer-reviewed scientific journal articles.							5
Total Organization							25

Delivery

Category	5-Excellent	4-Good	3-Fair	2-Poor	1-Grim	0-Missed	Total
Work is presented in a scientific tone, using appropriate scientific language, recognizing audience reaction and adjusting delivery accordingly, fielding questions with poise and intellectual honesty.							5
Presenters are poised, well-rehearsed, dressed appropriately, respectful of time limit, and meet conventions of oral presentation.							5
Total Delivery							10

Thoroughness of Interdisciplinary Research

Category	5-Excellent	4-Good	3-Fair	2-Poor	1-Grim	0-Missed	Total
Speakers show expert knowledge of the subject, cite recent and appropriate peer-reviewed primary journal articles as well as secondary sources.							5
Speakers can define all terminology, understand and articulate the scientific mechanisms behind their topic (i.e., molecular, cellular, biochemical level, statistical, depending on the topic).							5
Speakers can relate their topic to concepts covered in chemistry such as properties of elements and compounds.							5
Speakers relate the topic to concepts covered in biology including the formulation of hypotheses and valid predictions.							5
Presenters can correctly interpret all information presented including units and rates of change for graphs and data tables.							5
Total Research							**25**

Collaboration

Category	5-Excellent	4-Good	3-Fair	2-Poor	1-Grim	0-Missed	Total
Evidence of well-coordinated teamwork, smooth transitions from speaker to speaker, equal division of labor. (If presenting alone, this is an automatic 10-point deduction.)							5
All presenters are present, well-prepared, and capable of fielding questions.							5
Interpersonal group issues handled appropriately throughout the semester according to team contract.							5
Total Collaboration							**15**
Total Interdisciplinary							
Project Score							

6

IMPLEMENTING A LINKED COURSE REQUIREMENT IN THE CORE CURRICULUM

Margot Soven

T his chapter begins with a history of the La Salle University linked course program. The "Background" section is followed by discussion about how we overcame staffing and scheduling constraints. The middle of the chapter is devoted to curriculum guidelines, the implementation and the value of writing and dual classes in linked courses, and a section on faculty development. A syllabus and examples of writing assignments and a dual class schedule are included as well. The chapter includes samples of instructor and student surveys as vehicles for assessment. I end with my conclusions about the future of the Doubles program at La Salle University.

Background

In 1998, the faculty at La Salle University approved a new core curriculum that stipulated that all freshmen would have the opportunity to participate in "Doubles courses," a linked course program in which two courses in different disciplines were connected thematically. These courses were limited in size to twenty students, with the same cohort of students in both courses. To enhance the potential for these courses to serve as a learning community, a one-credit section of the freshman orientation program (The Freshman Odyssey) was attached to each link and taught by one of the instructors of the two linked courses.

The challenge we set for ourselves was ambitious. Although many schools have linked course programs, very few attempt to develop linked courses for all freshmen in a school of our size, with an average entering class of 800 freshmen. Furthermore, in many linked course programs, one course is typically a content-based course (e.g., science, religion, or history, etc.) and the other is an application course (writing or speech). When this is the case, the content-based course is actively supported by the skills course. Our program was not tied to this model. We believed, and still do, that if students are to see the relationship between different courses, then we should encourage all kinds of pairings.

At the time, I did not foresee all of the challenges that lay ahead. Although La Salle had considerable experience with linked courses through its honors program, which for many years had provided a "triple" for all honors students (English, history, philosophy), the honors program was modest in size compared with the new linked course program for all freshmen except those in the honors program.

It soon became obvious that implementing the "Doubles" would be my greatest challenge as core director. A core advisory board to help the core coordinator oversee the core, composed of faculty representing different departments as well as representatives from the registrar's office and the dean's offices, were also appointed. At the time, I didn't realize the important role that the core advisory board would play in the evolution of the Doubles. I now recognize that an advisory group composed of administrators and faculty is crucial when it comes to making decisions about issues related to linked courses.

We began with a pilot program with ten linked courses staffed by instructors eager to participate. They partnered with faculty whom they knew beforehand. The only criterion for a course to be included in the program was that it had to be a core course typically offered during the freshman year, because students were required to take their linked courses during their first year at La Salle.

The original intention was to include courses at all levels from all departments in the Doubles program. We soon realized the contradiction in the core requirements. Because students were required to enroll in a Double in their freshman year, the Doubles had to be constituted from courses students typically take in the freshman year. The original intent provided much more freedom for developing linked courses than we found to be practical, given other core requirements.

Despite this constraint, at the end of the pilot year, we came to the conclusion that students and faculty seemed, on the whole, to like linked courses. Several faculty reported that they were energized to rethink their courses and pedagogy as a result of having to link their course thematically with a course in another discipline. Among the data we gathered from students, we learned that many students believed that linked courses challenged them to think more critically than traditional courses. The links were varied: biology and philosophy, psychology and religion, philosophy and English, and so on. Students reported that among other benefits, they were able to understand the connections between courses in different disciplines more easily as a result of being in the Doubles program.

We also learned that some disciplines are not as easy to "double" as others. Although many faculty members were eager to try to link their courses, some Doubles were not successful. Physics and foreign languages, for example, were not a successful pair.

Staffing and Scheduling

The following year (2000) we launched the Doubles program to accommodate all freshmen. We soon learned that developing forty pairs (eighty courses) was a mega-change from scheduling ten pairs (twenty courses). We no longer had the luxury of giving faculty the opportunity to choose their partners; departments had to agree to offer the number and kinds of Doubles set by the registrar at the times scheduled for them, and to identify faculty willing to teach linked courses at the times scheduled by the registrar. This approach required faculty to be willing to teach with a colleague who they might not even have met, and who might teach in a discipline that was not necessarily their first choice when they thought about linking courses. Neither chairs nor faculty were happy about this change. For chairs, it meant that they had to schedule department courses "around" the Doubles in their department, because the schedule for the Doubles was set by the registrar.

We developed a formula for the number of courses a department had to dedicate to the Doubles program. The formula was based on the number of core courses the department controlled. For example, because students were required to take two philosophy courses as part of the core, and only one course in political science, the Philosophy Department provided a greater number of sections to the doubles program than the Political Science Department. Needless to say, this approach required a great deal of collaboration among department chairs with each other, as well as with the registrar.

Some faculty, understandably, flatly refused to teach a Double under these circumstances. If they couldn't choose their Doubles partner, or the course with which they would like to "Double," they were not about to take their chances with someone they did not know.

However, the school culture at La Salle was on our side. Most faculty are committed to the idea of a "La Salle community" as well as to their department community, and, although some chairs grumbled more than others, they went along with this policy. We created several incentives for faculty to "volunteer." We offered a modest stipend ($500.00) to faculty who were teaching a Double for the first time, and offered day-long training sessions, for which they also received a stipend to attend.

Some of our most successful Doubles were taught by an adjunct instructor paired with a full-time, tenure-track faculty member. These Doubles produced an added benefit for the instructors. Adjunct faculty who taught in the Doubles program seemed to feel more strongly connected to the La Salle community than those adjuncts that did not have the opportunity to teach in the program. Another secondary positive outcome of staffing Doubles is the advantage of pairing new faculty with a senior faculty. The new faculty member often brings fresh ideas; at the same time, the new faculty member also benefits from the senior faculty member's experience teaching at La Salle.

Some faculty pairs became known as the "dream teams." They produced imaginative syllabi and assignments that became models for other Doubles. For example, a number of these Doubles worked particularly well because of the dynamics between the two instructors who taught them: art history and religion, psychology and religion, composition and accounting, and philosophy and nutrition.

However, things did not always go smoothly. After the first wave of enthusiasm (the honeymoon period), chairs had some difficulty recruiting enough faculty for the program. Some faculty pairs did not work well together. Other faculty had a hard time reconceptualizing their courses to connect with courses from other departments.

Another staffing problem occurred: high turnover. We discovered that it takes several semesters to create a good "Double," to work out effective approaches to collaboration, to experiment with assignments, and to discover how to relate to students in the linked course situation. However, full-time faculty often could not be spared by their Departments to teach introductory courses on an ongoing basis. Furthermore, adjunct faculty might leave or require schedules that did not conform to the Doubles roster.

Staffing became the number one issue. To alleviate the staffing problem, the provost approved six full-time, non–tenure track positions in the departments that contributed the largest number of courses to the Doubles program: English, philosophy, religion, history, and psychology. Their job description included teaching four Doubles each semester and serving as leaders in the ongoing development of the Doubles program.

Once the non–tenure track, full-time faculty were hired, a large percentage of the Doubles were taught by these faculty members whose main focus was teaching linked courses. Paired with one another, they taught two thirds of the Doubles courses. We were now able to assign the remaining Doubles to instructors who were enthusiastic about teaching in the program and were successful Doubles instructors.

These six faculty met as a group frequently throughout the semester in addition to meeting individually with their partners. They had a major effect on the Doubles curriculum, as they developed new assignments and new approaches to assessment. In the excerpts from syllabi that follow, notice how the same instructors pair with partners from different disciplines and are capable of designing Doubles in different disciplines. All six faculty had been adjunct faculty at La Salle prior to their new appointments. This was a plus; they had taught conventional introductory courses prior to their Doubles teaching assignment. They had indeed become a faculty community.

Two of these instructors left La Salle for reasons unrelated to the Doubles. At this point a hiring freeze prevented us from replacing these two positions. Staffing problems once again became an issue, which we never quite solved. We experimented with several staffing plans, but none succeeded as well as the plan for hiring instructors whose teaching responsibilities were dedicated to the Doubles program.

Important Revelation 1

The number of meetings, e-mails, and personal conversations during the start-up period of any integrative learning community should not be underestimated. Finding solutions to scheduling and staffing procedures requires patience, tact, and sometimes the intervention of senior administrators. One chair at La Salle refused to participate in the Doubles. The dean of arts and sciences argued that because the core program was approved by the faculty, the chair really did not have much choice.

Student Scheduling: Placement and Grades

The original intention when the Doubles program was first conceived was to have all freshmen enroll in a Double coupled with a first-year orientation (FYO) course in the fall semester. This scenario turned out to be impossible for staffing and scheduling reasons. Students who were required to enroll in the Double in the spring semester created another set of problems. By that time, many of them had chosen a major and were obligated to take certain courses in the spring. The registrar now had to schedule students in a Double with this additional constraint in mind.

Another complication was that as more students gravitated to the professional majors, more freshmen elected majors that required them to take introductory courses in the major, such as in business, nursing, and education or prerequisites for the major during their freshman year. For example, nursing—which grew to be our largest major during these ten years—requires students to begin their science courses as freshmen. We had to create some Doubles with courses in the major.

We also had some concern about student placement. Because of scheduling limitations related to the large number of Doubles that had to be rostered, students were no longer able to choose their Double, as they were during the pilot phase of the program. However, the registrar did try to place students into a Double composed of courses they had indicated an interest in taking during their freshman year.

Another policy decision we had to make because the Doubles were a requirement was what to do when students failed one of the courses, or in some cases both courses. We decided that students should be required to repeat the Double in either case. Invariably, as with any requirement, we needed to waive the requirement occasionally when it interfered with the major.

There were other constraints as well related to the possible success or failure of the Doubles program. We tried to schedule the courses back to back to give instructors the option of having an extended dual class if they chose, or if they wanted to attend each other's classes. This was not possible in all cases, but we learned that it was a vital part of the program. In assessment surveys, dual classes are rated very highly by students.

We also tried to "connect" the FYO course to the Double. Ideally, one member of the linked course team would teach the one-semester FYO course with the same student cohort as were in the Double. However, not all Doubles faculty were interested in teaching this one-credit course required of all freshmen. Therefore, we scheduled stand-alone FYO courses for approximately one third of the freshmen. These sections were taught by faculty and student affairs staff. We were curious to find out if the FYO courses connected to the Doubles were rated more positively than the stand-alone FYO courses.

Important Revelation 2

Students' positive evaluations of the FYO course correlate more closely with the person who teaches the course than the connection of the course to a Double.

The Doubles Curriculum

The linked courses had to do double duty. The Doubles courses had to conform to department guidelines for each course as well as the special guidelines for the Doubles. To meet this dual role, the following guidelines were designed for instructors to develop Doubles syllabi, submit the syllabi for review, and introduce the Double to the students.

What should a Doubles syllabus include?
1. The Department's objectives for the course
2. A description of the Doubles program and the theme that connects the two courses
3. On a separate sheet, a list of the assignments, readings, dual classes, trips or other activities related to the Doubles component of the course, and grading policy
4. The course schedule
5. Contact information, attendance policy, texts, and so on

When should the syllabus be submitted?
Both Doubles partners should submit their syllabus to the Core Director and the department chair by *mid-August* electronically as well as in hard copy.

How should the syllabus be introduced to students?
The syllabus should be discussed the first day of class in a joint session with both instructors present. The objectives of the Doubles program should be reviewed at the same time.

The following Double (accounting and composition) conforms to the Doubles description guidelines and demonstrates that students will be studying the accounting principles required by the major, the writing skills required in the composition course, and the thematic focus of the Doubles course.

Accounting–Composition Doubles

To the Students:

These two courses are participating in the Doubles Program, a required component of the core curriculum at La Salle University. A *Double* is a thematically linked pair of courses taught by two faculty partners from two different disciplines. In our case, Business 101, taught by Kristin Wentzel, is paired with English 108, taught by Margot Soven.

The primary aims of this Double are as follows:

- *To foster cross-fertilization between our two disciplines.* Modern education has become so specialized that each discipline tends to become isolated. Our goal is to show the connections between our disciplines. Accounting is primarily about communicating information to decision makers using figures as the primary source of information. Composition is learning about how to communicate using words as the medium. Both disciplines are concerned with conveying appropriate information to the desired audience.
- *To help create a miniature learning community within the larger community of La Salle University.* In regular courses, classmates often do not get to know each other as well as they could. However, in this Double, we have designed the class to be small to allow each person to get to know his or her classmates better. In such a learning community, each student gets to know and respect his or her peers and each student becomes a really important part of that class. When students depend on each other and learn from each other, they learn more effectively. The Double allows you to share many experiences together and form a mini-community together because you are in class together for six hours each week.
  Over the course of this semester, we will be studying accounting and composition. Some of the learning activities will be confined to one class or the other; however, we will be watching movies, using common readings, writing one common writing assignment, learning how to write an executive summary, meeting together for class discussion about Enron, and taking a class trip together. In the composition class, we will be reading about the individual people who were instrumental in the history of several corporations (Disney, Walmart, Microsoft, Enron, and Home

Depot) and writing essays about them. These same corporations will be used for analysis and discussion in the accounting class, and they will be used as the framework for the five quizzes in accounting.

Doubles Pedagogy: Dual Classes and Writing Assignments

Instructors experimented with a variety of methods to achieve the purposes of the Doubles, including writing assignments, jointly held classes (dual classes), collaborative projects, trips, and study groups. Dual classes and writing assignments were identified as the most powerful pedagogies for achieving the purpose of the Doubles.

Dual Classes

Students consistently rated dual classes as the most effective strategy for communicating the intellectual connections between two disciplines. With both teachers in the classroom, students see first-hand a model of discussion in which different disciplinary perspectives can be integrated in solving a particular problem. They see their instructors model a discussion that brings both disciplines to bear on a particular subject. For example, how can biology and political science contribute to solving the global warming crisis?

Within this instructional model, instructors were encouraged to distribute a separate schedule for the team-taught sessions. As demonstrated in the following schedule, in one Double (philosophy–nutrition) the instructors describe the five two-hour sessions, spaced through the semester, in which both classes participated. Other classes on the syllabus are shown on each instructor's syllabus.

Dual Classes Schedule

Biology 1561: Human Genetics
Philosophy 151: Moral Inquiry and Moral Choice
Theme: Genetics and the Quality of Life

Doubles Session 1: The Complete Life

Readings from Aristotle, Sophocles, Campbell Lewis, Human Reproduction
"Never Say Die" PBS Broadcast

Doubles Session 2: The Meaning of Suffering

"Lorenzo's Oil" film
Readings from Buddha, Victor Frankl, Robert Novak

Doubles Session 3: Genetic Screening and Privacy

Readings from Sisela Bok, Resnick, and Rothstein

Doubles Session 4: Eugenics

Readings from John Stuart Mill, Edward Wilson, Michael Bayles, Aldous
  Huxley

Doubles Session 5: The Hazards of Genetic Engineering and Genetic Therapy

Articles from *Scientific American, Newsweek,* Ruth Macklin, and Thomas
  Nagel

The instructors of this Double distributed their own student survey in addition to the student survey distributed in all of the Doubles courses (see the following). Many instructors created similar class surveys.

Student Survey of the Philosophy–Nutrition Double

1. Do you believe that your understanding of human genetics was improved by association with your moral inquiries course? Can you explain or illustrate your answer?
2. Did application to issues in human genetics help you understand or appreciate moral principles presented in your moral inquiries course? Can you explain or illustrate your answer?
3. What did you find most helpful about the interdisciplinary linkage between the courses?

Writing Assignments and Linked Courses

Richard Light (2001) has argued,

> The relationship between the amount of writing for a course and the students' level of engagement [in the course] . . . is stronger than the relationship between students' engagement and any other course characteristic. The simple correlation between the amount of writing required in a course and the students' overall commitment to it tells a lot about the importance of writing. (54–55)

Light's research corroborates the findings of the value of writing in the Doubles. Our Doubles student surveys indicated that writing assignments are powerful vehicles for enacting the purpose of linked courses. Depending on the courses included in the Double, the kinds of writing assignments employed differed. The following section offers several examples.

Writing Assignments in Composition Doubles

Writing assignments in Doubles, in which one of the courses is in composition, may differ from writing assignments in other Doubles. The structure of the assignments may reflect the kinds of papers typically taught in the composition class, although the content for the assignments may be based on the readings in the other class. For example, three assignments in a composition and history Double assume that the readings will be from the history class. These assignments include the following: assignment 1, a summary of a primary text assigned as a reading in the history class; assignment 2, a comparison of two texts in the history class; and assignment 3, a short research paper related to a topic in the history course.

Another strategy includes assigning separate writing assignments for a shared reading. In a composition and political science Double, students read the courtroom drama *Twelve Angry Men.* In the political science course, they write about the play as an illustration of the jury system. In the composition course, they write a character analysis based on one of the main characters. The instructors grade the papers independently. However, they conduct a joint class discussing the two perspectives on the play.

In another composition and history Double, students write about the same issue from the perspective of different readings and different assignments. In this case, the readings in one class may inform the papers in the other class if the assignment is constructed to give students that opportunity. For example, in the composition class students write about the role of women in ancient India as compared with the role of women in modern India. They read an ancient text in the history class. In the composition class, they read a short story, "Orbiting," by Bharati Mukherjee, who emigrated from India to the United States in the 1960s. We found that for writing to have the desired effect, writing must be viewed as an integral, ongoing part of both courses. Several short papers spread throughout the semester rather than one long paper are more effective for connecting the courses.

Ungraded Writing: Reflections on Connections

Nongraded, informal writing that asks students to reflect on the connections between their linked courses is another method for reinforcing students' awareness of the relationship between the two courses. These "journal writings" urge students to periodically think about how the two courses relate. Students may be asked to identify the main idea of a particular class session or to describe how two sessions related to one another.

The benefits of such periodic writing are many. Students may pay more attention to possible points of connection when they know they will be writing about them frequently. These writing reflections also focus student thinking and can be used to initiate class discussion. Furthermore, they give important feedback to instructors who may want to reinforce certain strategies for increasing student awareness of the contact points between courses. Richard Light (2001) points out that "reflections document for students that they are indeed learning something substantial about the ways their experiences interrelate" (68–69). Light suggests that students will be less likely to forget the connections they themselves have drawn.

To make nongraded writing work, a certain amount of course credit should be allotted for completing the writing tasks. Instead of grades, instructors can write brief comments indicating their responses, and can give credit for responses being submitted on time. My own solution to the "credit" problem is to incorporate credit for ungraded writing into the class participation grade.

Faculty Development

In any program that develops over a period of years, faculty development programs must remain fluid to meet the different needs of an evolving staff. Furthermore, the schedule for any faculty development dedicated to a school-wide program needs to be attended to throughout the academic year as well as after the academic year in preparation for the following year.

At La Salle we conducted day-long workshops in the beginning of the summer, shorter meetings during the summer and academic year, and one-on-one meetings with faculty pairs who were often teaching together for the first time. These workshops were well attended. In September, we began the semester with a "Doubles Breakfast" at which faculty would share their new Doubles syllabi.

Our workshops often focused on pedagogical techniques. Other sessions focused on the special group dynamics of the linked course classroom.

Another group of meetings were declared "open agenda" meetings at which faculty could share and discuss successes and problems.

Many workshops and discussions were conducted by the La Salle Doubles faculty themselves. Others were conducted by the campus learning specialist and the director of institutional research. Occasionally, we invited an outside expert on freshman pedagogy, linked courses, or assessment, for example, Gillian Kinzie (National Survey of Student Engagement).

Important Revelation 3

Request top administrators, such as deans, the provost, and the president, to "meet and greet" workshop participants and possibly participate in some workshops. It is important to show administrative support for the "rank and file" who are carrying out curricular innovation.

The Doubles and Assessment

La Salle designed both a faculty and student survey to judge the value of the Doubles as perceived by its participants. As with most linked course programs, the results have been positive. These are administered at the end of the fall semester. On the whole, students and faculty strongly support the benefits of the Doubles. Versions of both surveys appear here. Both surveys were periodically modified as emphases in the program changed. (See Chapter 8 for more information on assessment of linked course programs.)

Doubles Program Faculty Survey

Date _____

Name _____ Department _____

Doubles Partner _____

Course No. and Title: _____

Course No. and Title: _____

Have you taught in the Doubles program prior to this semester? _____

Is this the first time you are teaching this specific Double? _____

If not, how many times have you taught this Double? _____

Does this Double include an FYO section? _____

1. Briefly discuss the methods used to link the courses (e.g., common readings, how many joint classes, common writing assignments, field trips, etc.). Please explain.

2. Can you estimate the amount of time you spent planning with your partner?
    a) Previous to this fall semester _____
    b) During this fall semester _____
    Explain.
3. When was the Doubles experience at its best?
4. How would you describe student outcomes?

Student Doubles Course Evaluation

1. Course Title and Section: _____ Instructor: _____
2. Course Title and Section: _____ Instructor: _____

Directions: Please circle the number corresponding to your answer.

1. Please indicate your degree of agreement with the following statements about the Doubles courses.

		Strongly Disagree	Some-what Disagree	Neither Agree nor Disagree	Some-what Agree	Strongly Agree
a.	My instructors clearly explained the purposes of the Doubles courses.	1	2	3	4	5
b.	The Doubles courses were a good learning experience.	1	2	3	4	5
c.	Professors in the Doubles sections seemed to work well together.	1	2	3	4	5
d.	Connections between the Doubles courses were clear.	1	2	3	4	5
e.	I would recommend the Doubles experience to incoming students.	1	2	3	4	5
f.	The Doubles program is achieving its goals.	1	2	3	4	5
g.	In my opinion, the goals of the Doubles are clear.	1	2	3	4	5
h.	The Doubles format helped me learn the subject matter.	1	2	3	4	5
i.	In the Doubles courses I got to see relationships that I would not have realized if I took each course separately.	1	2	3	4	5

j.	My Doubles courses helped me understand connections between subjects.	1	2	3	4	5
k.	The Doubles are a good idea.	1	2	3	4	5
l.	Activities outside of class helped to achieve the goals of the Doubles.	1	2	3	4	5
m.	Reading and writing assignments helped to achieve the goals of the Doubles.	1	2	3	4	5
n.	Joint classes helped to achieve the goals of the Doubles.	1	2	3	4	5

2. Compared with other *required* courses you have taken at La Salle, how would you rate your Doubles courses on the following aspects?

		Much Worse	Some what Worse	About the Same	Some what Better	Much Better
a.	Allowing you to think critically	1	2	3	4	5
b.	Made learning a pleasant experience	1	2	3	4	5
c.	Allowing you to interpret ideas	1	2	3	4	5
d.	Teaching you how to solve problems	1	2	3	4	5
e.	Helping you retain what you learned	1	2	3	4	5
f.	Challenging your thinking	1	2	3	4	5
g.	Capturing your interest	1	2	3	4	5
h.	Helping you integrate ideas	1	2	3	4	5
i.	Helping you evaluate ideas	1	2	3	4	5
j.	Allowing you to appreciate different perspectives	1	2	3	4	5
k.	Engaging you in the learning process	1	2	3	4	5
l.	Helping you work in with your fellow students	1	2	3	4	5
m.	Helping you work more closely with the instructor	1	2	3	4	5
n.	Fostering student interactions	1	2	3	4	5

o.	Making the material relevant to your everyday concerns	1	2	3	4	5
p.	Deepening your interest in the subject matter	1	2	3	4	5

3. What did you like the most about the Doubles courses?
4. What did you like the least about the Doubles courses?
5. What should be done differently to enhance the Doubles experience?

Demographic Information

(Purpose: To help us understand if there are any differences in opinion by demographic characteristics)
a. Your major: _____
b. Your gender (circle one): *Female Male*
c. Your living arrangement (circle one): *Resident on Campus   Commuter*
d. Your anticipated grades in the Doubles: *Course 1:____ Course 2:____*
e. Did you plan to take *both* of the courses composing the Double?
   1 Yes   2 No
f. Was your FYO class connected to one of the courses in the Doubles? *1 Yes   2 No*

A summary of the findings of Student Surveys given over a period of eight years is found in Chapter 9, "The Nuts and Bolts of Evaluating Linked Courses."

The Future of the Doubles at La Salle University

As we go to press, the La Salle Doubles program has been indefinitely suspended. The main reason for this suspension of the program: cost. Doubles courses were limited to twenty students. As the University experienced economic constraints, the caps for all Core courses were raised to thirty-five students. Also, the difficulty in staffing and scheduling this large number of Doubles played a part in their demise. The strain on the registrar, the chairs, and the faculty was considerable.

Where do we go from here? We have proven, beyond a doubt, that the Doubles are a worthwhile experience. Eight years of data cannot be ignored. We have tried to develop "mini-links" consisting of an FYO one-credit course and a three-credit course either in the core or the major. Most of the FYO courses are now attached to a three-credit course. The others are still taught as stand-alone one-credit courses. In this version of two linked courses, the same cohort of students is taught by the same instructor. Some of the benefits of the Doubles program are beginning to surface, especially in the School of Business Administration (SBA). Instructors demonstrate how the orientation to La Salle and the city of Philadelphia has a connection to the major.

The concept of a faculty learning community is also "salvaged" as students in the SBA FYO program meet together to develop FYO projects connected to the major in business. For example, SBA students take a trip to the Philadelphia Zoo, learn about the finances of this institution, and then write a report about the Zoo that focuses on both the population it serves and its budgetary matters. The faculty becomes part of a learning community as they plan these and other projects.

It is too soon to assess the outcome of these new minilinks. A new survey has been developed to understand their effect. However, the curriculum is always changing. A task force has been appointed to revise the core curriculum. The current core advisory board will recommend that they seriously consider a version of a linked course program that is more modest in scope than the Doubles program, from which we learned that it is well worth the effort to create linked course programs.

Reference

Light, R. (2001). *Making the most of college: Students speak their minds.* Cambridge, MA: Harvard University Press.

7

ACADEMIC PARTNERSHIPS WITH RESIDENTIAL LEARNING COMMUNITIES

Maggie C. Parker and Alex Kappus

The University of Georgia (UGA) believes in the importance of engaging students both inside as well as outside of the classroom. The UGA Learning Community Initiative demonstrates the commitment of forming a seamless learning environment by forging partnerships between academic and student affairs divisions. Connecting students to faculty and with the resources they need to succeed remains a challenge for all universities, but especially for a large, comprehensive flagship state university like UGA. As this book demonstrates, learning communities encourage student involvement, development, and learning by helping students make connections across disciplines, fostering a closer interaction with faculty, and tapping into student interest to promote learning. This chapter provides some history and background of the UGA Learning Community Initiative, as well as the current status and envisioned future of the program. The chapter focuses on the partnership aspect of the program and, in particular, why UGA believes that learning communities take on an even more important role when intentionally designed as living–learning communities. The UGA Learning Communities Initiative provides students with a platform for shared experiences both inside the classroom and within a residential community.

History and Background

The UGA Learning Communities Initiative was a direct result from a recommendation following the National Survey of Student Engagement (NSSE) administered in 2003. The NSSE annually gathers information about student participation at colleges and universities and provides insight into student learning and development. (For more information on the NSSE, see http://nsse.iub.edu/.) From the UGA report results, the Office of the Vice President for Instruction began collaborating with the Department of University Housing to create a living–learning community initiative. UGA was certainly not the first institution to build a living–learning community initiative through strategic planning, and in fact looked to similar programs offered at peer institutions for guidance. After a year of data collection and preparation, and identifying the specific learning outcomes for the UGA Learning Communities (see http://learningcommunities.uga.edu/about/), UGA enrolled the first cohort of students into the program.

The UGA Learning Communities are groups of up to twenty students who share similar academic interests, are enrolled in several linked courses, and live together in Creswell Hall (a first-year residential facility). Through this program, students are immersed in a collaborative learning environment that allows them to live among peers who have similar academic goals and promotes a greater interaction with faculty and upperclass students. Students are also exposed to university resources and activities, leadership development opportunities, as well as service-learning within the Athens community.

The partnership between these two offices affects the student experience in the Learning Communities because each side is responsible for certain aspects in terms of execution of the initiative. The director of the UGA Learning Communities is a position located within the Office of the Vice President for Instruction. The Office of the Vice President for Instruction's charge is to continually improve student learning on campus. This mission is enacted through the organizations that report to this office as well as teaching initiatives undertaken directly with schools, colleges, and individual faculty members. The director of the UGA Learning Communities currently shares responsibilities with other academic initiatives on campus and supervises an administrative associate position that takes on many administrative responsibilities for the UGA Learning Communities. The Department of University Housing is a mission-driven office that seeks to "provide comfortable, affordable and secure on-campus housing options in residential communities where the academic success and personal growth of residents are encouraged and supported" (Mission, Values and Principles, 2011). The senior coordinator for Academic Initiatives, responsible for maintaining and building academic partnerships across campus, works with the director of the program to ensure proper communication and collaboration. The Office of the Vice President for Instruction works to coordinate the faculty members and provides significant assistance to recruitment efforts. University Housing ensures living space for the residents, assists in recruitment efforts, trains and supervises undergraduate resident advisor staff, and coadvises the undergraduate student staff members called *peer advisors*. The senior coordinator for Academic Initiatives supervises a graduate student who works on various partnership tasks, including planning for organizing various receptions and working with the peer advisors.

Purpose

Research has shown that the more students—especially first-year students—are academically and socially engaged, the more likely they are to learn and develop and remain in school (Astin, 1999; Tinto, 1993). Universities that promote first-year programs, such as learning communities, have been linked to enhancing student success (Kuh, Kinzie, Schuh, & Whitt, 2005). Learning communities blend students' living and learning together through coordinated partnerships between student and academic affairs departments. On a practical level, the living–learning communities help students meet peers with similar interests, create more intimate interaction with faculty members, and provide the support of staff and peer mentors. The students entering our program have the high standards in achieving at UGA, but have the added benefit of making their experience in the first year more intentional. Students, especially those at a large institution, might become overwhelmed at the thought of the size of UGA. The Learning Community Initiative creates a stronger and more tight-knit community for the residents of the building.

Composition of the UGA Learning Communities

Course Requirements

Each Learning Community has three course requirements that students must register for in order to participate. Each course is centered on the theme of the specific Learning Community. The required courses are defined in this program as First Year Odyssey Seminar (FYOS 1001), First Year Composition (ENGL 1101 or ENGL 1102), and a theme-related course. FYOS 1001 serves as the backbone and centralizing course for each community. The instructor for this course is considered to be the lead instructor for the Learning Community. He or she coordinates with the other faculty and staff to create a holistic experience for the participating students. The composition of this seminar is based on the concept of small groups and encourages faculty–student interaction. The seminar includes the twenty Learning Community students, the lead instructor, and the peer advisor (who is discussed in a later section). The format of the seminar is largely discussion-based and geared toward encouraging interaction among the students and with the faculty. The other two required courses are centered on the topic of FYOS 1001.

Each student is required to take an English course as well, either ENGL 1101 or ENGL 1102. Because of the increased number of students who exempt out of ENGL 1101 via advanced placement (AP) testing or joint enrollment, students are allowed to take ENGL 1102 as well. Each class is taught toward the overarching theme of the Learning Communities, correlating the material and subjects covered in the other two Learning Community courses. The English instructors are selected by the department because they have an interest in the area or subject of a particular Learning Community. In this course, students read and write about topics related to their Learning Community theme, instead of the general curriculum of most composition courses. Students have emphasized that having this directed course work has allowed them to succeed in improving their writing skills by maintaining their interest. Another technicality to note is that each Learning Community's ENGL 1101 and 1102 sections are taught in the same classroom, in efforts to keep students together within their courses. What has affectionately been dubbed the "school house model" keeps all 20 students together and with the same instructor. The instructor is aware of who gets 1101 and 1102 credit, and adjusts his or her assignments and expectations accordingly.

The third course requirement is the theme-related course. This course varies for each Learning Community but is a general education course that ties into the theme of the Learning Community. These courses can range in size and format. If the course has a lab or break out session attached to it, all of the Learning Community students are in that section together as well. All of the theme-related courses fulfill one of the core general education requirements set for all students at UGA (see "General Education Requirements" later in this chapter). By maintaining courses in the general education curriculum, it allows any student to participate in a Learning Community based on an interest, not necessarily a major. All the courses taken count toward graduation, regardless of major.

Exemptions and Exceptions

As mentioned previously, there are a rising number of students who exempt out of specific college credit courses through AP tests and joint enrollment credits. If a student has exempted one of the required courses for his or her specific Learning Community, then the student takes the remaining courses. Students can sometimes exempt both English courses and the theme-related course, and in that case, the students only need to take FYOS 1001. This is not the ideal; however, that choice is left up to the students.

Another exception that can occur is if a student has placed into a UNIV English course. Courses with the prefix UNIV are designed to better prepare students for the required entry-level courses. Many international students take UNIV English courses to learn the language and usage better, prior to enrolling in ENGL 1101. If students did not score well enough on their English Placement Test, they are encouraged to take a more entry-level course. If this is the case, the students are allowed to remain in the Learning Community, simply taking the other two courses with the Learning Community students.

Sample Course Structure for 2011–2012 UGA Learning Communities
Fall Semester
FYOS 1001—First Year Odyssey Seminar
ENGL 1101 or ENGL 1102—First-Year Composition
Theme Related Course (dependent on Learning Community theme)

- GEOG 1101—Human Geography
- SPCM 1100—Introduction to Public Speaking
- CHEM 1211—Introduction to Chemistry
- MUSI 2060—History of Rock and Roll
- POLS 1101—American Government
- HACE 2100—Family Economic Issues through the Life Course

Spring Semester
- FRES 1020—Service Learning Project (Spring Semester)

General Education Requirements

As per the University System of Georgia's core curriculum requirements, UGA implements general education curriculum requirements on all students for graduation. A summary of UGA's general education requirements can be seen at www.bulletin.uga.edu.

One of the main considerations of the UGA Learning Communities in regard to the general education requirements is that students do not fall behind by participating in the program during their freshman year. Keeping all the UGA Learning Community courses within the general education curriculum, students can remain on track for graduation, regardless of their major. The specific section of the requirements that each course fulfills varies for each Learning Community, but the English composition course is a standard across the board as a required foundation course.

First Year Odyssey Seminar and Freshman Seminar

Another requirement for all first-year students at UGA is FYOS 1001. This seminar is also included in the Learning Community course load; however, the shape of this course within the Learning Communities has changed over the years.

In the initial implementation of the UGA Learning Communities, a freshman seminar was included as the centralizing course of the program. The concept was that if first-year students were exposed to a smaller environment with a familiar group of peers and with access to a faculty member, their engagement with the University and with each other would be greater than students not involved in such a program. Freshman seminars have been included in the Learning Community course load for the entirety of the program. Until fall 2011, these seminars had been coded as a one-hour elective (nonrequired course).

UGA underwent its reaffirmation of accreditation in the fall of 2010, and as a result, the Quality Enhancement Plan proposed was approved for what would eventually be called the *First Year Odyssey Seminar (FYOS)*. Essentially, the FYOS is a required course that puts each first-year student in a seminar with a small number of students and a tenured or tenure-track faculty member. Because of this requirement, the Learning Community seminar was adjusted to fit the FYOS criteria, but still remains in the core for the UGA Learning Communities program. For more information regarding the FYOS, please visit www.fyo.uga.edu.

Service Learning

Another building block and key component of the Learning Communities is the focus on service learning. In addition to the course work in the fall semester, Learning Community students participate in another one-hour seminar in the spring with a focus on service learning. The origin of the Learning Communities was based on the idea that engagement with the university and the community is an important value that is often missed with students in larger universities. The Office of Service Learning, also a stem of the Office of the Vice President for Instruction, started around the same time as the UGA Learning Communities Initiative and has been expanding and growing as well.

During the spring semester, the Learning Community students meet with their group, lead instructor, and peer advisor to develop and implement a service learning project of their choice. There are no preset projects and this allows the students to develop projects based on their interests, both individually and as a group. The instructors and peer advisors both serve as supervisors and to provide resources, if their guidance is needed. They also lead the class in reflections and discussions in the classroom based on the experiences of the service learning projects. It is that correlation and tie-in with the course work that is the epitome of the service learning mission.

Some examples of previous service learning projects follow:

- Participating in Habitat for Humanity
- Creating a presentation on money and time management for high school students
- Raising money for Nets for Nets
- Holding a benefit concert for a local food bank
- Creating an organization on campus that creates and sends educational materials to Africa
- Selling of Ugandan women's beads to send money back to them
- Raising money and creating a team for Relay for Life

Implementation and Administration

Recruitment

One of the areas in which the UGA Learning Communities has morphed and grown since its inception is in its recruiting of students. Initially, only physical mail (letters and brochures) was used to advertise the program and to let students know how to register. Because of this process, the bulk of the sign-ups were occurring during the summer orientation sessions. Over the last three years, recruitment has taken a more active approach. Not only is information about the UGA Learning Communities included in every student's admissions packet, but an e-mail is also sent to the student and their parents with information about what the Learning Communities are and how to sign-up. With every wave of admissions (approximately three per year), e-mails are sent to the newly admitted students. Additionally, in mid-spring a contact from the Learning Communities requests the names and e-mails of all currently admitted students so that another informational e-mail can be sent. In addition to the more technological approach of e-mail correspondence, the Learning Communities Initiative also began participating in "Explore Georgia" resource fairs. These are opportunities during the summer, fall, and spring semesters for upcoming or current high school seniors to come to UGA and learn more about the campus and what it has to offer. At the resource fair, representatives of the Learning Communities Initiative are able to give out information and answer questions about the program and get students excited about it, even before they decide to come to UGA.

The last major, positive change that was made to the recruitment strategies of the UGA Learning Communities is the purchasing of promotional items for both Explore Georgia fairs and summer orientation sessions. From summer 2009 through the current school year, red Frisbees, black lanyards, and carry bags, all with the Learning Community logo and website, have provided another way for students and parents to get information about the Learning Communities. There has been great feedback from these promotional items and the Learning Communities Initiative is gaining steam and acknowledgment across campus.

Orientation

Another area that has improved significantly within the Learning Communities Initiative is its participation in the summer orientation for all first-year students. Over the past three years, the Learning Communities have been gaining a larger presence at orientation in a few different ways. There are two small sessions about the Learning Communities Initiative, one on the first day for the students and one on the second day for the parents. At these sessions, people who have already signed up for the Learning Communities learn how to register for their courses, and those who have not signed up yet learn more about the program and are able to sign up if there are still spots available. It is also a place where parents and students can ask questions and get to know the Learning Community staff.

The Learning Communities Initiative is also improving recruitment efforts at the resource fairs, where departments and programs across campus have tables. The Learning Communities have a table to hand out information and promotional items, and to answer any questions parents or students might have. This presence at the resource fair has significantly increased our visibility not only to the students but also to other departments on campus, thus further legitimizing the program.

Logistics—Registering for the Learning Communities

There are two different ways that students are able to register for the Learning Communities. There is a form on the website that can be filled out, printed, and mailed in, or submitted via e-mail. Adding the e-mail component has increased the accessibility of the program to the more technologically savvy generation of students. The Learning Communities program operates on a first-come, first-served basis and is free for any first-year student. So when registration forms are received, the student's information is entered into a database and the student is sent a confirmation–acceptance e-mail. If students sign up for a Learning Community during summer orientation, they simply fill out a hard copy form and then are given the appropriate information for registration.

Communications

The main correspondence between Learning Communities students and staff prior to orientation is via e-mail and phone. Once registration forms are received, students receive a confirmation e-mail along with other informational e-mails leading up to the summer orientation sessions. Once a student is enrolled in a Learning Community, he or she is added to a specific distribution list for that community that includes all of the students, the lead instructor, peer advisor, other course instructors, and Learning Community staff. This serves as a great communication tool throughout the school year.

Registration for Courses

Course Coding

Because Learning Community students are required to take specific courses to participate, the Learning Community contact in the Office of the Vice President for Instruction works with the various departments throughout the spring to set aside seats in each of the required courses. To do this, those specific seats are taken out of the general population course, given a unique call number, and coded "LCOM." This coding is similar to a Permission of Department (POD) or Permission of Major (POM) course in that only students who have been coded can register for it.

Student Coding

To code students participating in the Learning Communities program, first, permissions must be granted from the Registrar's office for the contact in the Office of the Vice President for Instruction to be allowed to code. Otherwise, a staff member in the Registrar's Office would need to do the coding. Each student registered for the Learning Communities must be coded with a community specific code. These codes were preset by the Registrar when the program began, and as new Learning Communities have been added, codes for them have been added as well. Once students have been coded correctly and approved by their advisor during orientation, they are given the appropriate information (call numbers) to register for their required Learning Community courses.

Block Call Numbers

All call numbers, as mentioned previously, are specifically created just for the Learning Community courses. To make the process easier and quicker for the students, all of their specific Learning Communities courses are then grouped into one "block call number." This allows students to enter in one five-digit call number into UGA's online registration system and have all three of their courses loaded onto their schedule. This allows the students to focus more time on scheduling their other courses around their Learning Community courses.

Faculty and Peer Advisor Selection

Faculty members for the Learning Community lead instructor positions are selected based on a few specific criteria. Lead instructors are asked to lead a Learning Community if they are well respected in their fields, both by peers and students. Also, a passion for improving first-year students' academic and university experience is a must. The majority of the current Lead Instructor faculty members have been with the program for at least three years, and the rest have come highly recommended over the last few years. With the implementation of the FYOS in fall 2011, the requirements for faculty shifted slightly. These seminars are now to be taught by tenured or tenure-track faculty; however, because some of the Learning Community instructors are lecturers only, they have been granted an exception and have been able to remain with the program. Every year, new lead instructors are provided with a faculty guidebook to aid them with the process of leading a Learning Community. Because the experience is so much more than a single class-room experience, it is helpful for them to have some guidance and suggestions from previous or current instructors.

The peer advisors for each Learning Community are interviewed and selected by staff both in University Housing and the Office of the Vice President for Instruction. A request for applications is sent out and posted early in the spring semester and interviews are conducted mid-spring. Peer advisors are chosen based on specific qualifications and it is preferable for them to have participated in the Learning Communities previously. Faculty often suggest or recommend specific students they have had in the past who they would like to work for them as a peer advisor, and those requests are taken into consideration when choosing the peer advisors.

Future of the Program

The future of the Learning Community Initiative at UGA appears bright. One goal for the future is expanding the program to include more students. A challenge for this initiative is in conveying the benefits of joining a Learning Community to new students and their families. The program comes at no additional cost, but some deterrents include some perceptions about join-ing, like additional time commitment. The benefits are clear and when explained to students and their families, many students are interested. If the initiative does see growth, the partners will need to work to bring the same structure to other residence halls on campus. Some additional funding would need to be directed to pay the lead instructors of the special seminar class. The FYOS program is seen as an initiative that can trace its groundings in the success of the Learning Communities at UGA. With hard work and coordination, the program should expect to see growth and continued success.

References

Astin, A. W. (1999). Student involvement: A developmental theory for higher educa-tion. *Journal of College Student Development, 40*(5), 518–529.

Kuh, G. D., Kinzie, J., Schuh, J. H., & Whitt, E. J. (2005). *Student success in college: Creating conditions that matter.* San Francisco: Jossey-Bass.

Mission, Values and Principles. University Housing. Retrieved August 15, 2011, from http://housing.uga.edu/about/mission-values-principles

National Survey of Student Engagement. Retrieved August 14, 2011, from http://nsse.iub.edu

Tinto, V. (1993). *Leaving college: Rethinking the causes and cures of student attrition* (2nd ed.). Chicago: University of Chicago Press.

8

LEARNING COMMUNITIES IN THE NEW UNIVERSITY

Siskanna Naynaha and Wendy Olson

This chapter describes a learning community project piloted within the College of Liberal Arts at a land-grant research university, Washington State University (WSU), during fall 2006. Supported by a Provost's Teaching and Learning Grant, the project was designed as an alternative learning community model to the university-wide and top-down administered Freshman Focus experience. Enrolling students in a pair of classes that they share with a number of other students assigned to their same residence hall during their first year, *Freshman Focus* promises students a "living–learning" experience. One premise behind this program is that these socially-based learning communities grow to nurture students' academic success organically. In this model, linked faculty are encouraged to collaborate, yet the university provided little apparatus to support this organic collaboration and, in most cases, faculty were not asked to substantially rethink how their own pedagogical approaches affect student learning experiences.

In contrast, we proposed a learning community project wherein courses were linked by a common theme, shared course content, instructor collaboration, and common learning goals that emphasized interdisciplinary learning and alternative pedagogical approaches. In doing so, our assumption was that, for a learning community to significantly affect student learning in a positive way, the formation and cultivation of the learning community itself needed to rethink traditional approaches to both disciplinary boundaries and pedagogical methods. As such, this chapter addresses the pedagogical challenge of how to create meaningful learning community experiences for students in the increasingly fragmented and bureaucratized environment of the new university.

Intended to meet the objective of the President's Teaching Academy to improve the learning experience of first-year WSU students, our proposed learning communities encompassed many of the other university-wide learning goals, including an emphasis on understanding the individual as fully contextualized within both local and global societies; the development of writing, listening, and speaking skills across disciplines; and real-world practice in discipline adaptability. The learning communities, which took place during fall 2005, involved six courses and three links: three sections of English (ENG) 101: Introduction to Writing (administered by the English department), a course required of all entering freshmen, were linked to American Studies 216: American Culture, Comparative Ethnic Studies (CES) 151: Introduction to Chicano/Latino Studies, and Women's Studies 200: Introduction to Women's Studies, respectively. The ENGL 101 and CES 151 link was specifically proposed to target incoming Latina/o, Chicana/o students, aimed at addressing the particular experiences of this student population within the context of an increasingly diverse local and global society. Course content and assignments across links were integrated based on instructor collaboration and all students were required to sign up for both courses, creating "closed" learning community links. Another supplementary goal of the project was to create enhanced professional development opportunities for participating instructors.

In what follows, we share the timeline of the project, outline the methodology used to assess the project, and present the major findings of our assessment of the pilot. The chapter closes with conclusions and recommendations from the project, information we believe can be used to further enhance future learning community projects across institutions. We outline the major findings briefly here:

1. Learning communities provide a positive effect on students' first-year learning experiences. Benefits as reported by students and teachers include more time on task with course material, a better grasp and understanding of course material, more explicit understanding of expectations of course assignments, and, in general, a more clearly articulated academic learning environment.
2. Learning communities positively affect teacher professional development, including providing opportunities for curriculum and assignment collaboration, space for pedagogical discussion and reflection to occur, and support for coteaching activities.

3. Additional, complementary benefits for student life and the university environment in general were also noted. Some of these benefits include a supportive social network for students, an enhanced commitment to studies by students, a tangible sense of belonging to an academic community by students, and his student retention.

Background

In an earlier project as part of a programmatic initiative under a revamped first-year composition program in the English department, five learning community links with General Education 110 and ENGL 101 were piloted in fall 2004. Financial support of $1,000 per instructor was supplied by the General Education department. Links were adopted to enhance student learning and retention. Projected benefits for instructors and faculty involved included expansion of teaching repertoires and approaches, continual revision and reflection on course content, and the acquisition of new scholarly interests. Assessment of the links during spring 2005 focused on the effectiveness of the piloted learning community links to affect student learning.

Data collected from student surveys and informal discussions with linked instructors suggested that more attention to teacher collaboration and crossover assignments were needed for the success of future linked and learning community projects. Although surveys revealed that some students did enjoy the social aspect of having some of the "same people in both classes," students also consistently commented on their disappointment in the lack of academic connections across the linked courses. Recommendations for future linked and learning community projects included the following:

- Scaffold teacher training and support for linked teaching partners.
- Provide one semester of preparation workshops, as well as continued support meetings, for teachers throughout the teaching semester.
- Explicitly explain and reinforce for students shared course material, assignments, and so on in syllabi.
- Use assessment-friendly assignments to assess students' (and teachers') evolving perceptions and reflections about the learning environment.
- Encourage instructors to experiment with alternative teaching strategies (e.g., service learning, coteaching) by providing examples and models during training.

Committed to continuing this worthwhile pedagogical experiment, we collaborated with the chair of the English department and drafted the proposal "Exploring Learning Communities as a Site for Improving Students' First-Year Experience," which was fully funded in spring 2005 by a Provost's grant through the Office of Undergraduate Education at WSU. This proposal targeted Chicana/o and Latina/o students, linking ENGL 101 courses with introductory courses in American Studies, Contemporary Ethnic Studies, and Women's Studies. The following reports on the project and its findings.

Assessment Methodology

Assessment of the fall 2005 Learning Community Links included both formative and summative data collection and evaluation. The process focused on assessing three primary objectives: the effect the learning communities had on the first-year learning experiences of students at the university, the pedagogical and scholarly influences on teacher professional development, and the overall role learning communities might play in the undergraduate curriculum at a research-intensive university. This study involved collaboration among six courses that composed three links (ENGL 101 and AM ST 216, ENGL 101 and CES 151, and ENGL 101 and W ST 200); six instructors (four teaching assistants [TAs], one adjunct instructor, and two faculty members); and the following academic departments: American Studies, Comparative Ethnic Studies, English, History, and Women's Studies.

To assess the objectives, we surveyed both participating students and instructors. These surveys asked participants to rate their learning community experiences via four markers:

- How well the nonwriting course informed students' understanding of course material in the writing course
- How well the writing course informed students' understanding of course material in the nonwriting course
- How well teacher collaboration enhanced students' learning experience
- Whether participants (both students and teachers) would participate in another linked course based on their experiences with this linked course
- The effect the experience had on participating instructors' professional development as teachers and scholars

Written comments were also solicited for each of these queries in the surveys, including a request for participants to describe what they considered to be the strongest and weakest element of the linked course experience. In addition to surveys, we collected course syllabi, course assignments, student portfolios (from the ENGL 101 courses), and critical reflections from instructors. Comments and suggestions from an end-of-project, roundtable discussion, in which instructors reflected collectively on the project, were also used in the assessment process.

The following section provides a narrative account of the project over the course of three terms (spring 2005, summer 2005, and fall 2005), followed by a discussion of the major findings from the assessment of the project.

Spring 2005

In spring 2005, the proposal for "Exploring Learning Communities as a Site for Improving Students' First-Year Experience" was fully funded. The initial plan had been to contact partner units, select appropriate courses, and assign instructors to the linked sections before the beginning of spring semester. However, funding was not approved until after the beginning of the term, which made meeting those goals impracticable. Contact with partner departments was made in early February, and meetings with department heads took place shortly thereafter.

At these initial meetings, department chairs (English, Women's Studies, Comparative Ethnic Studies), interested faculty (Women's Studies), and the learning community (LC) coordinators (Wendy Olson and Siskanna Naynaha) discussed the proposal, which all in attendance had received via e-mail prior to the meeting. (Director of the university's Multicultural Student Services [MSS] and Acting Director of American Studies were also invited but unable to attend.) The purpose of the meeting was to address any questions and concerns that partner units had about the proposal—which ranged from the logistical to the political—and to set a timeline for the rest of the semester. All present agreed to participation in the project and instructors were to be selected and assigned by each department within a two-week timeline, one each from Women's Studies and Comparative Ethnic Studies (ENGL 101 instructors were chosen and assigned in the prior fall semester). Contact with the director of Multicultural Students Services was an important component of the project because distributing information on the links through MSS was one of the primary advertising strategies planned. In addition, we still needed to contact the third partner unit, American Studies, to verify participation and request the assignment of an instructor to the project. Phone calls and e-mails were the primary means of follow-up with the units not in attendance at the initial meeting.

In preparation for conducting training in learning community pedagogy, the LC coordinators attended a national conference on learning communities entitled "Pedagogies of Engagement: Deepening Learning In and Across the Disciplines," hosted by the Association of American Colleges and Universities. Upon the return of the LC coordinators, participation by all partner units had been accomplished (with the exception of MSS; contact could not be established with this unit at that time) and instructors had been assigned.

It should be noted that at this point the project was considerably behind schedule with regard to the spring semester schedule outlined originally in the proposal. Consequently, in place of the originally planned four workshops to undergird and support the project, two extended instructor meetings were scheduled to take place before the end of the semester. In the first meeting, the LC coordinators discussed the proposal itself, goals, and projected outcomes of the project, and provided an introduction to various learning community models. A packet of information was also distributed to all instructors, which include the following:

- Contact information
- A copy of the project proposal
- Literature on the foundations for developing and means of sustaining learning communities
- Course descriptions and objectives for ENGL 101
- Copies of English course evaluation surveys
- Literature on writing assessment in general and assessment of learning communities in particular
- A copy of the University's Latina/o faculty document "Proposal for Becoming a Hispanic Serving Institution (HSI)"
- Sample syllabi and assignments for courses linked in learning communities

At the second meeting, LC instructors discussed and planned strategies for integrating their curricula, assignments, and pedagogical approaches. Instructors shared past syllabi, assignments, and required texts. In addition to the larger group meeting, instructors were also given time to pair off and work on their links independently, the results of which they presented to the entire group before parting for the summer.

Summer 2005

Because of conflicting schedules and summer vacation, no group meetings were scheduled during the summer 2005 term. Individually, linked partners worked together intermittently via phone conferences and e-mail to continue work on syllabi and share course particulars. Much of the summer was concerned with the administrative issues of advertising the links and getting students enrolled in the courses; a number of complications arose in the process. The majority of this logistical work was coordinated with and assisted by the efforts of staff and faculty associated with ALIVE! (the university's orientation and registration event for incoming freshmen), the university's Student Advising and Learning Center (SALC), and the university writing programs. The following faculty and staff members assisted in brainstorming and developing advertising avenues and opportunities from which to make contact with students:

- Acting assistant vice president of educational development director, SALC
- Assistant director of SALC for advising
- Associate professor and vice chair, department of English
- Writing assessment director, writing programs

Coordinators and support staff from participating departments provided much-needed assistance in the logistics of enrolling and dropping students from the links. A particular complication with the enrollment process was that university registration software lacked the capability to enroll and drop students from the linked courses simultaneously. For this reason, course line numbers had to be blocked and distributed manually, in essence to interested students individually through alternative advertising means. Our main mechanism for advertising the links and attracting students to them became the distribution of flyers through liberal arts advisors during ALIVE! sessions. Interested students were given course line numbers and notified that participation in the link depended on maintaining enrollment in both courses. Throughout this process, LC coordinators had to monitor enrollments daily, calling students who enrolled in one course but not its linked counterpart, stressing students' need to either enroll in both or drop both. Moreover, as graduate students, the coordinators did not have administrative access to drop or enroll the students themselves. Therefore, any students that did not comply with registration reminders about the linked course requirement (dual enrollment) had to be added or dropped manually with the assistance of department coordinators. A mechanism for automatically linking course enrollment through registration software is decidedly recommended for similar linked projects.

Another enrollment complication concerned the student population targeted in the original proposal, Chicana/o and Latina/o students. As mentioned previously, contact with MSS, especially the Chicana/o and Latina/o (ChicLat) Student Center, was one of the primary advertising strategies called for in the development of the learning community proposal. The LC coordinators created flyers for the entire learning community project together, advertising all three links in one source, as well as flyers advertising each link individually. Flyers were distributed to the departments of Comparative Ethnic Studies, English, and Women's Studies, the program in American Studies, as well as to MSS. The staff in MSS helpfully took copies of the flyers and distributed one to each MSS counselor via their internal mailboxes and posted a flyer on the office bulletin board. However, much more consistent and pervasive advertising was needed to meet enrollment for the links in a timely manner. Multiple e-mail and phone messages to the faculty in MSS went unanswered, and the ChicLat Center remained closed entirely for this portion of the summer (approximately mid-July to the beginning of fall semester). Hence, the LC coordinators had serious difficulty reaching those students who were the primary focus of the original proposal. Enrollment in the ENGL 101 and CES 151 link remained low throughout summer ALIVE! sessions, forcing the need to open the courses up to nonlinked students near the onset of open enrollment at the beginning of fall semester to justify not closing the courses completely. Although each course was subsequently able to meet enrollment numbers to remain open, the number of linked students in each course was minimal at six students.

Half way through the summer term, we also lost one of the participating instructors, a faculty member who resigned from the university and took a position elsewhere. Women's Studies was able to appoint a graduate TA as a replacement. This last-minute change to the final teaching assignment put this particular link at a distinct disadvantage. Because one instructor was newly introduced to the project at the penultimate moment, that instructor had not had the benefit of the shared preparatory and collaboration meetings in the spring semester. Thus communication between the two instructors regarding their developing curricula and pedagogy was not a possibility at all over the summer.

At this point, the LC coordinators decided to focus the assessment of the project on a comparative analysis of the three links as they had developed: a partial link (ENGL 101 and CES 151) and two "closed" links in which the same students were enrolled in both of the two linked courses (ENGL 101 and AM ST 216 and ENGL 101 and W ST 200).

Fall 2005

During fall 2005, despite various setbacks and complications, learning community links were realized and the project was on task. Linked partners met throughout the term to discuss and shape their course implementation. The LC coordinators facilitated five meetings over the semester. Topics covered and issues discussed included the following:

Thursday 8/18/05: Coordinators shared assessment strategies and designs, drafts of student and instructor surveys were shared for feedback, and linked partners worked together to finalize syllabus and curriculum plans for the semester.

Friday 9/9/05: Instructors shared "best practices," discussing what was working and what was not in the linked courses thus far; instructors discussed and shared ideas for potential collaborative assignments and exercises to further embed into the courses over the semester.

Friday 10/7/05: Instructor partners presented collaborative assignments to the group; coordinators gathered a "next-time" list of suggestions for learning community preparation and training.

Friday 10/28/05: Coordinators distributed student surveys, and instructors coordinated times to administer surveys for one another's classrooms; instructors discussed plans for how they would (or would not) collaborate on final examinations and grading; and coordinators prepped instructors for critical reflection expectations.

Wednesday 12/14/05: Coordinators collected critical reflections from instructors and administered surveys, and instructors collectively discussed and reflected on the project.

At the end of the semester, writing samples from students were collected as well as copies of course assignments and exercises. The administered surveys asked participants to rate their experiences from "scant" to "substantial" on a continuum of one to six, with three visually representing the mid-range score. From this visual ranking, one to two represented a "low" score, three represented a "medium score," and four to six represented a "high" score. As stated previously, participants were also asked for written comments to accompany each score. Examination of surveys from participating students and instructors, along with the supplementary material mentioned earlier, were then used to identify key patterns that emerged in the project.

Major Findings

Analysis of student surveys revealed that students reported considerable benefits from the linked course experience. Of all student participants, including both linked and nonlinked students, 63 percent (percentages averaged to the nearest whole number) ranked significant positive experiences. Commenting on how one course informed the learning in the other course, one student remarked, "The material covered in both classes was easy to relate and helped me to understand the material better. I think I understand it [more] than I would have if I just took one class." Another student commented on how the link enhanced critical reading skills: "The ENGL 101 material helped one to analyze and better understand the readings for AM ST 216." Widening this percentage to include medium to high responses raised the positive response rate to 77 percent. Only 6 percent of student participants rated their experiences as in some way unsatisfactory.

Low responses from students across categories proved minimal: an average of 4 percent across the linked courses. Nonlinked students from both ENGL 101 and CES 151 (the only nonlinked students in the study) represented the largest percentage of students rating their experiences as low or "non-applicable" across the spectrum of questions, although it is significant that even this response rate included only about half of the nonlinked students (an average of 53 percent combined, only 5 percent of which falls under the low category). Thus even responses from nonlinked students involved in the links speak to the appeal of the links overall as an innovative learning opportunity. For example, one CES student remarked that she had never taken a linked course but, based on her experience in CES 151, would be willing to take one in the future. A number of nonlinked students in the linked ENGL 101 course made similar comments.

Furthermore, nonlinked ENGL 101 students noted that their experience provided them with a deeper understanding and appreciation for Chicana/o and Latina/o culture, which also benefited their writing skills. One student mentioned "studying a specific, in-depth topic throughout the semester" as a strength that developed analytical skills in ENGL 101. Another student commented that the linked curriculum brought more "structure and direction" to the English course because "all assignments were interrelated" throughout the semester. Speaking of the potential benefits of the course, another student astutely observed, "With any course, different instructors can teach the very same class and have completely different outcomes. Two instructors working together would bring different ideas and different techniques, helping both the instructors and the students." In short, even for those students who were not in both linked classes, the learning community experience provided them with an increased sense of coherence and purpose in their individual courses.

Additional comments about the linked experience from nonlinked participants spoke to the potential disadvantages for nonlinked students. When asked to share what they perceived to be the weakest element of the linked course from their experience, a number of nonlinked ENG 101 students commented on what they thought they were missing from the experience. "It kinda sucks for students who aren't in the linked class," wrote one student, "b/c they almost feel left out. I think if they do link, both classes should be mandatory." Other students noted the potential for confusion and a lack of understanding for nonlinked students. For example, one student wrote that "having a difficult time understanding all of the topics discussed if not in the linked class" was a weakness. Thus, although these findings speak to the success of learning community experiences in general, they also suggest that student learning and experience is, perhaps, further enhanced for participating students when links are designed as closed links, or links in which all students in each class are enrolled in both courses.

Another pattern that emerged in analysis of student surveys was the level of collaboration among linked instructors and its influence on students' learning experiences. More articulated and comprehensive collaboration between instructors, as indicated by higher rankings on the collaboration question on the student survey, corresponded to increased perceived learning and student fulfillment, as indicated by student comments and desire to repeat the experience. Based on instructor reflections and student surveys, the ENGL 101/AM ST 216 link emerged as the most collaborative link in the project. Unlike the ENGL 101/CES 151 link, in which only six students were linked, all twenty-one ENGL 101/AM ST 216 students were enrolled in both courses, making it a "closed link." In contrast to the other closed link,

ENGL 101/W ST 200, the instructors of the ENGL 101/AM ST 216 link benefited from the full range of preparation time and training afforded by the project (as noted earlier, the W ST instructor was replaced mid-project, which significantly reduced the training and preparation potential for this link). And according to instructor reflections and comments, the ENGL 101/AM ST 216 instructors met weekly throughout the semester, whereas scheduled curricular meetings for the other participating instructors were less formalized. The ENGL 101/AM ST 216 instructors also collaborated on student conferencing, all major assignments in both classes (including a final portfolio), and cotaught a number of class sessions.

Consequently, students in the ENGL 101/AM ST 216 link consistently rated the level of collaboration between their instructors as high. As one student put it, "The collaboration was excellent and was a huge positive in my experience." Seventy-five percent of students rated instructor collaboration as very high (scoring a 5 or a 6 on the survey continuum), with 20 percent rated high. Only 5 percent rated the collaboration in the medium range, and no scores ranked the instructor collaboration as low. In contrast, 11 percent of participating students in the ENGL 101/W ST 200 ranked instructor collaboration low, with 24 percent ranking it medium whereas the remaining 65 percent ranked collaboration high. Among the ENGL 101/CES 151 linked students, 17 percent ranked instructor collaboration in the mid-range, while the remaining 83 percent was spread across the high range (no scores ranked the instructor collaboration as scant or insubstantial). Benefits of such collaboration, according to students, included more time on task to better understand class material: "The homework and papers are relevant and linked to both classes. This makes more time spent with the topic."

Analysis of instructor surveys and reflections found that instructors' scholarly interests and pedagogical strategies also benefited from the learning community linked experience. One instructor commented, "We put a lot of collaborative support into this link and it helped my development as a teacher/scholar by giving me a different environment and situation—a pretty unique one—that will carry over into future work." Another instructor remarked on how the experience had affected her pedagogy: "It was enlightening to see how . . . my partner and I approached teaching and course material with both similar and different pedagogical strategies. This collaboration made me reflect on my pedagogy and try different things with assignments and class discussion." Data suggests that even difficulties in collaboration offered a critical avenue for teacher reflection. "Although a collaborative relationship never fully formed," one instructor wrote, "my awareness of classroom management styles and content versus process pedagogy and learning community evolution was pretty enhanced. The 'collaboration' was an invaluable experience."

As implied in the previous comment, one issue that arose for participating instructors over the course of the semester was how to negotiate potentially incongruous pedagogies. Introduction to varying pedagogical strategies is, arguably, an advantage that linked courses provide for both students and instructors. Differences, however, need to be made explicit. The potential for incompatible pedagogies is compounded when linking courses as distinct in goals from one another as writing courses and nonwriting courses. With regard to the learning community links in our project, the primary goal of the introductory writing courses was practice in and production of academic writing, whereas the primary goals of the nonwriting courses concerned covering a breadth of discipline-specific material. The means instructors enacted for reaching these goals, in part because of their distinct differences, varied accordingly. Thus writing pedagogy often relied on drafting workshops, peer response sessions, and process, whereas pedagogy styles for introductory, nonwriting courses more often than not relied on a combination of lecture, presentation (of visual information or video), and discussion. As one instructor explained, "Content area teaching and process-oriented pedagogy [were] a little difficult to coalesce." If these differences are not acknowledged, discussed, and managed by instructors beforehand and throughout the link, unnecessary dissonance can occur for both students and instructors. This issue became a particular concern for the ENGL 101/W ST 200 link in its already disadvantaged position—perhaps in part because of it.

Lastly, analysis of data suggests that the links as practiced in this project resulted in a number of complementary benefits for students that stretched beyond just improving their learning experiences with course content. Additional patterns that emerged included the development of a supportive social network for students, an enhanced commitment to studies by students, and student retention. As one instructor observed, "The community that developed among the students and the instructors over the semester was amazing."

At the same time, students across the links commented on their appreciation of the community the linked course offered them. For example, one student believed the strength of the linked experience to be "the relationships you get to build with peers because of the close environment" and another student noted similar benefits in that "you get to have the same students in the same classes to help you with assignments."

Although longitudinal data about participating students is not available, it is encouraging to note that drop rates across the linked courses remained quite minimal. Instructors also reported consistently high attendance. Furthermore, instructors noticed a higher level of commitment to course work from student link participants than from students they had taught in previous sections of the same courses. Comparing the linked course to other incarnations of the course she taught, one instructor remarked,

> Most students read everything and many students read almost everything. . . . Students held each other accountable in ways that other classes have not. Students were aware of who was or was not in class, who did or did not do the day's work or reading, and they often encouraged/ embarrassed each other into being more committed to their class work.

Another instructor noted that her students "came to class more prepared, challenged, ready to engage, and excited about how a discussion from one class could continue in another space, with a different facilitator and continue to be critically evaluated, this time through writing."

Conclusions and Recommendations for Employing Linked Courses

1. Although varying kinds of learning community or linked course structures exist to meet distinct educational goals and objectives, "closed links," in which participating students enroll in both classes, were the most beneficial to student learning in our project. These links received overall higher ratings with respect to students' perceptions of how the linked experience affected their learning in both courses.

2. Higher levels of collaboration among linked instructors (including shared assignments, coteaching, and set curriculum meetings) resulted in a higher level of both student learning and student satisfaction with the linked course experience. As such, we recommend that other linked course projects both require and support a minimal level of collaboration and shared course material from participating instructors and faculty.

3. For links to successfully meet the goals of positively influencing student learning and first-year experience, participating instructors need training and preparation beforehand. Furthermore, this training

should occur over time to best ensure that a sound understanding of learning community philosophy develops among participants and to allow linked partners the time and space to develop a substantial relationship with one another. Benefits to such preparatory training include better-prepared instructors and a higher level of embedded interdisciplinary curriculum in links.

4. Ongoing teacher training and support needs to occur throughout the length of the linked term as well. Instructors in our project consistently commented on the positive effect group meetings had on their overall experience, providing a space to discuss pedagogy, to gather and share assignment ideas, and, among other things, to talk through difficulties and challenges as they came up over the course of the semester. In fact, some instructors offered useful suggestions for further support, including a shared online space to trade materials and draft syllabi and assignments collaboratively.

5. The planning, logistics, and implementation of successful linked experiences rely on backing and buy-in from a number of stake holders, some more readily visible than others. Our project suggests that a top-down administrative approach is less successful than approaches that invite and unite interested parties, taking into consideration the vested interests of all affected parties as it does so. This is not to suggest that we believe such learning communities might grow organically; on the contrary, our experiences from this project illustrate that upper administrative support is absolutely necessary to success and without it complications in implementation are compounded. Instead, we suggest a flexible administrative approach that provides a supportive framework—including appropriate funding, time allocation, and resources—to grow a project that adapts to the needs of various stake holders while also utilizing in-house expertise at all levels.

6. Finally, we recommend that more research and data collection within universities be committed to support (through both funding and resource distribution) and analysis of learning community and linked course models. The assessment results presented here cover student and teacher perceptions of learning community experiences. Also collected but not yet analyzed are student writing samples, instructor syllabi, and course assignments. These materials, combined with similar materials collected from other university learning communities, can provide deeper insights into potential benefits of various learning

community models as well as make available a substantial wealth of teacher training materials.

Though certainly envisioned as programs that provide a number of beneficial attributes, including improvement of retention rates and academic success among students, the rise of learning community offerings across institutions of higher education cannot be separated from the ongoing corporatization of the university and a focus on the "entrepreneurial potential" that drives the "new university" model (Crow, 2008). We invoke the language of the "new university" in our title to capture this tension. Increasingly, learning communities are seen institutionally as not only as useful vehicles for enhancing student learning and student learning experiences, but also recruitment tools for students and tuition dollars. In the ever-increasing competition for students, it is important that we don't lose sight of our original impetus for, and philosophy behind, learning communities: the opportunity to create meaningful and substantial learning environments for students. Top-down learning community models that ignore or de-emphasize the role of faculty and the need for faculty support and training in contributing to successful learning communities can inadvertently miss this opportunity.

Reference

Crow, Michael (2008, June). Building an entrepreneurial university. Paper presented at the *Third Annual Kauffman Foundation-Max Planck Institute,* Munich, Germany.

PART THREE

ASSESSING LINKED COURSES

9

THE NUTS AND BOLTS OF EVALUATING LINKED COURSES

Michael Roszkowski

P rogram evaluation is the systematic collection of data about a program's characteristics, activities, and outcomes that allows one to make a judgment about whether the program is working (Weiss, 1998; Worthen, Sanders, & Fitzpatrick, 1997). There is a growing demand for accountability in education (Allen, 2003), and a program evaluation can provide the necessary evidence that linking courses is an effective pedagogical method. As with the planning for any sort of evaluation, the two overriding preliminary issues to be addressed with an evaluation of linked courses are (a) what to assess and (b) how to assess it. The aim of this chapter is to offer the reader some suggestions on both matters. It is not intended to be a detailed guide, but it should provide the reader with enough background to understand the basics and to pursue more intensive sources on this topic if needed.

Questions to Be Answered by Process and Outcomes Evaluations

To carry out a comprehensive evaluation of linked courses, one may need to conduct both a process evaluation and an outcomes evaluation. An outcomes evaluation will tell one whether the project has achieved its goals, whereas a process evaluation can inform about why such results occurred. That is, in outcomes evaluation, one determines whether the expected benefits occurred, and so the focus is on the results of the program. In a process evaluation, on the other hand, one considers the descriptive characteristics of the program, so if the outcome data indicate that the expected benefits are not evident, process data can be used to help determine the reasons for this. Obviously, process evaluation is particularly relevant if the expected results do not materialize, providing clues as to deficiencies in the program, but one may want to conduct a process evaluation even with positive outcomes because process data on successful programs can be insightful if others want to replicate the program.

Process Evaluation

In process evaluation, one focuses on materials and activities. The core dimensions of effective linked courses have been identified by Visher, Wathington, Richburg-Hayes, and Schneider (2008) as (a) integration, (b) active learning, (c) faculty engagement, (d) student engagement, (e) supplemental support services, and (f) institutional and structural transformation. Moreover, these researchers have developed a comprehensive list of key indicators for each dimension. A process evaluation needs to examine the extent to which the key indicators shown in Table 9.1 describe one's linked course program.

Unfortunately, it is not clear what features are most critical for achieving success in linked courses (Price, 2005), but the greater the number of these features are present, the more likely it is that the program can be successful. If an outcomes evaluation shows that one's linked course program is not achieving the desired results, one should definitely examine in detail whether the program had the critical characteristics. Sometimes it may be a good idea to consider a process evaluation even before launching a linked course program because whenever only a few of these characteristics are present in the program, one has to question whether benefits can reasonably be expected to realize. If enrollment in linked courses is voluntary, one may benefit from comparing and contrasting the attitudes and background characteristics of students who choose to enroll from the ones who do not as part of the process evaluation.

Outcomes Evaluation

Outcomes are the favorable results that are meant to come about from some action, such as the linking of courses. To conduct an outcomes evaluation,

TABLE 9.1
Indicators of Core Dimensions of Linked Courses

Core Dimension: Integration
Description: Course content organized around common themes or topics
Key Indicators:

- Course syllabi are merged, blocked, or aligned.
- Joint assignments, projects, and grading are given.
- Commonalities and differences between disciplines are indicated.
- Seminars, special topics lectures, or research and field study sessions are linked to courses.
- Multiple perspectives are given for the description, analysis, or explanation of phenomena.

Core Dimension: Active-learning pedagogy
Description: Teaching techniques that involve experiential, collaborative, and reflective learning that relate the course content to real-world issues and thereby foster critical-thinking skills.
Key Indicators:

- Project- and problem-based activities are presented in the classroom.
- Active discussions occur among students and instructors.
- Reflective or responsive writing assignments are given.
- Interactive labs and field work are completed.
- Instructors respond proactively to students experiencing problems.

Core Dimension: Faculty engagement
Description: Instructors collaborate in designing linking activities and assignments.
Key Indicators:

- Instructors participate in scheduled meetings and other systematic communication during the term.
- Team teaching or coteaching occurs.

Core Dimension: Student engagement
Description: Students play an active role in the learning process, which creates peer networks that can provide academic support and promote social integration.
Key Indicators:

- Same cohort of students are enrolled in the linked courses.
- Dyads or study groups are formed, either informally or created by the instructor.
- These study groups are characterized by diversity in terms of demographic and cultural characteristics.

TABLE 9.1 (Continued)

- Cocurricular activities such as field trips, service learning, or community-based projects occur.
- Students interact outside of class in informal social situations, such as at meals.
- Students in linked courses have meaningful relationships with each other.
- Students become independent learners.

Core Dimension: Supplemental student support services
Description: Students use campus resources that can promote academic and social development.
Key Indicators:
- Student are aware of the support services available to them.
- Students are encouraged to make use of these services.
- Faculty actively refer students experiencing difficulties to appropriate support services.
- Support services are integrated with classroom activities (e.g., representatives from the offices offering support services make presentations in the classroom regarding the services available from that office).
- Instructors and student services representatives meet on a regular basis to discuss student academic and social needs.
- A collaborative relationships exists between instructors and student services staff.

Core Dimension: Institutional and structural transformation
Description: Institutional support exists for learning communities from the larger campus community.
Key Indicators:
- Linked courses are aligned with the overall institutional mission.
- Linked courses are publicized.
- Adequate funding exists for linked courses.
- Regular communication occurs between administrators and linked courses staff.
- Professional development is provided to faculty to learn linked course pedagogical practices.
- Incentives are provided to faculty to teach linked courses.

Note: Adapted from Visher et al. (2008).

one first needs to articulate the major goals or objectives of one's program. In the present case, these are general statements regarding the benefits that linking of courses intends to produce. (Some authors restrict the term *outcomes evaluation* to short-term goals, preferring the term *impact evaluation* for long-term goals.) Next, for each goal, one has to specify the indicators, or observable measures, that can inform whether the objective is being met. Unlike the goals, which are broadly stated, the indicators must be stated in measurable terms.

In the outcomes evaluation, one then needs to compare the intended consequences of linked instruction to what actually happened. Of course, aligning goals and evidence requires one to be clear about goals. The literature on the benefits of linked courses provides one with a list of potential goals for one's linked course program based on reported benefits at other institutions. It has been claimed, with varying degrees of credibility, that linked courses show superiority to nonlinked courses in terms of (a) intellectual interaction among students, (b) participation in class discussions, (c) attendance, (d) discipline problems, (e) student satisfaction, (f) sense of community, (g) understanding of the construction of knowledge, (h) camaraderie among students, (i) academic coherence, (j) writing with greater depth and more critical insight, (k) seeking connections between nonlinked courses, (l) joy for learning, (m) less redundancy in assignments among courses, (n) fostering faculty–student relationships, and (o) knowledge of interdisciplinary connections (for reviews, see Price, 2005; Taylor, Moore, MacGregor, & Lindblad, 2003; Tinto, 1998). These positive experiences are believed to engage students more fully than traditional courses and thereby are claimed to improve the ultimate measures of academic success such as (a) grades, (b) persistence, and (c) time to degree completion. Supposedly, faculty benefit as well from linked courses by learning from each other and through the fostering of a sense of community among faculty (Creamer & Lattuca, 2005).

These positive results identified in the literature on linked courses can inform the reader regarding what indicators to select when evaluating one's own program. However, the caveat is that with a few exceptions, most reports on the benefits of linked courses (a) have been based on experiences at a single institution, (b) with students who volunteered to take them, (c) lacked control groups, (d) considered only a small number of outcomes, and (e) looked at these outcomes over the short run and not the long run (Price, 2005; Taylor et al., 2003). Also, not all attempts to link courses have led to positive results (e.g., Levine & Guy, 2006), and the number of failures may be underestimated in the published literature, given the bias by journals against the acceptance of studies failing to show statistically significant differences between groups (Rosenthal, 1979).

The best design for collecting data for an outcomes evaluation has the following features, which can demonstrate the "value added" of linked instruction (Scrivener & Coghlan, 2011): (a) a pre- and a posttest to measure the amount of change, (b) a control group of students not participating in the linked course program to allow for benchmarking against traditional instruction, and (c) random assignment of students to the treatment (i.e., linked courses) and to the control group (i.e., traditional courses) to avoid attributing any outcomes to participation in the linked program that may instead have been due to self-selection (student characteristics that increase or decrease learning of any type, such as motivation).

If random assignment is not feasible, as most often is the case, statistical control for differences between students is possible, but it is less credible than random assignment. A good example of statistical control in learning community evaluations is the analysis reported by Borden and Rooney (1998). In looking at outcomes, it is necessary to consider the time frame. For instance, in the early semesters, linked courses may show an advantage on course passing rates and number of credits earned, but these advantages may not translate to higher graduation rates (Scrivener & Coghlan, 2011).

If one wants a model of best practices in the evaluation of linked courses, then she or he should take a look at the process employed in assessing the outcomes of a demonstration project named *Opening Doors,* operated by MDRC at Kinsborough Community College in Brooklyn, New York (Bloom & Sommo, 2005; Scrivener & Coghlan, 2011). Developmental students took three linked courses during their first semester. The study had a control group and used random assignment. A two-year window was used for the evaluation. The results, however, are mixed. Positive effects were observed on course pass rates and credits earned during the first semester, including completion of the developmental English course. Compared with students in the control group, students in linked courses also reported feeling more integrated and more engaged. Surprisingly, however, no differences in persistence occurred.

The interdisciplinary nature of linked courses should also offer some benefits in terms of the learning of certain unique skills. According to several authorities, the distinctiveness of interdisciplinary learning is the development of the student's ability to synthesize and integrate (Boix-Mansilla, 2005; Klein, 1990). An analysis of interdisciplinary education at liberal arts institutions by Rhoten, Boix-Mansilla, Chun, and Klein (2006) concluded that determining the appropriate mechanism for judging the effect of inter-disciplinary courses and programs on the development of such skills consti-tutes the biggest hurdle facing proponents of "interdisciplinarity." These researchers contend that in most cases, interdisciplinary courses are evalu-ated, by default, with the same approaches as used for traditional courses. Thus few programs are able to capture the outcomes unique to "interdisci-plinary learning," that is, the skills that cannot be gained (or not as readily) through any type of liberal education. However, in a program evaluation of linked courses, one should strive to assess whether this unique benefit is occurring.

The Four Levels of Outcomes

A good framework for analyzing the diverse outcomes data that can accrue from linked courses is an intuitively appealing four-level model initially pro-posed in 1959 by Donald Kirkpatrick for evaluating industrial training pro-grams, a model which remains immensely popular (Lee & Pershing, 2000; Tamkin, Yarnell, & Kerrin, 2002). More recently it has been suggested as a system to be applied to the evaluation of university programs as well (Antheil & Casper, 1986; McLean & Moss, 2003; O'Neil, Wainess, & Baker, 2005; Rajeev, Madan, & Jayarajan, 2009; Roszkowski & Soven, 2011), including interdisciplinary learning (Cooper, Carlisle, Gibbs, & Watkins, 2001).

Kirkpatrick's first level is called *Reaction,* and here one measures how students felt about the course in a questionnaire such as a course evaluation form, a focus group, or an interview; these are frequently called *indirect measures* in the assessment literature. At the second level, called *Learning,* actual content mastery is measured, preferably in terms of a pretest and posttest design. The third level, termed *Behavior,* requires an analysis of whether the knowledge generalized from the classroom by observing the performance of the student in real life. The final level, which Kirkpatrick called *Results,* considers the effect of the outcomes in the broader context of the organization's goals.

Kirkpatrick contends that a comprehensive evaluation of an instruc-tional program needs to consider all four levels, but the complexity and usually the cost of the evaluation increases as one moves from level 1 through level 4. Consequently, in industrial training contexts most evaluations of outcomes do not advance beyond the first level (Ruona, Leimbach, Holton, & Bates, 2002; Sugrue & Rivera, 2005), despite the fact that reliance on reactions alone has come under intense criticism (Newby, 1992). Specifically, according to the American Society of Training Development's 2005 "State of the Industry" report (Sugrue & Rivera, 2005), a survey of organizations showed that 91 percent evaluated their training programs at level 1, 54 percent at level 2, 23 percent at level 3, and only 7 percent at level 4. Cooper et al. (2001) conducted a metaanalysis of studies focusing on the interdisciplinary education of undergraduate health professions students, and classified the outcomes in terms of Kirkpatrick's four levels. Not surprisingly, they reported, "Interprofessional educational interventions seemed to be most effective in relation to two areas: 'reaction' and 'learning.' Much less apparent were effects upon 'behaviour' and 'results,' but this reflected the fact that the majority of the interventions had not focused upon measuring these outcomes" (p. 233). This claim is supported by a survey of liberal arts colleges regarding interdisciplinary programs, in which it too was determined that the two most common outcomes measures are student grades and opinion surveys, respectively (Rhoten et al., 2006). According to Taylor et al. (2003), the most commonly used outcomes indicators for learning communities, which includes linked courses, are course performance, grade point average (GPA), and retention into the third semester.

The dominance of level 1 measurement is also evident in the "Learning Communities Directory Report" published by the Washington Center for Improving the Quality of Undergraduate Education (www.evergreen .edu/washcenter/natlc/dir/showQuest.asp?qid = 26), which reports answers to a survey that asked institutions with learning communities the following question: "Overall, how are you assessing the effectiveness of your learning community initiative?" Of 311 institutions, 266 responded, with the percentage using each measure being as follows:

- Student satisfaction: 87 percent
- Analysis of retention within the program: 72 percent
- Analysis of year-to-year retention at institution: 72 percent
- Faculty and student affairs satisfaction: 64 percent
- Annual program enrollment: 61 percent
- Studies of GPAs: 60 percent
- Student learning as demonstrated in projects and portfolios: 48 percent
- Rates of course or program completion: 46 percent

- Graduation rates: 36 percent
- Student progress toward degree: 36 percent
- National instruments such as the College Student Experience Questionnaire, the Community College Student Experience Questionnaire, the National Survey of Student Engagement (NSSE), or others: 36 percent
- Entry into or graduation from certain majors: 13 percent

One troubling finding revealed in a metaanalysis of industrial training by Alliger, Tannenbaum, Bennet, Traver, and Shotland (1997) is that reactions (level 1) do not necessarily correlate highly with learning (level 2). However, as pointed out by Kirkpatrick and Kirkpatrick (2005), measuring reactions shows participants that their opinions matter and, perhaps more importantly, it provides ideas on how to improve the program. Reactions can be valuable because even though positive feelings about a course do not ensure learning, it is probable that negative reactions stifle learning such as when the participant drops the course, does not take further coursework of this sort, or discourages others from doing so (Brown, 2005; Light, Singer, & Willett, 1990; Long, DuBois, & Faley, 2008).

Level One Measures

Despite some of the obvious shortcomings of reactions, it is nonetheless productive to measure outcomes for linked courses at level 1. Placing potential linked course outcomes into Kirkpatrick's framework means that at level 1, one could survey students about their perceptions of the linked courses, asking about characteristics such as satisfaction, relevance, difficulty, enjoyment, level of engagement, self-assessed learning, and so on. At La Salle University, in addition to the standard course evaluation, reactions to the linked courses, which we called *Doubles,* were sought with a Likert scale asking for level of agreement with the following statements:

- My instructors clearly explained the purposes of the Doubles courses.
- The Doubles courses were a good learning experience.
- Professors in the Doubles sections seemed to work well together.
- Thematic connections between the Doubles courses were clear.
- Doubles faculty seemed to learn from each other.
- I would recommend the Doubles experience to incoming students.
- The Doubles program is achieving its goals.

- The number of joint classes was sufficient.
- In my opinion, the goals of the Doubles are vague.
- The Doubles format interfered with my learning of the subject matter.
- The theme around which the Doubles courses are organized is appropriate.
- The joint classes in the Doubles courses were well coordinated with each other.
- In the Doubles courses I got to see relationships that I would not have realized if I took each course separately.
- My Doubles courses helped me understand connections between subjects.
- The Doubles are a good idea.
- Activities outside of class helped to achieve the goals of the Doubles.
- I cut fewer classes in the Doubles courses than in my other courses.
- Reading and writing assignments helped to achieve the goals of the Doubles.
- Joint classes helped to achieve the goals of the Doubles.

Attempting to capture the benefits of "interdiscipliniarity" (Klein, 1990), La Salle's questionnaire also had a section on which the student was asked to compare her or his Doubles courses with non-Doubles courses in terms of aspects on which interdisciplinary courses have been reported to be superior, using the following scale: 1 = *much worse*, 2 = *worse*, 3 = *about the same*, 4 = *better*, 5 = *much better*. Table 9.2 summarizes La Salle's experiences over seventeen semesters. It reports the mean ratings on each item aggregated over this time span. The standard deviations indicate that the variation over the semesters was small. Moreover, the values of the coefficient of variation (which is simply the standard deviation divided by the mean) were quite uniform across items, falling in the range of 3 percent to 4 percent. On average, the linked courses were seen as superior to the non-linked courses the student was taking that semester on all aspects, with the top benefit being student camaraderie, although integration was also among the more commonly perceived strengths.

A similar set of items worth considering in an evaluation at level 1 was used in a cross-institutional survey conducted in 2010 and 2011 by the Washington Center for Improving the Quality of Undergraduate Education and Skagit Valley College's Institutional Research Office. Respondents from 22 colleges and universities (n = 3,706) reported on their experiences in various

TABLE 9.2
Benefits of Doubles (Linked Courses) Relative to Nonlinked Courses
at La Salle University

Item	Mean	SD	CV
Helping you work with your fellow students	3.74	0.13	0.03
Allowing you to appreciate different perspectives	3.68	0.10	0.03
Fostering student interactions	3.65	0.10	0.03
Challenging your thinking	3.62	0.12	0.03
Allowing you to interpret ideas	3.61	0.13	0.04
Helping you integrate ideas	3.58	0.11	0.03
Making learning a pleasant experience	3.56	0.11	0.03
Allowing you to think critically	3.55	0.11	0.03
Helping you evaluate ideas	3.54	0.13	0.04
Engaging you in the learning process	3.53	0.10	0.03
Helping you retain what you learned	3.51	0.13	0.04
Helping you work more closely with the instructor	3.51	0.10	0.03
Deepening your interest in the subject matter	3.45	0.12	0.03
Capturing your interest	3.44	0.13	0.04
Making the material relevant to your everyday concerns	3.36	0.10	0.03
Teaching you how to solve problems	3.28	0.14	0.04

types of learning communities, which consisted primarily (82 percent) of combined classes. One of the questions asked students to compare the amount of time spent in various tasks in the learning community courses relative to traditional courses ("In my learning community, compared with other classes, I spend more, less, or about the same amount of time"). The items and the percentage of students indicating "more" for the learning community courses are in the following list. (The Washington Center for Improving the Quality of Undergraduate Education is recruiting participants for repetitions of this study. Participants will be able to compare their results to the overall data, providing a valuable benchmark. Readers interested in participating in future surveys should write to Washington Center at washcenter@evergreen.edu.)

- Analyzing elements of an idea, experience, or theory: 60 percent
- Evaluating information, methods, and arguments: 60 percent
- Integrating ideas, strategies, and skills from multiple sources: 60 percent

- Thinking through my assumptions: 59 percent
- Synthesizing ideas, experiences, or theories: 58 percent
- Applying theories or concepts to practical problems or new situations: 55 percent
- Memorizing facts and figures: 38 percent

An evaluation of linked courses at George Mason University (Office of Institutional Assessment, 1997) likewise asked for comparative data between linked and nonlinked courses. The items addressed whether the expected curricular connections existed and if a greater sense of community resulted. The percentage of students agreeing with each statement is shown here.

Curricular Connections in Linked Courses

- When enrolling, I expected many curricular connections: 85 percent.
- Faculty views and opinions may differ depending on their academic discipline: 79 percent.
- The number of curricular connections were appropriate: 73 percent.
- My linked courses did make curricular connections: 71 percent.
- Curricular connections helped me see subject matter relationships: 70 percent.
- As a result of the link, I was more comfortable in my larger, non-English courses: 55 percent.
- Because of the links, I began to make curricular connections in other, nonlinked courses: 49 percent.

Academic and Social Community

- It was easier to achieve community in my English class: 81 percent.
- A social community developed in my linked courses: 79 percent.
- I experienced closer relationships with linked faculty than with faculty teaching other courses: 68 percent.
- Linked courses helped ease transition to college: 60 percent.
- A sense of community carried over to my non-English class: 57 percent.
- Academic community formed between students: 56 percent.
- As a result of the link, I was more comfortable in my larger, non-English courses: 55 percent.

It is always a good practice to include some open-ended questions. For example, the following questions, used in the University of Southern Maine

evaluation of linked courses in 2004, are worth asking (http://usm.maine
.edu/sites/default/files/Office%20of%20Academic%20Assessment/assess-rep
linked_spring04.pdf):

- In what ways has the linking of this course assisted your learning?
- In what ways has linking of this course hindered your learning?
- Do you have suggestions for improving the link?

If participation in the linked program is voluntary, one may also want
to determine what motivated students to enroll in these courses as well as the
reasons for not undertaking linked courses. For instance, at George Mason
University (Office of Institutional Assessment, 1999) the reasons for enrollment were that the student expected to learn more (47 percent), because it
was the only course open at registration (27 percent), because of someone's
recommendation (24 percent), because the student felt that he or she would
get to know other students better because of smaller class size (23 percent),
because the student anticipated a lighter workload (21 percent), to get to
know faculty better (12 percent), and to ease transition from high school to
college (8 percent). Research at some institutions suggests that one should
find registration problems to be a common answer on reasons for not enrolling (Baker & Pomerantz, 2001).

Finally, one should not forget the reactions of faculty teaching in the
linked courses are valuable, and may offer another perspective on the matter,
especially for formative evaluations meant to improve the programs. For
example, at Seattle Central Community College, postprogram interviews are
held with faculty and administrators involved in learning communities (Bystrom, 2005). In the discussions, the following questions are addressed:

- What did you set out to do and what did you expect?
- What went well? (What in your teaching and in your colleagues'
  worked well for students?)
- What would you change about the program if you did it again? How
  would you set it up next time?
- What suggestions do you have for other CSP teams?
- What have you learned from this that you will take back to your
  stand-alone classes?

Level Two Measures

At level 2, one should examine actual learning. Thus one can look at course
grades, which are direct measures of mastery, but course withdrawals are also

valuable. Although Kirkpatrick prefers a pre- and a posttest design because it takes into account what the student knew before the course, it may not always be feasible. Besides content mastery as reflected in course grades, one may also want to assess the extent to which linked course participation develops critical thinking skills by relying on one of the standardized tests in this area, such as the Collegiate Learning Assessment, the Measure of Academic Proficiency and Progress, or the Collegiate Assessment of Academic Proficiency.

One may also want to assess whether the student's writing demonstrates *interdisciplinary understanding,* which is defined as the ability to combine knowledge from multiple disciplines or areas of expertise to create something new that would have been difficult or impossible to craft through a single discipline (Boix-Mansilla & Dawes Duraisingh, 2007; Boix-Mansilla, Dawes Duraisingh, Wolfe, & Haynes, 2009; Boix-Mansilla, Miller, & Gardner, 2000).

Operationalizing this construct has proven to be extremely difficult (Mansilla, 2005; Stowe, 2002; Stowe & Eder, 2002), but Boix-Mansilla and Dawes Duraisingh (2007) have developed a rubric called the *Targeted Assessment Framework* that is meant to capture this ability. In the *Targeted Assessment Rubric for Interdisciplinary Writing,* the assessor judges the product on four dimensions: (a) purposefulness, (b) disciplinary grounding, (c) integration, and (d) critical awareness or metacognition. A rating from 1 to 4 is assigned on each dimension, reflecting four levels of sophistication: naïve, novice, apprentice, or master. The rubric looks promising, and although some evidence for validity was presented by its authors, it needs further validation.

Level Three Measures

In Kirpatrick's model, level 3 is the use of skills taught on the job. Unless the student is in a co-op program, how well the student applied the knowledge from the classroom to real life may not be available for assessment until the student graduates and starts to work. As noted by Acharya (2002), student performance on the job provides the prima facie demonstration that the skills taught in college are being applied in the workplace. Job placement rates and feedback from alumni and employers can be used to determine this (Hoey & Gardner, 1999), with the latter being a more direct means for capturing this information.

However, some real-life benefits of linked courses may be observed while the student is still on campus. Although this means stretching the construct as originally formulated by Kirkpatrick, I contend it is a logical extension because the person's job while in school in a sense is being a student. Behaviors that enhance that role and that result from participation in linked courses are therefore legitimate considerations at level 3. Thus retention and time to degree rates are behaviors that in my opinion can be subsumed under Kirkpatrick's levels. Another aspect worth examining is degree of involvement in campus and community activities, which has been claimed to be a benefit of learning communities. For assessing level of engagement, one may take an actual inventory of student involvement or rely on self-reports in surveys such as the NSSE. Overall adjustment can be captured with a standardized scale such as the Student Adaptation to College Questionnaire.

Level Four Measures

Level 4 evaluation involves an assessment of the return on investment. Here, one should consider how the outcomes of the linked courses benefit the organization and society. At this level, one can conduct a cost-benefit analysis, considering factors such as improved graduation rates and time to degree completion. If linked courses are just a demonstration project, then in this analysis one may want to explore a scenario in which there is a university-wide adoption of linked courses. One may also want to assess the broader effect on society at this level. To society, the benefit may be that students with interdisciplinary exposure may be better performers in jobs requiring navigation between cross-functional and cross-sectional teams (Business-Higher Education Forum, 1999). Feedback from employers would be a source of data about whether this benefit was realized.

Bottom Line

Try to conduct both a process and an outcomes evaluation. If the outcomes are successful, then the process evaluation can serve to identify program features that should be replicated. On the other hand, if the outcomes assessment shows that the program did not meet its desired goals, the process evaluation may offer hints as to the reasons for the failure. Attempt to evaluate at all four levels of the Kirkpatrick model, but unless resources are available for a comprehensive evaluation (such as a grant), most likely your evaluation will be restricted to level 1 and level 2. If possible, attempt to build in a longitudinal perspective, although most likely given budgetary constraints at most institutions, your evaluation will focus more on the short-run outcomes. Under ideal circumstances, one would want an evaluation with an experimental design that incorporates both a control group and random assignment to the linked course (treatment group) and the control group, but in reality that may not be practical, so you may have to be satisfied with a less rigorous design. Unfortunately, this can raise questions as to what really accounts for any observed outcomes, and so you should be prepared for some healthy skepticism. Finally, realize that there are gaps in our understanding of what makes linked courses effective, so not all benefits may be realized by your program. The most probable benefit seems to be greater camaraderie and satisfaction, followed by better grades in the linked courses, and perhaps an appreciation of the interdisciplinary nature of knowledge. Whether these benefits translate into better grades in nonlinked courses and longer-term outcomes such as improved retention is a more open question.

References

Acharya, C. (2002). Employers' feedback: A source of information on students' learning outcome. *CDT Link, 6*(1). Retrieved from http://www.cdtl.nus.edu.sg/link/mar2002/feedback2.htm

Allen, M. J. (2003). *Assessing academic programs in higher education.* New York: John Wiley & Sons.

Alliger, G. M., Tannenbaum, S. I., Bennet, W., Jr., Traver, H., & Shotland, A. (1997). A metaanalysis of the relations among training criteria. *Personnel Psychology, 50,* 341–358.

Antheil, J. H., & Casper, I. G. (1986). Comprehensive evaluation model: A tool for the evaluation of nontraditional educational programs. *Innovative Higher Education, 11,* 55–64.

Baker, S., & Pomerantz, N. (2001). Impact of learning communities on retention at a metropolitan university. *Journal of College Student Retention, 2*(2), 115–126.

Bloom, D., & Sommo, C. (2005). *Building learning communities: Early results from the Opening Doors demonstration at Kingsborough Community College.* New York: MDRC.

Boix-Mansilla, V. (2005). Assessing student work at disciplinary crossroads. *Change, 37*(January/February), 14–21.

Boix-Mansilla, V., & Dawes Duraisingh, E. (2007). Targeted assessment of students' interdisciplinary work: An empirically grounded framework proposed. *Journal of Higher Education 78*(2), 215–237.

Boix-Mansilla, V., Dawes Duraisingh, E., Wolfe, C. R., & Haynes, C. (2009). Targeted assessment rubric: An empirically grounded rubric for interdisciplinary writing. *The Journal of Higher Education, 80,* 334–353.

Boix-Mansilla, V., Miller, W. C., & Gardner, H. (2000). On disciplinary lenses and interdisciplinary work. In P. Grossman & S. Wineburg (Eds.), *Interdisciplinary curriculum: Challenges to implementation* (pp. 17–38). New York: Teachers College Press.

Borden, V. M. H., & Rooney, P. M. (1998). Evaluating and assessing learning communities. *Metropolitan Universities, 9*(1), 73–88.

Brown, K. G. (2005). An examination of the structure and nomological network of trainee reactions: A closer look at "smile sheets." *Journal of Applied Psychology, 90,* 991–1001.

Business-Higher Education Forum. (1999). *Spanning the chasm: A blueprint for action.* Washington, DC: American Council on Education and National Alliance of Business.

Bystrom, V. (2005). Post-program interviews for learning community faculties: An assessment strategy which builds our expertise and improves our programs. In J. MacGregor et al. (Eds.), *Assessment in and of collaborative learning.* Available at http://www.evergreen.edu/washcenter/resources/acl/index.html

Cooper, H., Carlisle, C., Gibbs, T., & Watkins, C. (2001). Developing an evidence base for interdisciplinary learning: A systematic review. *Journal of Advanced Nursing, 35,* 228–237.

Creamer, E., & Lattuca, L. R. (Eds.). (2005). *Advancing faculty learning through interdisciplinary collaboration: New directions for teaching and learning, no. 102.* San Francisco, CA: Jossey-Bass.

Hoey, J. J., & Gardner, D. C. (1999). Using surveys of alumni and their employers to improve an institution. *New Directions for Institutional Research, 101,* 43–59.

Kirkpatrick, D. L. (1959). Techniques for evaluating training programs. *Journal of American Society for Training and Development, 13*(11), 3–9.

Kirkpatrick, J. D., & Kirkpatrick, D.L. (2005). *Transferring learning to behavior: Using the four levels to improve performance.* San Francisco, CA: Berrett-Koehler.

Klein, J. T. (1990). *Interdisciplinarity: History, theory and practice.* Detroit, MI: Wayne State University Press.

Lee, S. H., & Pershing, J. A. (2000). Evaluation of corporate training programs: Perspectives and issues for further research. *Performance Improvement Quarterly, 13,* 244–260.

Levine, M. F., & Guy, P. W. (2006).Freshman linked cohort classes in the study of business: Results of performance and graduation in business. *Journal of College Teaching and Learning, 3*(1), 55–64.

Light, R. J., Singer, J. D., & Willett, J. B. (1990). *By design: Planning research on higher education.* Cambridge, MA: Harvard University Press.

Long, L. K., DuBois., C. Z., & Faley, R. H. (2008). Online training: The value of capturing trainee reactions. *Journal of Workplace Learning, 20,* 21–37.

Mansilla, V. B. (2005). Assessing student work at disciplinary crossroads. *Change,* *37*(1), 14–21.

McLean, S., & Moss, G. (2003). They're happy, but did they make a difference? Applying Kirkpatrick's framework to the evaluation of a national leadership program. *Canadian Journal of Program Evaluation, 18*(1), 1–23.

Newby, A. C. (1992). *Training evaluation handbook.* San Francisco: Jossey-Bass/ Pfeiffer.

Office of Institutional Assessment at George Mason University. (1997). Assessing GMU's fall 1996 linked courses. *In Focus, 2*(2). Retrieved from https://assess ment.gmu.edu/Results/Other/1997/LinkedCourses1996.cfm

Office of Institutional Assessment at George Mason University. (1999). Fall 1998 linked courses report results from pre- and post-course questionnaires. *In Focus, 4*(3). Retrieved from https://assessment.gmu.edu/Results/Other/1999/Linked Courses1998.cfm

O'Neil, H. F., Wainess, R., & Baker, E. L. (2005). Classification of learning outcomes: Evidence from the computer games literature. *The Curriculum Journal, 16,* 455–474.

Price, D. V. (2005). *Learning communities and student success in postsecondary education: A background paper.* New York: MDRC. Retrieved from http://www.mdrc .org/publications/418/full.pdf

Rajeev, P., Madan, M. S., & Jayarajan, K. (2009). Revisiting Kirkpatrick's model: An evaluation of an academic training course. *Current Science, 96,* 272–276.

Rhoten, D., Boix-Mansilla, V., Chun, M., & Klein, J. T. (2006). *Interdisciplinary education at liberal arts institutions.* Teagle Foundation White Paper. Retrieved June 13, 2007, from http://www.teaglefoundation.org/learning/pdf/2006_ssrc_ whitepaper.pdf

Rosenthal, R. (1979) The "file drawer problem" and tolerance for null results. *Psychological Bulletin, 86,* 638–641.

Roszkowski, M. J., & Soven, M. (2011). Did you learn something useful today? An analysis of how perceived utility relates to perceived learning and their predictiveness of satisfaction with training. *Performance Improvement Quarterly, 23*(2), 71–91.

Ruona, W. E. A., Leimbach, M., Holton, E. F., III, & Bates, R. (2002). The relationship between learner utility reactions and predicted learning transfer among trainees. *International Journal of Training and Development, 6,* 218–228.

Scrivener, S., & Coghlan, E. (2011). *Opening the doors to student success.* New York: MDRC.

Stowe, D. E. (2002). Assessing interdisciplinary programs. *Assessment Update, 14*(3), 3–4.

Stowe, D. E., & Eder, D. J. (2002). Interdisciplinary program assessment. *Issues in Integrative Studies, 2,* 77–101.

Sugrue, B., & Rivera, R. J. (2005). *State of the industry: ASTD's annual review of trends in workplace learning and performance.* Alexandria, VA: American Society for Training and Development.

Tamkin, P., Yarnell, J., & Kerrin, M. (2002, October). *Kirkpatrick and beyond: A review of models of training performance* (Report 392). Brighton, England: Institute for Employment Studies, Sussex University.

Taylor, K., Moore, W. S., MacGregor, J., & Lindblad, J. (2003). *Learning community research and assessment: What we know now.* National Learning Communities Project Monograph Series. Olympia, WA: The Evergreen State College, Washington Center for Improving the Quality of Undergraduate Education.

Tinto, V. (1998, January). *Learning communities and the reconstruction of remedial education in higher education.* Presentation at the Conference on Replacing Remediation in Higher Education at Stanford University, Palo Alto, CA.

Visher, M. G., Wathington, H., Richburg-Hayes, L., & Schneider, E. (2008). *The learning communities demonstration: Rationale, sites, and research design.* An NCPR Working Paper. New York: National Center for Postsecondary Research.

Washington Center and Skagit Valley College Institutional Research Office. (2011). *Online learning communities' student survey highlights from the 2010–11 surveys.* Retrieved from http://www.evergreen.edu/washcenter/resources/upload/2010–11_Highlights.pdf

Weiss, C. H. (1998). Have we learned anything new about the use of evaluation? *American Journal of Evaluation, 19,* 21–33.

Worthen, B. R., Sanders, J. R., & Fitzpatrick, J. L. (1997). *Program evaluation: Alternative approaches and practical guidelines.* New York: Longman.

10

USING PROGRAM ASSESSMENTS AND FACULTY DEVELOPMENT TO DEEPEN STUDENT LEARNING

Lynn Dunlap and Maureen Pettitt

A relatively small community college district in Northwest Washington State, Skagit Valley College (SVC) includes a main campus in Mount Vernon, a campus on Whidbey Island, and several centers in outlying areas. Of the approximately 6,500 students (3,900 full-time equivalent students) enrolled in credit courses, 45 percent intend to seek a university transfer degree. The student body is primarily White (75 percent), with a growing Hispanic population; approximately one-third are first-generation college attendees. Since 1986, the College has been offering learning communities, generally pairs of courses in which students enroll as a cohort, and has required learning community participation as part of its general education program for transfer degrees since 1993.

The direct transfer agreement (DTA) between public four-year universities and community colleges in the state of Washington is a distribution model of general education that emphasizes breadth. The DTA specifies that one half to two thirds of transfer degree credits must be divided among the three traditional distribution areas (e.g., physical and biological sciences, social sciences, and humanities) and a smaller percentage among skills courses such as math and communications. Students select courses from a menu of choices to satisfy these requirements. This structure results too easily in piecemeal, fragmented education composed primarily of 100-level introductory courses.

When the College was reconsidering its general education program between 1987 and 1993, it recognized that numerous benefits (e.g., better retention, increased student involvement with the college, and faculty revitalization) could accrue from learning communities. The rationale for requiring them, however, was the desire to create curricular coherence. The national literature at that time (Boyer, 1987; Commission on the Future of Community Colleges, 1988; Erickson, 1992; Gabelnick, MacGregor, Matthews, & Smith, 1992; Gaff, 1991) argued for a more coherent general education curriculum. Similarly, at the College, faculty claimed that students did not see connections among courses and were not transferring skills from course to course. The faculty also believed that students needed deeper engagement with their learning and a clearer understanding of education as a dynamic process of exploration and discovery.

To address these issues, the College sought a strategy that would connect areas of students' learning within the constraints of the statewide DTA. Thus, initially, the requirements were for students to take two required college-level composition courses and at least one course in each of the required distribution areas in learning communities. Student transcripts indicated which courses met the requirements of the DTA, but an internal coding system signaled that their study of those subjects was linked. Within two years, the college was offering about 70 learning communities each year, an effort that involved over half of the full-time faculty, dozens of adjunct faculty, and almost every academic department at the College.

Since implementation of the general education reforms in 1993, Skagit has conducted three general education reviews. The first two were shorter reviews of internal assessments that led to minor modifications to the program in 1997 and 2001. From 2004 to 2006, a more comprehensive review of the national literature and Skagit's own assessments resulted in a major reform. Consistent with the literature (Altieri & Cygnar, 1997; Eaton, 1993; Project on Strong Foundations for General Education, 1994; Ratcliff, Johnson, La Nasa, & Gaff, 2001), the College shifted its emphasis from content, that is, fundamental skills and breadth of disciplinary knowledge, to learning and habits of thought. The College is still bound by the relatively unchanged DTA; now, however, instead of using this distribution model as an organizing principle, the College has adopted a set of eleven learning values, each with a set of specific outcomes for student learning. In the spirit of the

American Association of Colleges and Universities's "Statement on Integrative Learning" (March 2004), application and integration were placed at the center of these dramatically reframed general education learning outcomes.

In each of these revisions, the learning community requirements were streamlined and the options for course combinations expanded, for instance to include developmental and college success courses. However, the College retained learning communities as a core requirement for general education. Studies of the program's effectiveness had consistently confirmed that learning communities served multiple purposes, including its original goal of creating curricular coherence. The description of learning communities in a 1997 SVC General Education handbook articulated our goals and the outcomes we believed could be met based on the research conducted to date:

> One of the major goals of the revised general education degree is to counter educational fragmentation and to help students learn how to integrate studies in different fields, particularly fields that might not otherwise seem related. Learning communities reinforce interdisciplinary connections and foster increased collaboration, communication, and critical thinking. The sense of community also promotes increased student support and study groups and thus retention. Finally, since students study the disciplines in a broader context and through multiple, sometimes conflicting perspectives, they learn to apply their studies to new situations and wider communities and to examine ethical dimensions of issues.

Although the program aspirations have remained consistent, from the vantage point of today, it is possible to see Skagit's learning communities working as a series of transitions in emphases that has brought us closer to our ideal of creating meaningful curricular connections. The earliest phase of our assessments had focused on determining the effect of learning communities. Once they were required for the degree, the focus shifted to identifying program successes and problem areas and to supporting effective coordination of courses that were linked in learning communities. As the program became established, the focus shifted again to identifying student learning within the context of learning communities, and ultimately to the nature and quality of students' integrative learning.

In reflection, we can see how these stages reflect what Boix-Mansilla (2008/2009) describes as "productive shifts." Each stage has been informed by changes in our assumptions about disciplinary expertise and integration, about what can and should be measured, and about student learning and, of course, teaching. This chapter explains how our assessments guided our efforts to strengthen our learning communities program and deepen students' learning through these productive shifts. The sections that follow include a brief description of Skagit's learning community program, an explanation of how our assessment and faculty development efforts evolved from an emphasis on course coordination toward integrative learning outcomes, an explanation of our current assessment efforts, and a description of the effect of these assessments on faculty development activities and student learning.

Learning Communities at Skagit Valley College

To accommodate student and faculty scheduling and department needs, Skagit Valley College offers learning communities in a variety of structures— fully coordinated (i.e., team-taught), linked, and federated, each with specific expectations for shared syllabi, outcomes, and integrative assignments.

About half the learning communities are *fully coordinated learning communities* with the course work (readings, activities, and assignments) thoroughly integrated and both faculty in the classroom at all times. These include a wide range of combinations, for example, "Pathways to Sustainability" (chemistry and global issues), "Outlaws and Outcasts" (literature and composition), and "His/Her/My Story" (interpersonal communication and pre-college English).

Linked learning communities, like "Music Makes the World Go 'Round" (world history and music) and "Reading between the Numbers" (pre-college math and reading), are pairs of courses with one or more overlapping assignments. Faculty collaborate to determine the extent of integration, which can be minimal, for example, with only a single culminating project, or extensive, with shared readings and a series of coordinated assignments. At minimum, however, linked learning communities must share at least one integrative assignment that both faculty evaluate and that counts as a significant part of the final grade in both courses.

In *federated learning communities,* small groups of students from several different "federated" courses co-enroll in a core course, and together explore the relationships in the two fields of study. For example, in "Celluloid Science," science majors enroll in a film course and one of the science courses required for their major with the explicit purpose of exploring how films portray scientists, scientific practices, and concepts. Students in "Decoding Science" co-enroll in "College Success Skills" and one of several science courses, with the objective of learning the reading, analytical, and test-taking strategies specific to their field of study. In federated learning communities, faculty collaborate to define the issues and relationships to be explored in the learning community and to establish the extent to which faculty in the federated courses will be involved in course activities and assignment design. At least two of the assignments in the core course must provide students the opportunity to integrate their learning from both courses.

Although the level of integration varies, the expectation remains that all learning communities emphasize collaborative, integrative learning and that students will work together in groups to prepare projects, panels, or papers that show their understanding of the connections between the two fields of study.

Rethinking Program Effectiveness

From the beginning, faculty at Skagit were aware of the importance of assessing learning communities and using the results to make decisions about the program and practices. As we began to understand the effect of learning communities and strengthened the program, we wanted a more precise understanding of what students learn in their learning communities and whether it could be improved. The next three sections describe the progression of assessments and faculty development, from an emphasis on coordinating courses to an emphasis on integrative learning.

Improving Course Coordination

Assessments done at the time of the 1987–1992 general education review and in the early years of implementation indicated positive results for student retention, student satisfaction, and faculty perceptions of student gains, all of which matched findings in the emerging national literature on learning communities (Goodsell, Maher, & Tinto, 1992; Hill, 1985; MacGregor, 1987).[1] The assessments revealed that most learning community students and faculty were generally positive about the opportunities for strengthening students' interpersonal skills, sense of academic community, critical thinking, and independent learning. Students in composition-based learning communities appreciated how writing about a discipline helped deepen their understanding of it and of its relationship to current events and other fields of study. The studies also indicated that, although some students resisted active learning pedagogies and the expectation of synthesizing multiple perspectives, most valued the experience of exploring diverse points of view in an academic setting. They also valued the opportunity to observe faculty model academic discourse. However, students were explicit about their need for faculty to provide greater direction in how to connect the courses.

Interestingly, the assessments suggested that, although learning communities supported academic success for students in developmental courses and persistence for all students, there appeared to be no overall gain in terms of their grade point average (GPA). In fact, students who took writing in learning communities early in their college course work tended to receive lower grades than those who took composition as a stand-alone course. Faculty suggested that in designing activities and assignments that integrated their separate disciplines, they were, of necessity, asking for higher-order thinking skills from students. They also noted that, as they collaborated to develop outcomes and reach agreements about what constitutes good work from students, they often held students to higher standards than they used in stand-alone sections of the same courses.

The research also provided important information about the effectiveness of the design and teaching of the learning communities. On the one hand, the assessments suggested that learning communities provided opportunities for faculty engagement with their own disciplines and with colleagues, particularly around sharing pedagogy. However, they also indicated that the success of these courses was uneven and depended in a large measure on faculty understanding of the rationale for learning communities, on their ability to communicate that rationale to students, and on their expertise in collaborating with each other and coordinating their teaching and assignments. The most successful learning communities were those in which faculty articulated a clear purpose for linking their courses, communicated effectively with each other and students, demonstrated mutual respect, and balanced organization and flexibility.

As a result of these assessments, faculty professional development during this period focused on the challenges of course design—how to combine different teaching approaches, address very different disciplinary demands, and make explicit connections between disciplines. Faculty handbooks and workshops provided suggestions for how to design a course that would be experienced as a unified whole rather than side-by-side lecture, how to foster community through active and collaborative learning pedagogies, and how to orient students to the program goals and their learning community experience. The suggestions for composition-based learning communities also discussed how to share responsibilities for teaching writing and for designing and grading writing assignments.

Although the assessments done between 1993 and 2000 informed us about the complexities of assessing programs and student learning and about what was and was not working in the program itself, we did not learn as much as we would have liked about student learning in learning communities, an effort that has since become became the major focus of our learning community assessment efforts.

Understanding Student Learning in Learning Communities

After the first round of assessments and subsequent changes to strengthen the program, the College continued to assess program effectiveness but also stepped up its efforts to understand the effect of learning communities on student learning. To do this, we employed a variety of methods with varying degrees of success.[2] The studies were not definitive, but they did show that Skagit students performed well once they transferred and that they believed that their experiences in learning communities contributed to their success once they transferred. They also revealed consistent patterns: learning communities result in greater levels of student effort and engagement and appear to support gains in students' critical thinking, collaboration, engagement with diverse populations, and willingness to use multiple perspectives.

Until recently, our understanding of student learning was primarily through surveys and focus groups that assessed students' satisfaction and perceptions of their learning. Through fall 2009, the primary learning community assessment tool was a brief student survey, administered quarterly in each learning community; the survey consisted of two questions—with two additional questions about writing for composition-based learning communities—and a comment section. The survey was used to monitor program success in terms of student satisfaction with the combined course format and to provide feedback to faculty members about their own learning communities. Results for individual courses were shared with—and only with—the instructors for purposes of course improvement, although aggregate data was shared with counselors, the General Education Coordinators, and the Learning Community Advisory Committee to assist with advising and curricular decision making. Results were also shared with the administration and Board of Trustees to provide general awareness of how learning communities were serving students.

Our assessment efforts also encompassed looking at the effect of learning communities on students' performance after transferring to a four-year institution. The most comprehensive research was conducted jointly with Western Washington University (WWU), thirty miles north of the Mount

Vernon campus, in Bellingham, Washington. The research included student focus groups designed to explore the extent to which transfer students' learning experiences in learning communities at Skagit supported their academic progress at WWU, as well as an examination of student performance at the four-year institution based on the students' academic experience at Skagit.

Consistent with other study results, students' positive comments on the quarterly surveys and in the WWU transfer study tended to focus on two aspects that support their learning: the collaboration among faculty and students and the interdisciplinary structure. The experiences in learning communities that were not well designed frustrated students who felt, as one observed, that instead of "cross-discipline exposure . . . what we're getting is two disciplines jammed together and duct taped." In contrast, students observed that when the collaboration and integration worked, they were challenged to "think more abstractly, and think more about concepts and how they would fit" and to recognize connections, even when they were not clear or explicit. Comments also indicated that students understood how learning communities helped deepen their learning, generating what one called "a true and comprehensive understanding of ideas." Some recognized that the learning community experience revealed gaps in the traditional approach of taking isolated courses: "Both of these courses would be strong alone but together they unify concepts that would otherwise be left untouched." Some students even identified this gap: "If they had been separate, I would have known what and where, but not the why, and the why is always the most important question."

To get a clearer sense of students' educational experiences, we administered the Community College Student Experience Questionnaire in the 1990s but switched to the Community College Survey of Student Engagement (CCSSE) in 2003 because it (a) mirrored very specifically the College's concern with student learning and engagement; (b) included a question that identified students who had participated in, were planning to participate, or had not nor had plans to participate in learning communities; and (c) had established national benchmarks against which the college could measure its performance. The college has administered the survey four times and has used the data to analyze the effect of learning communities on student engagement and learning activities.

The CCSSE results indicated that students who take learning communities are significantly more likely to do the following:

1. Engage in activities that increase their time on task (and thus their chances for meeting their educational goals).

2. Assume responsibility for their learning.
3. Interact with faculty members.
4. Work with other students both in and out of class.
5. Prepare two or more drafts of an assignment.
6. Work on papers or projects requiring integration of ideas or information from various sources.
7. Have serious conversations with students of a different race or ethnicity than their own.

In addition, when compared with other colleges of the same size, Skagit's benchmark scores on the CCSSE for "active and collaborative learning" and "student–faculty interaction" were substantially higher, affirming that the College's pedagogical and collaborative approaches were reaping benefits for students. The CCSSE results helped the college to better understand the effect of learning communities on student engagement with their course work, instructors, and peers, as well as their perceptions of intellectual gains. However, the results did not give us a clear sense of the level of integration taking place in learning communities.

Zeroing in on Integrative Learning

During the 2004–2006 review of general education, the College's desire to be more intentional about student learning and, as one faculty member expressed it, to "move to the next level" in our teaching in learning communities led to the decision to participate in a national project that we hoped would help us sharpen the focus of our work. Thus Skagit Valley College agreed to participate as one of twenty-two teams from two- and four-year institutions in the national research project, "Assessing Learning in Learning Communities," which was launched in fall 2005. The express purpose of this two-year project of The Washington Center for Improving the Quality of Undergraduate Education was to develop collaborative assessment practices that focus on the quality of student learning made possible by learning communities.

Project participants read some of the emerging research about interdisciplinary studies and, over the course of several retreats, focused on developing shared definitions of—and purposes for—integration and interdisciplinary integration as well as an understanding of how these can be assessed. One of the major activities of this project was learning to use a structured conversation protocol targeted specifically for interdisciplinary work. This version of the "collaborative assessment protocol," developed by Veronica Boix-Mansilla for the project, is based on the work described in *The Evidence Process: A Collaborative Approach to Understanding and Improving Teaching and Learning* (2001), a publication of the Evidence Project, Harvard Graduate School of Education.[3] Project participants were asked to use student work to consider the core elements of disciplinary understanding: Faculty "discerned the *purpose* that the student pursues in the piece of work examined, the ways in which two or more areas of expertise and *disciplines* informed the work, the ways in which different forms of expertise were *integrated*, and the *reflections* students shared about the nature and limitations of their work" (Boix-Mansilla, 2008/2009). As the national project evolved, faculty teams developed integrative assignments using the Washington Center's integrative assignment heuristic and refined them using the collaborative assessment protocol.

Our participation in the project clarified several issues. For starters, it provided us with a definition of *interdisciplinary integration,* which was subsequently incorporated in the newly established general education learning outcomes for integration. The three proposed integration outcomes had included (a) recognition of the strengths and limitations of different fields of study, (b) evaluation of relationships among those fields of study, and (c) use of concepts and frameworks from different fields of study to analyze situations and develop comprehensive approaches and responses. On the basis of the project, we refined the third outcome for greater precision and added a fourth—reflection on the learning students gain from integration. In our definition, which draws heavily from the work of Boix-Mansilla and her colleagues (Boix-Mansilla, 2005; Boix Mansilla & Dawes, 2007; Rhoten, Boix-Mansilla, Chun, & Klein, 2006), *interdisciplinary integration* now means the integration of concepts and analytical frameworks from multiple perspectives to develop one or more of the following: more comprehensive descriptions, multicausal explanations, new interpretations, or deeper explorations of issues. The core of interdisciplinary integration is that it is *disciplined*—grounded in the purposes, methods, knowledge, and performance expectations of the disciplines—and that it *leverages* those disciplinary dimensions to advance understanding.

During the project, we differentiated two additional kinds or levels of integration. In contrast to interdisciplinary integration, *tooling,* a concept developed during the project retreats, is the use of one or more elements of one discipline to deepen understanding in another one, for example, teaching anatomy and physiology students to shape and fire clay to form and connect ceramic "bones" to reinforce their understanding of the human skeletal system. This kind of integration can provide invaluable opportunities for students to strengthen their understanding of a discipline. The most general kind of integration, what Boix-Mansilla (2005) calls "common sense" integration, draws on people's personal experience and knowledge. In academic settings, this kind of integration can be used as an intentional strategy to help students draw on and also reexamine their own and their peers' prior experiences and knowledge as they explore issues and new fields.

These definitions and our examination of student work helped us distinguish between *integrated courses*—the work of faculty in designing collaborative courses and assignments—and *integrative course work*—the intellectual work of students as they engage with assignments and classroom activities and begin to learn how to integrate different disciplines and multiple perspectives. This recognition contributed to the revision of our learning communities proposal process. In the past, proposal forms required information about how faculty planned to integrate their courses into a seamless whole. In contrast, the new forms emphasize student learning by requiring that faculty specify which of Skagit's four integration learning outcomes their learning community is intended to meet and to describe how it will help students meet those outcomes.

Finally, participation in the project led to insights about how course and assignment design can enhance student learning. Faculty at the College had often observed that students' learning community work was promising but not consistently strong. Students might offer subtle interpretations without providing sufficient disciplinary support or, in contrast, provide "side-by-side" insights specific to each discipline without fully synthesizing them into more meaningful understanding. The revision of existing assignments to make disciplinary and integrative evaluation criteria explicit produced better and more consistent student performances. Equally importantly, faculty realized that integration is a specific skill and, as such, must be taught. Not all college students have already learned how to integrate disciplinary concepts and perspectives. With more intentional focus on integration—sequenced design of assignments and classroom activities, opportunities for faculty to model and explain integration, and opportunities for students to practice and receive feedback—learning community students who enrolled in introductory courses and who had no prior experience with either discipline were able to demonstrate more sophisticated and substantive interdisciplinary integrations.[4]

The insights from the learning community project were subsequently reinforced and expanded when Skagit Valley participated in a second project on integrative learning sponsored by the Washington Center and funded by Washington Spark. This one-year "Reaching College Readiness" project provided faculty teaching developmental classes the opportunity to analyze the skills students need for rigorous academic work. Using the principles of *Redefining College Readiness* (Conley, 2007) and *The Teaching for Understanding Guide* (Blythe et al., 1998), faculty designed integrative assignments that asked students to build college readiness skills while simultaneously applying them in meaningful ways to compelling and relevant social issues. The major outcomes for the College, aside from several carefully crafted integrative assignments for developmental learning communities and stand-alone courses, were to reinforce the importance of being guided by student work and of emphasizing purposefulness. In other words, establishing why the study of each discipline matters, connecting that study to relevant social issues, and creating connections in readings, activities, and assignments.

The project also helped clarify the role of three of the four facets of college readiness as defined by Conley (2007): key cognitive strategies (such as reasoning and inquisitiveness), academic behaviors (such as self-monitoring and study skills), and contextual skills and awareness (such as knowledge of the norms, values, and conventions that operate in higher education). These abilities, which are often the responsibility of student development faculty, are crucial for success in college. As a result, we have begun to explore how these skills align with the general education program and can be integrated throughout the curriculum. Currently, we are in the process of defining the disciplinary grounding (i.e., the purpose, knowledge, methods, and performance criteria) for student development courses. A curriculum retreat about college success skills in summer 2010 was based on the frameworks used in the "Reaching College Readiness" project. The differences between *understanding* and *knowing* were examined and the ensuing discussions led to the initial identification of desired students' understanding in three areas—thinking and learning, college readiness and success strategies, and application of knowledge and skills in context. We are continuing to refine these understandings and revising the course outlines and developing common activities for our college success skills courses, many of which are taught in learning community format.

Assessing Conditions for Integrative Learning

As our participation in the two projects helped us refine our focus on student learning, a pair of subsequent assessments revealed gaps in our practices. The next two subsections describe these two assessments and what we learned from them.

Assessing Integrative Assignment Design

In 2006, to provide program consistency for the integration outcomes, Skagit established specific syllabus and assignment requirements for learning communities. These requirements are dependent on the structure, a fact reflected in the proposal process. On the learning community proposal form, faculty who wish to teach a linked or federated learning community may signal that the course meets any of the College's four integration learning outcomes. Fully coordinated learning communities, however, must include the third outcome—that students will integrate the concepts and analytical frameworks of the disciplines into a more comprehensive analysis or interpretation. Fully coordinated learning communities must also provide students a shared syllabus and assign a minimum of three major integrative assignments as part of the evaluation of student learning in both courses. Federated learning communities must assign at least two integrative assignments, and linked courses must assign at least one.

These syllabi and assignments have become part of the evidence of how learning communities foster the new integration learning outcomes. In spring 2010, the College conducted a preliminary analysis of assignments from 101 learning communities—both classroom and online—taught from fall 2008 through winter 2010. The analysis was undertaken to determine what kind of evidence the assignments provide about the nature and extent of disciplinary integration in each learning community.

Because this was a preliminary study, the analysis was an open-ended exploration of how faculty communicate to students that an assignment requires purposeful integration of what they are learning from the two different courses. Because this information could be (and was) signaled in a variety of ways, each assignment was coded for two elements:

1. Statements of purpose or learning outcomes specific to each discipline
2. Evaluation criteria that were grounded in the concepts, methods, and competencies of each discipline

The first steps of this preliminary analysis revealed some basic gaps in our practices and the need for clearer communication with faculty (including adjuncts, who were somewhat less likely to meet submission criteria). There was no common system for identifying electronic documents from different courses (or even within a single course), and the print versions of many assignments contained no information identifying the learning community, courses, or assignment number. In addition, instead of assignments, some faculty submitted a syllabus that referred to assignments, a list of assignments (sometimes with brief descriptions), a course notebook, or links to online materials. Some faculty provided an abundance of information about how classroom and online activities were used to support students' ability to integrate the disciplines; however, it was difficult to determine which materials were scaffolding for learning and which were major assignments. It was equally impossible to determine whether assignments were early ones, designed to introduce students to integrative skills, or culminating projects, designed to evaluate students' ability to integrate concepts, skills, or analytical frameworks.

With respect to student learning, the information gleaned from assignments was limited. Although the assignments often used imaginative approaches that might be integrative in nature, they did not contain enough information to determine whether learning communities provide students with effective opportunities for demonstrating the general education learning outcomes related to integration. The majority of the assignments focused on describing the tasks and sometimes steps in the process for completing them. Very few provided specifics about the purpose or intended outcomes or how the student work would be evaluated, either in terms of separate disciplines or their integration. Even within single learning communities, some assignments were well detailed and others vague.

As shown in Table 10.1, of the 63 learning communities with assignments that could be analyzed, one-third provided no information about assignment outcomes or evaluation criteria. Assignments from five learning communities specified outcomes or evaluation criteria that were not specific to either discipline but focused on completion or performance skills (i.e., organization, presentation quality, or control of writing or speech skills).

Assignments from the remaining 36 learning communities provided some information about outcomes and evaluation criteria. Half focused primarily on criteria from one discipline. Of these, 15 identified integration outcomes or criteria from only one of the courses in the learning community, and three indicated *outcomes* for both disciplines but specified evaluation criteria for only one. Interestingly, most of the assignments with evaluation criteria for just one discipline were from learning communities with a composition course. These assignments tended to elaborate criteria for effective essays but few or no criteria for demonstrating competency in the second

TABLE 10.1
Learning Community Assignment Analysis

Number of Useable Assignments	63	
Assignments with information about assignment outcomes or evaluation criteria	41	(65%)
Assignments with information about assignment outcomes or evaluation criteria *relevant to disciplines*	36	(57%)
Assignments focused on outcomes and criteria for one discipline	18	(29%)
Assignments addressing integration or multidisciplinary outcomes or evaluation criteria	18	(29%)
Included interdisciplinary outcomes and criteria on all assignments	8	(13%)

course. Assignments from the remaining 18 learning communities explicitly or implicitly addressed integration or multidisciplinary outcomes or evaluation criteria based on both courses, but only eight met the desired goal of articulating this information on all assignments.

The report concluded that faculty need parameters for determining which of their many course assignments and activities should be considered evidence of "major" integrative work. It recommended that Skagit establish integrative assignment criteria—for instance, that assignments should expressly identify disciplinary and integration learning outcomes and the disciplinary and integrative criteria used to evaluate student work. Finally, the report recommended steps for faculty support, including publicizing best practices for integrative learning and assignment design, revising the general education handbooks, developing an archive of model assignments and assessment rubrics, and creating opportunities for faculty conversations about the practices that foster that integrative learning.

Assessing Classroom Practices

The creation of the web-based *Survey of Students' Experiences of Learning in Learning Communities* was the result of input from colleges and universities involved in the "Assessing Learning in Learning Communities" project, described in the earlier section, "Zeroing in on Integrative Learning." Although the assessment of student work—the focus of the project—

provided critical information about student outcomes with regard to disciplinary and interdisciplinary learning outcomes, project participants expressed the desire for a survey that assessed students' experiences and perceptions in the learning community as a companion to the assessment of student work. There would also be a clear advantage to having national data about the "what" and "how" of substantive learning in learning communities and opportunities to use that data to guide the creation of online resources and tools that help faculty to enhance students'—and their own—experiences in learning communities.

Subsequently, the Washington Center approached Skagit Valley College to help design and administer a web-based survey specifically for students enrolled in learning communities. As noted by Boix-Mansilla (2005), the challenges associated with assessing student learning are particularly evident in interdisciplinary learning where there is less clarity and definition about the indicators of quality. However, a review of existing surveys about learning outcomes, including integrative learning, helped to establish underlying learning principles for the survey, which in turn led to the focus on classroom activities and students' perceptions of their understanding and abilities.

A preliminary version of the survey was shared widely with colleagues across the country. In addition, Skagit instructors used a "think aloud" protocol, in which a small group of learning community students took the survey and then described to a faculty member what they thought each question meant as they tried to answer it. After a number of revisions, the web-based survey was piloted with 12 colleges and universities across the country in fall 2009, which resulted in 1,063 responses. Several conference calls were subsequently held with pilot colleges to solicit feedback about survey logistics and questions. The feedback informed the design of a revised survey that was used starting in the winter and spring of 2010.

The current survey contains 42 items divided into four sections as follows:

1. Students' engagement in classroom activities—13 items
2. Instructors' activities that support learning—13 items
3. Students' perceptions of gains made in their own understanding and abilities—10 items
4. Students' perceptions of cognitive activities in the learning community versus other courses—7 items

This survey offered Skagit Valley College an unprecedented opportunity for looking at our own learning communities' practices from the students' perspectives and for measuring some of the College's general education learning outcomes for integration. We have since adopted this survey as the primary learning community assessment tool to replace the very brief survey used through fall 2009. (See the earlier section, "Understanding Student Learning.") As with that earlier survey, course-level results are provided only to the general educator coordinator and to the faculty teaching in that particular learning community. However, aggregated results are provided to the Learning Communities Advisory Committee and the General Education Committee.

We use the survey not only to assess the program but also to identify faculty professional development activities. Skagit's survey results suggest some interesting implications for faculty development. As shown in Table 10.2, the results from the 2010–2011 academic year administrations of the survey indicated that three quarters of the students are likely to connect or integrate ideas, strategies, or skills in their learning community, and a similar number report they reflected on how these connections led to new insights or understanding. On the other hand, a smaller percentage of the students (64 percent) reported that their instructors demonstrated how or assigned work that asked students to integrate concepts and skills from different classes in a meaningful or novel way.

Students in learning communities that included developmental (precollege) level courses were more likely to report that their instructors encouraged them to use their own experience to learn new things and to explore their ideas. These same students were also more likely to indicate that the instructors demonstrated how to integrate concepts and skills from different classes, to assign work that asked them to connect concepts and skills from different classes, and to show them how to evaluate the strengths and weaknesses of their work so they could improve.

As noted in Table 10.3, compared with their other classes, students in learning communities reported that they were more likely to use analysis, synthesis, evaluation, and integration, and were more likely to apply what they had learned to practical problems or new situations.

Our analyses of the survey data over six quarters reveal that most learning community faculty are adept at creating an environment that supports active and collaborative learning: students are being asked to participate, work collaboratively, and address complex issues. Results about faculty classroom practices are less encouraging, however. That only 64 percent of students report that faculty show them how to integrate concepts and skills

TABLE 10.2
**Skagit Student Responses to the Survey of Students' Experiences
in Learning Communities, 2010–2011**

	Percent Reporting Often or Very Often		
	All LCs (N = 686)	*LCs with a Precollege Course* (N = 191)	*LCs with Only College-Level Courses* (N = 495)
1. Student Behaviors in the LC Work with other students to solve problems or examine complex issues during class.	71.9%	70.7%	71.3%
Work on connecting or integrating ideas, strategies, or skills from classes (or disciplines) included in this learning community.	75.8%	71.2%	77.8%
Reflect on how these connections lead to new insights or understanding.	73.5%	70.1%	74.4%
Use what I am learning to contribute to another class or seminar.	63.9%	71.7%	60.6%
2. Instructor Behaviors in the LC Encourage me to explore my ideas.	71.2%	80.1%	68.0%
Help me use my background knowledge and experiences to learn new things.	60.6%	62.8%	58.4%
Demonstrate how to integrate concepts and skills from different classes in a meaningful way.	64.4%	73.9%	61.1%
Assign work that asks me to connect concepts and skills from different classes to reach new understandings and applications.	68.6%	71.8%	67.3%
Show me how to evaluate the strengths and weaknesses in my work as a basis for improvement.	68.6%	82.8%	63.6%

LC, Learning community.

TABLE 10.3
Students' Use of Thinking Skills in Learning Communities
Compared to Other Courses

Prompt: "In my learning community, compared with other classes, I spend more, less, or about the same amount of time:"

	% Reporting "More"
Memorizing facts and figures	37.8
Analyzing elements of an idea, experience, or theory	59.8
Thinking through my assumptions	52.2
Synthesizing ideas, experiences, or theories	56.8
Evaluating information, methods, and arguments	56.5
Integrating ideas, strategies, and skills from multiple sources	57.2
Applying theories or concepts to practical problems or new situations	51.4

from different classes in a meaningful way and that only 70 percent assign work with the expectation that students will connect concepts and skills from different classes to reach new understanding and application are particularly disturbing because these activities are critical to students' meeting Skagit's general education learning outcomes for integration. Finally, although students see themselves as critical thinkers, the results presented in Table 10.1 suggest that less than 60 percent of the learning community students report they are doing *more* analyzing, synthesizing, evaluating, and integrating than in their other classes.

Our analyses also suggest that results for a number of items are dependent on the learning community faculty and course level (precollege only, precollege and college level, or college level only). In addition, results from learning communities taught by faculty who participated in the two national projects suggest that more of these students believe they are being oriented to and using integrative skills and using higher-order thinking skills in their learning community compared with other classes.

Although we are just beginning to gather and analyze this data, these preliminary results suggest several directions for faculty professional development. We expect that the professional development focus might change based on a more thorough exploration of the differences by type of courses (e.g., those that include composition courses), the level of coordination (fully coordinated versus not fully coordinated), and faculty status.

Using Assessments to Improve Integrative Learning

On the basis of these recent research projects, Skagit is sharpening the focus of professional development activities for learning community faculty. We are developing an online collection of resources for faculty—model syllabi, assignments, and proposals, as well as articles and handouts and materials from workshops. And we have organized orientation sessions and a two-year workshop series on integrative assignment design and best practices.

As a first step, the Mount Vernon campus has begun to mandate attendance at an orientation for any faculty—veteran or new—who wish to propose a learning community. Based on the assignment analysis, the Learning Community Advisory Committee concluded that new faculty need an introduction to the general education program and veteran faculty would benefit from a review of the most recent changes to the general education program. These changes included the proposal process and the ways that the College now assesses and documents work, including the integrative assignments and online survey. The first orientation in fall 2010 reminded faculty that Skagit's integration outcomes are the core of all its learning communities and that in fully coordinated learning communities, faculty are expected to help students learn to integrate concepts and analytical frameworks from multiple perspectives to develop more comprehensive explanations, new interpretations, or deeper explorations. This reminder provided a segue into the faculty development workshops planned for the year.

The next two subsections describe the first year of workshops in the two-year districtwide faculty development series intended to provide more in-depth training for integration learning outcomes. In the three workshops offered during the first year (2010–2011), the emphasis was on the design of integrative assignments; the focus for the second year (2011–2012) is on classroom practices that support integrative learning. Deans were invited to join the participating faculty, whose experience ranged from those who had not yet taught in a learning community to those with decades of learning community experience.

Examining Integrative Assignment Design and Student Work

The first afternoon workshop in the series, "Integrative Assignment Design: Designing for Disciplinary Grounding and Integration," focused on analyzing integrative assignments. Using the collaborative protocol, faculty examined two assignments from learning communities taught at the College for evidence of how they communicate (a) the *purpose* of the assignment (particularly as it related to the general education outcomes), (b) the *disciplinary* grounding (i.e., methods, knowledge, and performances necessary to complete it successfully), and (c) the overarching *integration* outcomes. At each step of the analysis, faculty discussed possible ways that the assignment in question could be strengthened. Faculty observed that the two assignments were similar to or better than many that they themselves assigned. In many ways, the assignments appeared to be general enough for use in any number of different courses, an advantage for faculty who are always pressed for time. The drawbacks of this approach, however, were that the assignments sometimes used vague terms and were not, overall, as precise as they could be.

Because faculty were attempting to look at the assignments through students' eyes, they realized that a number of assumptions embedded in the assignments should be made explicit—for example, grading criteria, disciplinary grounding, expectations for levels of integration. One of the major assumptions appeared to be that students would comprehend all that was needed with a single explanation the day the assignment was handed out. Several participants pointed out that it is not easy to grasp assignment instructions all at once so they should be like a recipe that students revisit, rereading and understanding better with each reading.

More importantly, the participants pointed out that the handouts probably did not fully represent the faculty's expectations for the assignments, expectations presumably elaborated more in class and in other handouts. One of the assignments provided a wealth of information about outcomes for the composition course in the learning community but none for the history course. Nor did the assignment provide a framework for evaluating the work, neither in terms of each discipline nor in terms of integrating them. By the time the participants began to analyze the second assignment, which clearly identified outcomes for disciplinary grounding and leveraging, they had developed a critical stance with respect to integrative assignment design. Despite the assignment's strengths, they argued, it could be improved with more explicit and precise language about the kinds and extent of interpretations and analysis expected.

In the second afternoon workshop, "Evaluating Student Work: Looking for Disciplinary Grounding and Integration," faculty used the collaborative assessment protocol again, this time to examine student writing to see if they could discern (a) its purpose (in this case, whether the *student* was clear about the purpose of the work), (b) demonstration of disciplinary grounding, and (c) demonstration of integration of the disciplines into a meaningful analysis and interpretation. In their discussion of two short pieces of student writing, faculty found that, although students articulated thoughtful ideas and demonstrated a reasonable grasp of concepts and vocabulary, these tended to appear as disciplinary "chunks" rather than a carefully integrated, unified analysis. After discussing examples of support that would help the students synthesize their knowledge and better express their insights, the faculty began to explore the kinds of classroom practices that would help students produce more effective work.

Redesigning Assignments to Leverage Disciplinary Grounding

The day-long summer retreat, "Strengthening Design and Assessing Integration: Going Beyond Disciplinary Grounding," provided a more comprehensive look at the College's work before diving into design work. Participants were asked to read Boix-Mansilla's (2008/2009) "Productive Shifts" prior to the retreat. The retreat then opened with an overview that oriented newer faculty to Skagit's history of learning communities and general education reform and that positioned work in the context of national research on learning communities as well as on learning theory.

The overview also introduced the guiding framework for the workshop: the assumption that effective assignments, including integrative assignments, respond to what we know about how people learn. According to Donovan, Bransford, and Pellegrino (1999), research has established that learners (a) need to be able to draw on (and question) previous knowledge, (b) require cognitive maps to use new knowledge, and (c) need opportunities to reflect on their learning. The decision to emphasize this research was based on the Skagit data from the online survey, specifically those questions about whether students were asked to draw on prior experiences and whether they received sufficient formative feedback about their work.

The workshop then reviewed the College's working definitions of three kinds of integration that developed from our work during the "Assessing Learning Communities" project before introducing the core dimensions of disciplinary grounding. These dimensions include the *purpose* of the discipline (what value its inquiry provides), the *methods* practitioners in the field use to build and validate knowledge, the *knowledge* (concepts, accepted findings, and expert perspectives) essential to be able to perform effectively in the discipline, and the kinds of *performances* (analysis, interpretation, application, design) expected of practitioners. The introductory overview concluded with examples of how disciplinary grounding for two courses could be integrated in a single learning community.

In the first of two breakout sessions of the retreat, faculty identified the dimensions—content, methods, purposes, and genres of performance—of their own disciplines. Using their discipline as a whole, a unit in a course, or a specific assignment, faculty first identified their own disciplinary grounding and then worked in pairs to explain their disciplines to each other. Each team next used what they had established as appropriate disciplinary grounding to sketch out an assignment that might ask students to leverage these into an integrated performance of their disciplinary understanding. A performance could be, for example, a group or panel presentation, work of art, dramatic performance, academic paper, service learning project, or poster session.

In the afternoon session, faculty teams worked on the design of learning community assignments that would ask students to demonstrate disciplinary knowledge and methods and the ability to leverage those in a meaningful, relevant task. Using the framework from the morning sessions, they established the purposes for the integrative task and, on the basis of those, identified disciplinary dimensions that would be relevant for students to demonstrate in completing the assignment. The guidelines for this work were framed as a series of questions for faculty teams to answer:

1. What disciplinary and integrative purposes will the assignment serve? Is it an introduction to the disciplines or to integration, intended to build skills, or a final project intended to demonstrate achieved abilities?

2. What is an appropriate disciplinary and interdisciplinary performance for this task?

3. What methods and knowledge from both disciplines will students need to complete the work?

4. What are the performance criteria for each discipline and for the integration? What might be the characteristics of beginning, developing, and advanced disciplinary and integrative student work?

5. What kinds of scaffolding, formative feedback, and opportunities for students to reflect on their disciplinary and integrative learning will the course provide?

Over lunch and at the conclusion of the retreat, faculty reflected on insights, challenges, and questions that the activities raised. For many, the retreat was the first time they had tried to articulate their own disciplinary grounding, a task that some found challenging. Some faculty were concerned that in integrating a 200-level course, they might be lowering the standards of learning in the course. This is of particular concern in sequential courses, which traditionally emphasize coverage of content, and, as faculty pointed out, time spent helping students learn to *use* their knowledge and *integrate* it is time not spent on coverage. Other faculty worried that in providing explicit criteria and details, students might be deprived of opportunities for discovering connections and relationships on their own.

Many agreed with the faculty pair who stated that the hardest work of the retreat was writing the evaluation criteria for their integrative assignment. However, as daunting as the task was, they believed it was the most valuable work of the day because, at that level of detail, they suddenly saw clearly how their two disciplines came together. Another faculty team observed that they began the day with a general idea of the assignment they wanted to give students but didn't realize they hadn't done the critical foundational work. Once they established the disciplinary grounds for the assignment, decided on the appropriate disciplinary performance, and set up disciplinary and integrative criteria, they realized that their assessment of student work would be far easier.

These participants' reflections about next steps mirrored the results of the online survey of students' learning community experiences and thus will help shape the next year's focus on classroom practices that support integrative learning. Participants asked for sessions about how to assess what students already know and how to integrate students' experiences into the academic context, in terms of validating those experiences and of helping students to examine prior assumptions. They also wanted to discuss levels of disciplinary and interdisciplinary performance, particularly how to distinguish and assess different levels of mastery, how to design assignments and activities that help students move from novice to expert stages, and how to provide effective—but also, for faculty, efficient—formative feedback for students as they learn. In terms of evaluating student work, faculty also requested opportunities to explore interdisciplinary rubrics and grading as well as some shared language and expectations, especially around writing.

Reflecting on Productive Shifts

When Skagit Valley College proposed its general education reforms in 1992, many in the College community recognized that the program was ambitious and that implementation posed significant challenges. It's probably fair to say, however, that few of us foresaw just how complex the task of reform would prove to be and how much we would learn in the process of trying to understand what we had undertaken.

In her description of the "Assessing Learning in Learning Communities" project, Boix-Mansilla (2008/2009) describes the evolution of faculty perceptions about their work on interdisciplinarity as "a shift in the center of gravity of their focus and thoughts" about assessment, disciplinary expertise, and interdisciplinary learning (p. 26). This model of productive shifts is equally apt for describing the changes in our understanding of the potential of learning communities as levers for strengthening and deepening student learning.

Many of the College's early assessments of student satisfaction and learning were driven by concerns about the newness of learning communities and whether they would "stick." We focused on whether faculty coordinated their course assignments and activities and whether these efforts delivered GPAs as good as, or hopefully better than, those of stand-alone courses. Our work of the past decade, and in particular of the past four years, has helped us move toward defining program effectiveness in terms of disciplinary integration rather than course coordination and toward intentional support for effective student learning. This includes a shift away from thinking of grades as the definitive measure of student learning and program success toward searching for the best ways to understand how students make sense of what they learn about disciplinary concepts and methods and how they use those to understand the world.

Our assessments of student learning and our collaborative work in the national projects, in our teaching, and in faculty development activities have helped us reconsider the purpose of disciplinary expertise. In the first decade of our learning community work, many faculty recognized that disciplinary knowledge is a powerful lens for understanding the world, but they did not feel that the end result of students' education at the college reflected this. As a college, we are now engaged in a concerted effort to move away from teaching practices that reinforce disciplinary knowledge as an end in itself. We are also in the midst of a shift away from viewing our learning community themes as organizing principles "to which multiple disciplines speak often in a parallel fashion" toward understanding interdisciplinarity and "valuing students' articulation of a multifaceted topic that demands the integration of disciplinary forms of expertise" (Boix-Mansilla, 2008/2009, p. 25).

We know from our most recent assessments of student work at both the program and classroom level that students recognize that this shift in focus requires more from them. In reflective essays, they frankly admit to being hesitant about the intellectual demands of their learning community work, because, as one student pointed out, its "distinct and challenging nature was something I have not experienced from previous courses, as it forced me to think in ways I have not done before." Students are also clear about the nature of this challenge, that "combining two separate disciplines into one analytical work can be a daunting task." As community college students whose course work is still primarily in introductory general education courses, they are often intimidated by the expectation that they not only learn to manage two new sets of vocabulary but also *use* those in meaningful ways. This awareness is clearly articulated by the student who wrote in an essay that the "ability to use language from both [disciplines] at first was difficult because balancing both concepts . . . was hard to accomplish as a first-year college student."

But just as our assessments and project work helped us to reach a more nuanced understanding of interdisciplinarity, the presence of students' voices in those assessments has helped us to recognize integration as a distinct skill that can—and must—be taught. This necessary shift in faculty focus and practices has led to improvements in student performance. It is also reflected in students' discussions of their learning. Students express both wonder and pride in the changes they have seen in their own intellectual work and in their attitudes toward it. One student pointed out that previously he had "preferred being lectured in class, and discussing the concepts as a group. But the most rewarding thing about the class would have to be actually beginning to understand many of those complex ideas." Many are like the students who write that in the past their educational goal had been "to just get by." Certainly many share the view of the student who explained that her purpose for enrolling was "to cross a learning community off my requirements page." It is our goal, however, that our students will find, as she did, that the work of the quarter engages them and that, like her, they will become "enthralled" with the explorations of society made possible by the disciplines and be stunned by "the connections we were making."

Because learning communities emphasize that students synthesize their disciplinary grounding in meaningful integrations and that they do so as members of a community of learners, many find—as one young woman did—that the expectations "challenged [her] in every aspect as a student." For most of our students, the expectation that they will collaborate with their peers, learn to listen and respect others' views, and integrate those into their learning as well is sometimes the most challenging aspect of learning community work. It is not easy for them to feel comfortable organizing their ideas and understanding so that they "can properly articulate it to others." Nor is it easy to "have to listen to ideas or interpretations" that they "find disagreeable or uncomfortable." Yet, in retrospect, many decide that what they at first perceived as insurmountable challenges ultimately become the sources of their success. They find they have "learned to comprehend the challenging material that rose from the integration" not just through deepened analytical abilities but "the help of other class members who brought a variety of meaningful perspectives to the class's group oriented atmosphere."

We are still engaged in productive shifts in our learning communities efforts. As part of the most recent general education reform, we have committed to an increasingly public assessment of student work through course portfolios and student work. We are still developing a shared understanding of our goals, shared language around integrative learning, and effective assessment protocols. We are in the process of analyzing, understanding, and using the results of our existing assessments to develop greater faculty expertise in teaching integration. And we are working to develop a more comprehensive understanding of how we can support student development objectives, that is, helping students learn the skills and academic behaviors that will not only help them stay in college but also to thrive.

When we first considered reforming our general education program in the late 1980s, our goals were lofty. Beyond simply creating coherence, faculty had expressed the desire to create conditions in which students would not just *see* but also *seek* connections in the courses that they take and would furthermore embrace their college education as a process of exploration and discovery. If the general education program, and in particular the learning communities portion, is working, then more of our students will find, as one did, that disciplinary studies are "not just a way of formulating ideas about the human experience, but also a way of examining the experiences themselves in the hope of getting closer to truly understanding various cultures." And they would, hopefully, conclude as did one young woman who volunteered the following statement when she completed the online *Survey of Students' Experiences of Learning in Learning Communities:* "I gained insight to my own life and lives of those around me in the sense that I was reassured that there is more to learning than a letter grade or prescribed grade point average."

Notes

1. Details of these assessments are described in Stanwood and Dunlap (2003).

2. A more extended discussion of these studies can be read in Dunlap and Pettitt's "Assessing Student Outcomes in Learning Communities: Two Decades of Studies at a Community College," (2008).

3. The collaborative assessment protocol targeted for interdisciplinary integration can be found in the resources section of the project website at The Washington Center for Improving the Quality of Undergraduate Education (http://wacenter .evergreen.edu/natlproject/resources.html).

4. Details about how simple course and assignment revisions help improve student learning can be found in Dunlap and Sult's "Juggling and the Art of the Integrative Assignment" in the 2008/2009 special issue of the *Journal of Learning Communities Research.* This issue also includes Pettitt and Muga's "Templates and Rubrics," which provides a template for helping students and faculty identify connections between their assignments, expected learning outcomes, assessment tools, and general education outcomes.

References

American Association of Colleges and Universities. (2004, March). Statement on integrative learning. Retrieved from http://www.aacu.org/integrative_learning/ pdfs/ILP_Statement.pdf

Altieri, G., & Cygnar, P. M. (1997). A new model for general education associate's degree programs: Developing and teaching a core across the curriculum. *Community College Review, 25*(2), 3–19.

Blythe, T., et al. (1998). *The teaching for understanding guide.* San Francisco, CA: Jossey-Bass.

Boix-Mansilla, V. (2005). Assessing student work at disciplinary crossroads. *Change, 37*(1), 14–21.

Boix-Mansilla, V. (2008/2009). Productive shifts: Faculty growth through collaborative assessment of student work. *Journal of Learning Communities Research, 3*(3), 21–26.

Boix-Mansilla, V., & Dawes, E. (2007). Toward a framework for assessing students' interdisciplinary work: An empirically grounded framework proposed. *The Journal of Higher Education, 78*(2), 215–237.

Boyer, Ernest L. (1987). *College: The undergraduate experience in America.* New York: Harper and Row.

Commission on the Future of Community Colleges. (1988). *Building communities: A vision for a new century.* Washington, DC: American Association of Community and Junior Colleges, National Center for Higher Education.

Conley, D. T. (2007). *Redefining college readiness.* Eugene, OR: Educational Policy Improvement Center. Retrieved from http://www.aypf.org/documents/Redefining CollegeReadiness.pdf

Donovan, M. S., Bransford J. D., & Pellegrino J. W. (Eds.). (1999). *How people learn: Bridging research and practice.* Washington, DC: National Academy Press.

Dunlap, L., & Pettitt, M. (2008). Assessing student outcomes in learning communities: Two decades of studies at a community college. *The Journal of Applied Research in the Community College, 15*(2), 140–149.

Dunlap, L., & Sult, L. (2008/2009). Juggling and the art of the integrative assignment. *Journal of Learning Communities Research, 3*(3), 27–45.

Eaton, J. S. (1993). General education in the community college: Developing habits of thought. N. A. Raisman, (Ed.). *Directing general education outcomes. New Directions for Community Colleges, no. 81.* San Francisco: Jossey-Bass Publishers, 21–30.

Erickson, M. E. (1992). General and liberal education: Competing paradigms. *Community College Review, 19*(4), 15–20.

Evidence Project Staff. (2001). *The evidence process: A collaborative approach to understanding and improving teaching and learning.* Cambridge, MA: Harvard Graduate School of Education.

Gabelnick, F., MacGregor, J., Matthews, R. S., & Smith, B. L. (1992). Learning communities and general education. *Perspectives, 22*(1), 104–121.

Gaff, J. G. (1991). *New life for the college curriculum: Assessing achievements and furthering progress in the reform of general education.* San Francisco: Jossey-Bass.

Goodsell, A., Maher, M., & Tinto, V. (1992). *Collaborative learning: A sourcebook for higher education.* University Park, PA: Pennsylvania State University, National Center on Postsecondary Teaching, Learning and Assessment.

Hill, P. J. (1985). Communities of learners: Curriculum as the infrastructure of academic communities. J. W. Hall & B. L. Kevles (Eds.), *In opposition to the core curriculum: Alternative models of undergraduate education.* Westport, CT: Greenwood Press.

MacGregor, J. (1987). *Intellectual development of students in learning community programs.* (Washington Center Occasional Paper No.1). Olympia, WA: The Evergreen State College, Washington Center for Improving the Quality of Undergraduate Education.

Pettitt, M., & Muga, D. (2008/2009). Templates and rubric: Connecting outcomes, assignments, and assessment in interdisciplinary learning communities. *Journal of Learning Communities Research, 3*(3), 109–126.

Project on Strong Foundations for General Education. (1994). *Strong foundations: Twelve principles for effective general education programs.* Washington, DC: Association of American Colleges.

Ratcliff, J. L., Johnson, D. K., La Nasa, S. M., & Gaff, J. G. (2001). *The status of general education in the year 2000: Summary of a national survey.* Washington, DC: American Association of Colleges and Universities.

Rhoten, D., Boix-Mansilla, V., Chun, M., & Klein, J. T. (2006). *Interdisciplinary education at liberal arts institutions.* (Teagle Foundation Social Science Research

Council Working Group White Paper). Retrieved from http://www.teaglefoun
dation.org/learning/pdf/2006_ssrc_whitepaper.pdf

Stanwood, L., & Dunlap, L. (2003). The assessment chase: The changing shape of
assessment in shaping change at Skagit Valley College. J. MacGregor (Ed.), *Doing
learning community assessment: Stories from five campuses.* National Learning
Communities Project Monograph Series. Olympia, WA: The Evergreen State
College, Washington Center for Improving the Quality of Undergraduate Education, in cooperation with the American Association for Higher Education.

11

LINKED COURSE ASSESSMENT

The Problem With Quantitative Data

Bethany Blankenship

This is not the chapter I expected to write. I wanted to write about how linked classes for first-year students at my university produce higher retention rates from the freshman to the sophomore year. Of course, I knew I wouldn't be the first to make such as argument. Vincent Tinto's article, "Building Community" (1993), describes a longitudinal study of first-year learning communities (FLCs) at the University of Washington and Seattle Central Community College. Persistence rates from spring to fall for students enrolled in FLCs were markedly higher than those of students not enrolled. Hotchkiss, Moore, and Pitts's article, "Freshman Learning Communities, College Performance, and Retention" (2006), studies similar persistence rates at Georgia State University, though they factored in race and gender to show how FLCs aided retention, especially with Black men and women. Soldner, Lee, and Duby's article, "Welcome to the Block: Developing Freshman Learning Communities that Work" (1999), studies persistence rates at Northern Michigan University that, in keeping with most other articles about retention and FLCs, show that participation in such a community positively affects retention.

However, comparing retention numbers of students in linked classes with students in FLCs is an apples-and-oranges affair. Unlike FLCs, linked courses do not necessarily address the social and emotional needs of first-year students. In addition, although they tend to focus on first-year students like FLCs, linked classes tend to be more focused on students' academic well being.

Also, the current literature on retention rates and first-year students does not specifically discuss the effects of a linked class experience. Although most first-year learning communities provide opportunities for a cohort of students to take the same classes throughout the fall semester, not all FLCs offer thematically linked courses, such as those being discussed in this book.

Furthermore, there are virtually no articles that deal with assessment of FLCs at small (fewer than 2,500 students) colleges, like my university (University of Montana Western [UMW]), which has fewer than 1,500 students. Phrases such as "statistical significance" tend to lose their power when sample sizes dip below 1,500.

Finally, I ran into this snag. UMW is the only public institution in the United States to offer block scheduling or, as we call it, *Experience One (X-1)*. Students take one class at a time for eighteen days for three hours a day. Students take four classes or "blocks" each semester. With this unique scheduling system come unique problems. Though students tend to bond early on in their classes, once the class is over, students must readjust quickly to a new set of peers for another intense eighteen-day session. This is particularly difficult for first-year students who often feel adrift in a sea of new faces during their first semester.

So even though rising retention rates of students in cohorts is well-covered ground, I thought with UMW's small sample size and unique approach to course scheduling that I would be able to proffer a somewhat unique argument about retention of first-year students in linked classes at a small college that offers consecutive rather than simultaneous linked classes. However, after poring through years of statistics and other data from my university, I found I cannot make the quantitative argument that linked classes lead to higher retention of freshmen at UMW. The qualitative data, however, tells a very different (and perhaps more interesting) story.

The Quantitative Narrative

In recent memory, using a cohort experience (students staying with the same group during the fall semester) UMW succeeded in raising retention rates. In 2002, seventy-five first-year students self-selected into a cohort experience and were divided randomly into three groups of twenty-five. They took general education classes that were not thematically linked. The only common denominator among these classes was the students. In the spring, the groups were changed because of math remediation needs. One third of the students stayed in the same groups, but even with this change, the esprit de corps carried on throughout the spring semester.

This cohort experience was assessed as it was part of a Fund for the Improvement of Postsecondary Education (FIPSE) grant. Though the cohorts were assessed for the purpose of determining the success of block scheduling at UMW, the data accrued for the FIPSE final report also describes how students achieved while staying with the same group of students in each class over one semester. The final report noted that 90 percent of the students in the cohort returned for a second semester (Krank, 2005). Furthermore, UMW boasted increased retention after the spring semester cohorts. Roughly 70 percent of the cohort students returned in the fall, whereas only 54 percent in the traditional program returned (Krank, 2005).

The next fall, seventy-five first-year students self-selected into a cohort experience, but this time, the groups were segregated by math ability; that is, students who required math remediation were in the same cohort, students who were able to go into advanced math were in the same group, and so on. Because of this segregation, the students quickly identified themselves as being part of the "dumb" or "smart" group. Students were not the only ones to classify their academic abilities. According to the FIPSE report,

> The lowest ability group soon became identified as extraordinarily challenging in terms of both affective and cognitive characteristics. Concerted, focused academic support for the provisional students by the Dean of Students office failed to materialize and as a result the low ability group spun into an ever-downward spiral of failure. The impending demise of the low ability group cast a pall over the entire FIPSE project. (Krank, 2005, p. 23)

In fact, retention data shows that fall to spring semester dropout rates for students participating in the second year of the FIPSE project were the equivalent of the historic dropout rate (20 percent) for UMW (unlike the first year of the project, which boasted only a 10 percent dropout rate for students in the cohort). Unfortunately, we do not know how many students in the cohort returned in the fall, but the retention number for all first-year students dipped to 50 percent, the lowest since 1995.

The cohort model was abandoned the following fall semester. All students taking general education classes did so in block scheduling, but the classes were not linked thematically nor were the students with the same group throughout the semester. Retention rates from fall to spring during this third year improved from 80 percent to 85 percent and fall-to-fall retention rates improved from the historic average of 55.5 percent to 60.6 percent.

According to the study, "This finding is extraordinary in light of the characteristics of [this group of students]. Academic performance predictors indicated [they were] decidedly at-risk as a group. Contrary to that prediction, [these students] not only had higher than expected retention rates, [they] also achieved a GPA that fell between the average GPA for the first and second year of the program" (Krank, 2005). Such numbers certainly speak to the notion that block scheduling helps improve retention, but what does it say about students who are put together in semester-long cohorts? Do these retention numbers tell us of the success of block scheduling or of the failure of cohorts?

To the UMW faculty, the numbers told them to proceed with a full implementation of block scheduling in 2005 and to be wary of cohorts in the future. At small universities such as UMW, memories last long, so when the idea of cohorts emerged a few years later, it was met with grumbling and general distaste. As a supporter of such an experience for first-year students, I began discussing the benefits of FLCs by calling the classes "linked" rather than "cohorts." Such a rhetorical change actually did satisfy a few of the long-time faculty members, but what really got faculty motivated was the promise of creativity when developing linked classes.

Cross-curricular and thematically linked, these classes span the first two blocks of the fall semester. For example, during block one, I taught Writing 101 while during block two, my colleague in the history, political, and social science department taught Philosophy 101. The two classes were thematically linked and called "Bada Bing: The Composition" and "Philosophy of *The Sopranos.*"

Out of 222 students, only 57 participated in linked classes. Though the retention numbers of all first-year students rose from fall to spring (89.8 percent the previous year to 92.5 percent) they fell the following fall (from 69 percent to 65 percent). Unfortunately, the number of students who persisted and were part of the linked classes were not calculated separately from the remaining students; but as students in linked classes, counted only for 25 percent of the total number of first-year students, so perhaps the lower retention rate does not signify the failure of linked classes to aid retention.

However, because fall-to-fall retention rates are not calculated until the fifteenth day of the semester, the administration and faculty did not know of the lower retention rates before they decided to proceed with more linked classes. Instead, faculty and administration were offered an analysis of qualitative data I retrieved from participating students. The following year, nine linked classes were offered for a total of 198 students.

The Qualitative Story

Retention numbers only tell us that a student has returned; they tell us nothing about what the student has learned. This is what David Jaffee (2007) calls "the unintended consequences of freshman learning communities." Although Jaffee's article focuses on the sociological impacts of FLCs on students, his argument affects my own: Quantitative data alone cannot tell the story of student learning.

During the first year of these linked classes, I conducted an informal assessment to discover what students learned in their linked classes. Only one respondent out of each of the linked classes indicated that the disciplinary link was not beneficial. The students spent most of their writing time on the first question that asked them to think about their group interactions. Overwhelmingly, students believe they gained more confidence with working in groups. The following is a sample of responses from each class.

1. Describe your confidence and comfort with group interactions and sharing ideas as well as your comfort with cooperative efforts and problem-solving.

   > "Working in a group has made me better because I now work better with others. Working in a group I have learned to take two sides of the story, not just one."

   > "The first day of class was a little slow as far as interaction goes. Not many of the kids spoke to one another but the end of the second block it was almost like we had all grown up together. We have become a family and we all supported each other."

2. How did attending linked classes make you aware of how content and theme can be applied to different disciplines (i.e., math and biology, English and history)?

   > "Linked classes allowed us to use the skills we were taught in the previous class and bring them to another class."

   > "Coming from English class, I could see the difference from being in this sociology class. In English class it was more of expressing your thoughts in many ways. . . . [In sociology] our papers were also not so much about our opinion, more of what we know and learned."

   > "By attending this linked class I have learned that using a common theme to apply to disciplines works very well. I have a better

understanding of the content and I don't wake up every morning dreading class."

"Attending the linked classes helped me to realize that different subjects can cross over into one another. When the subjects are linked with a topic it makes it easier to form a connection."

3. To what extent has your linked class aided the development of your critical thinking skills?

"The linked classes aided our critical thinking skills because it allowed us to discuss subjects as a group rather than as individuals. The more brains put together the better a solution would be because the part it's made of are from different perspectives."

"It helped critical thinking by examining more aspects of the time period we studied instead of just looking at it from one angle."

"The linked classes force me to think outside of the box. It forces me to search for connections and correlations. It makes me look deeper into a topic and come up with ideas I didn't know I had."

"My critical thinking has been changed to the point that I can work in a group and I am confident that my ideas and thoughts contribute."

It is clear that students benefited from taking linked classes. They learned to work cooperatively and became confident during classroom interactions. Also, students understood the links between the classes as disciplinary connections that, as one student wrote, "forces me to search for connections and correlations." This outcome is perhaps one of the greatest strengths of linked courses: the ability to explicitly demonstrate how disciplines overlap and inform one another.

Interestingly, however, even this qualitative data had its limits. As one student put it, how would students know the difference between their experiences and other students' nonlinked class experiences? That is, what would happen to these students when they enter their block 3 classes?

To that end, during block 4, I wrote to students in two different linked classes and asked the following questions (responses follow):

1. How would you characterize your level of involvement in your regular eighteen-day block class versus in your two-block linked class? Which class engaged your attention more fully?

"Being in the linked class definitely kept me more involved. When you are in the same class with the same people for two blocks instead of one, you feel much more comfortable speaking up in class and participating."

"My level of involvement increased with the linked block class. I felt more comfortable with my peers and found it easier to open up. Group and class participation came easier for me and I enjoyed the atmosphere the class created."

2. How did your involvement in a two-block linked class help you or hurt you as you sought to make friends at the university?

"The two-block linked class helped me make friends a lot easier than if I were in the eighteen-day class."

"The linked block made the transition from high school to college so much easier. The friends I made in the first two blocks are the ones through whom I met many other people on campus. I feel that the linked classes make college less intimidating and much easier on the social aspect of a student's life."

3. Would you recommend two-block linked classes to next fall's incoming freshmen? Why or why not?

"I would highly recommend linked classes to incoming freshmen. I think overall it was a very good experience, and I thought the learning and friendship aspects were both very good."

"Yeah, it was fun having the two subjects put together by something common and having the same people in two blocks right after each other instead of having a bunch of new people in each class repeatedly."

"I would recommend it to incoming freshmen; however, I would caution them because I did not enjoy my second block at all. The writing styles were completely different and difficult for me to switch from one to the other, and the second block professor didn't agree with certain ideas that we had from the first block class, which made it difficult for him to accept or understand the point I was making."

Even though these responses were not entirely positive, they show that a number of participants felt they were more involved in their linked classes than in their traditional eighteen-day classes. Students also believed that linked classes aided in their transition from high school to college. However, as I mentioned in the previous section, retention decreased after the first year of linked courses, but this data was unknown at the time of implementation of the following year's linked classes. The qualitative story, it seems, was enough to convince faculty and administration to proceed.

The next year, almost two hundred first-year students took part in linked classes. At the end of the second block, students were asked to respond to a similar (from the previous year) set of questions. In an internal report that summarized the survey's finding, Brian Price, assistant provost, writes,

1. Students thoroughly appreciated being in the same cohort for two blocks, many stating that it helped their transition from high school to college.
2. Students enjoyed every opportunity they had to work collaboratively in small groups. For some, it meant that they could ask questions without fear that their faculty might interpret their question-asking as evidence of intellectual weakness. For others, it was a revelation that they could actually learn from their peers and rely upon them as intellectual aides.
3. In four linked classes, students easily identified the themes that connected their two courses. In the others, students often didn't recognize that their courses were linked until the start of the second block, and couldn't identify linking themes even then.
4. Though most students commented upon improvements in their *critical thinking* ability, it was clear that some students didn't really know what the term meant. With few exceptions, students did not indicate that critical thinking was taught explicitly as part of their courses.

As in the previous year, students gained confidence when interacting with one another in the classroom; however, many of the students did not fully understand the connections between their classes. This lack of understanding, Price shows, occurred because of lack of faculty communication, a problem that could be improved in subsequent years of implementation. Later, Price concludes that collaborative interaction in itself was the most commented upon and positively reacted to outcome by students.

> If linked courses amount to nothing more than simply keeping the same cohort of students together for two blocks, . . . the linked course initiative

should be kept going. Virtually every student commented positively upon the experience of working in small groups with their peers, the support they felt, . . . their ability to learn from their peers, and the increased comfort they now felt in speaking up in class. What the almost unanimously positive response to this item suggests is that when learning is social, students are much more comfortable than when the primary lines of interaction are between the (judging/grading) faculty and the students as monadic individuals. And students know it.

Price's conclusion mirrors Krank's FIPSE report, which showed that keeping students together, even in unrelated classes, benefits students.

The qualitative story of linked classes at a small university shows that it is the student himself or herself who is the most significant data point. Students at UMW believe that linked classes help them develop skills in working with small groups. Linked classes, students say, build their confidence so that they feel comfortable speaking up in class. No amount of statistical analysis can measure this intellectual growth: that of students taking responsibility for their own learning.

References

Hotchkiss, J., Moore, R., & Pitts, M. (2006). Freshman learning communities, college performance, and retention. *Education Economics, 14*(2), 197–210.

Jaffee, D. (2007). Peer cohorts and the unintended consequences of freshman learning communities. *College Teaching, 55*(2), 65–71.

Krank, M., U.S. Department of Education, Fund for the Improving of Postsecondary Education. (2005). *Immersion scheduling and experiential learning: Predictors of traditional age, first-time college student success.* The report can be requested through the FIPSE website at http://fipsedatabase.ed.gov/fipse/grantshow.cfm?grantNumber = P116B011439

Soldner, L., Lee, Y., & Duby, P. (1999). Welcome to the block: Developing freshman learning communities that work. *Journal of College Student Retention, 1*(2), 115–129.

Tinto, V. (1993). Building community. *Liberal Education, 79*(4), 16–22.

12

CONSTANT RECONNAISSANCE

Assessment for Validation and Change

Greg Smith and Geoffrey Mamerow

A ssessment has always been part of the higher education enterprise: Whether in stand-alone classes or in linked course environments, faculty have always worked to assess student learning as well as evaluate their own teaching and effectiveness. The concept of assessment, nevertheless, is broader than those classrooms and their faculty members' judgments and measures of how much an individual student has learned or not learned.

To be sure, although the idea of assessment is not a foreign concept to most educators, designing an effective assessment protocol that is appropriate for a specific program, especially one involving multiple classrooms and curricula, can be a daunting and confusing endeavor. It may be tempting to simply gather volumes of data, compile the resulting information into a report, and declare the process complete. All good assessment, however, needs to be born of a thoughtful process with a clear purpose—one that is anchored in the stated purposes of the program, measures intended outcomes, and provides guidance for future direction. As an added benefit, a well-designed assessment approach can help a program to develop relationships with campus partners that strengthen its standing, not just measure its success or effectiveness.

Today institutional budgets are continually tightening and resources are becoming more precious. In turn, program assessment has become increasingly important as a tool for leaders forced to make difficult decisions regarding the effectiveness of programs and the allocation of scarce resources. A program's survival may be contingent on whether it can demonstrate that it is achieving its goals to the benefit of students. As accountability becomes more and more of an influential force in higher education, we are often expected to conduct regular and ongoing programmatic assessments; some accreditation organizations themselves are even asking institutions to develop more rigorous protocols. With these imperatives in mind, it is incumbent on the smart practitioner to develop a culture of assessment—one that promotes excellence in learning, identifies opportunities for improvement, and justifies current support while building more.

In this chapter, we present a number of specific strategies, as well as the philosophical foundations of an assessment approach developed for a linked course educational program at the University of Wisconsin–Madison (UW-Madison). It is an approach that can be used by practitioners in higher education—administrators and faculty alike—to design from whole cloth or to adapt to various educational applications or programs, especially those that link courses together for the benefit of students. To illustrate our techniques, we use data and experiences collected from UW-Madison's first-year interest groups (FIGs), a program that has been linking courses together for over a decade. It is our hope that the rich experiences we use to describe FIGs can prompt discussion about the various approaches that can be used to assess linked courses, provide a starting point for those just beginning to plan, or illuminate new areas and approaches for the seasoned practitioner.

A Philosophy of Assessment

From its inception, the UW-Madison FIGs program has engaged in rigorous, systematic assessment to guide the administration of what started out as a unique linked course experiment, but has grown into a robust program serving nearly 20 percent of incoming freshmen. Although the exact protocols have shifted over the years in response to specific programmatic needs, evaluation of the UW FIGs program has been based, at its core, on a philosophy of assessment that incorporates the following principles:

> *Purpose*—Assessment should be based on the program's purpose and intended outcomes. Emphasizing program evaluation encourages planners to develop measurable learning outcomes, and assessment efforts are important in validating a program's efficacy.
>
> *Stakeholders*—Assessment must involve principal stakeholders. Those who are closely involved—students, faculty, campus partners—are

those best able to describe their experiences and make recommendations for improvement.

Multifarious—Assessment should be conducted on multiple levels using multiple measures: Summative and formative assessments utilizing both quantitative and qualitative data are important to portray a complete and accurate picture of how successful the program is in its attempt to achieve its goals.

Simplicity—Assessment plans should be simple and doable. Complex assessment protocols may prove to be cumbersome and inconvenient, and as such may be less likely to be fully implemented.

Useful—Assessment results should be useful. Program evaluations can be time and resource intensive, so results need to focus on data that can be analyzed and applied to best enhance the program.

Sharing—Assessment results should be shared with stakeholders, campus colleagues, institutional leaders, and others who might find them informative and useful. Sharing the results of program assessment may well lead to collaborations with colleagues and continued institutional support.

Constant—Assessment is constant. Continuous quality improvement should be part of program evaluation and planning. Situations and environments are in constant flux, so program administrators must engage in "constant reconnaissance" of the environment, measuring a program's strengths, examining areas of weakness, and looking for opportunities for collaboration and growth.

Some of these principles may seem self-evident: that assessments should be linked to a program's purpose, or that assessment plans be simple and useful. However, other principles may be easily overlooked, such as identifying stakeholders and finding ways to include their voices in the assessment process. The need to share assessment results may not be so obvious, and it can also be difficult to find creative ways to share data that demonstrate how evaluation has resulted in substantive and positive programmatic changes with critical audiences across campus. Finally, because assessment takes time, energy, and resources, creating a "culture of assessment" that recognizes the need for "constant reconnaissance" may also be met with some resistance.

FIGs Background

To best explain the various ways these principles can be applied to learning environments that utilize linked courses—as well as how to best harness the resulting data to improve programming—it is necessary to give a brief explanation of the UW FIGs program.

The FIG program at UW-Madison was created as a response to recommendations that the campus develop a first-year experience as one way to improve the academic performance, retention, and multicultural understanding of first-year students. The fundamental mission of the program is to enhance first-year student learning through the development of learning communities that foster academic and social connections. The program attempts the following:

- Provide diversity education for participating students.
- Contribute to general education goals and learning.
- Offer integrated learning across clusters of linked classes.

The structure of FIGs emphasizes faculty involvement, curricular integration, and social connections among students. Each FIG enrolls a small group of students (maximum of twenty) who co-enroll in three linked classes, including, in many cases, a class that fulfills one of the campus' general education requirements. Each FIG is designed, in partnership with program administrators, by a faculty member who teaches the core "FIG seminar" that enrolls just the twenty or so FIG students. These special topic seminars—typically three-credit classes—may be courses that are regularly offered but that have been tailored for a FIG environment (lecture-style pedagogy does not work well with a small group of twenty students); in many cases, however, they are truly special courses offered nowhere on campus but in the FIG. Occasionally, faculty who are interested in developing a new course for a department's curriculum will teach that course as a FIGs seminar first to "test it out" before submitting a formal proposal to a curriculum committee. Through planning and communication with other faculty, the instructor of the main class of a FIG integrates appropriate material from the two "linking classes" into the core seminar. Most faculty teaching the core seminar do so as part of their regular teaching loads, although some elect to do so as "unpaid overloads." Although faculty receive no extra salary compensation for teaching FIG seminars, they do receive a stipend for supplies and expenses, which allows them to, among other things, provide enrichment activities for their FIG students: field trips, guest speakers, meals linked to study sessions, and so forth. In addition, some FIGs also include service-learning opportunities, extending the out-of-class experiences of students into the surrounding community.

UW's FIG program is housed administratively in the College of Letters and Science, and although initially all faculty teaching the main FIG seminars came from departments within that college, the program has expanded to include faculty from virtually every school and college on campus, and now includes courses in dozens of departments and majors. Some FIGs are designed to appeal to students interested in pursuing specific majors, such as engineering and nursing. These course clusters in such cases may include either prerequisites for entry or courses that fulfill specific requirements for those majors. "Health Care Systems in Contemporary America," for example, is designed for students who intend to apply to the School of Nursing and includes courses required for admission to that major.

Most FIGs, however, are more general in nature and offer students opportunities to engage in thoughtful exploration of topics and disciplines in which they have interest or, in some cases, to which they have had little exposure. The experience often also allows students to see those areas of interest through a different lens and to begin understanding the interconnections of academic disciplines. The seminar course in a FIG entitled "Nature and Culture," for example, focuses on literature about nature and the environment, and it is linked to courses in both environmental studies and botany, thus allowing students to explore topics from multiple points of view. Other FIGs introduce students to topics and disciplines they may never have considered or even heard of before. A good example of this is a FIG titled "An African Cultural Expedition," which focuses on Yoruba life and culture and includes an introductory Yoruba language course. Few if any new freshmen have even heard of this language before enrolling in this FIG, yet for the past seven years this has been a popular option, demonstrating that students may be willing to "take risks" if they understand that they will be part of a supportive community of peers.

Figure 12.1 gives a visual representation of how a FIG is structured and how the 20 students are co-enrolled in three courses linked by a common theme.

Applying Assessment to FIGs: Summative Versus Formative

Different assessment efforts have different purposes and may be done at different times throughout a program's cycle. Summative assessments, on one hand, provide information about the effectiveness of a program: Is it doing what it was designed to do, and are program goals being achieved?

FIGURE 12.1
Nature and Culture: How Humans Interact With the Natural Environment

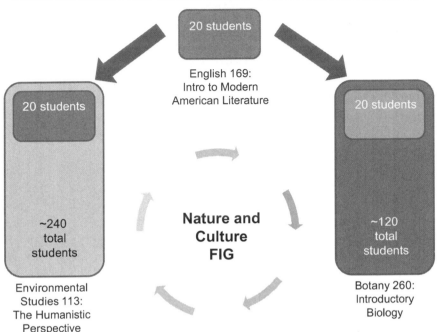

In other words, is the program working and is it worth keeping? Summative assessments are frequently done at the conclusion of a program cycle, for example, at the end of a semester or academic year.

Formative assessment, on the other hand, can be more complex. It is an ongoing process that provides a basis for program evolution and improvement: What seems to be working well and should be continued, and what changes should be implemented? Each type merits a place in the overall assessment plan of any program in higher education and can fulfill purposes as varied as providing a basic justification for the program, measuring its effectiveness or efficiency, and providing guidance when changing directions in how the program is run. Further on in the chapter we discuss appropriate times to use the various assessment types to their greatest benefit.

From the very beginning, assessment was a key element of the FIGs program. When it was launched as a tentative four-FIG pilot program in fall 2001, it was clear that rigorous summative assessment would be critical in determining whether the program was achieving its goals—and whether it would or should ultimately be allowed to continue. Unlike other FIG program models at other institutions, where small cohorts of students may simply be embedded together in clusters of large lecture classes, UW-Madison's program depends on significant faculty involvement, and faculty who might otherwise be teaching large lecture classes or graduate seminars instead are teaching small classes of just twenty first-year students. This distinction makes the UW-Madison FIG model a resource-intensive effort requiring that it demonstrate almost immediately that it was achieving its goals. Without clear, rigorous, and empirical evidence illustrating that linking courses together in this manner was productive and worth the expense and effort, academic departments would be reluctant to allow their faculty to participate and the program would wither. Campus data on student demographics, grade point averages (GPAs), and retention, coupled with data from surveys and focus groups, were critical in this effort to provide for these "summative evaluations." Fortunately, the results of our initial assessments validated the program's strengths. (We will explore those assessment results a little later.)

Additionally, formative assessment has been important as the program has continued to evolve; as with any new venture, the program needed to be responsive to recommendations for changes in structure and process. Formative assessment helps to evaluate process and procedure, logistics, and program delivery. It provides opportunities for stakeholders to help determine whether the program is meeting their needs and what improvements might be implemented. This aspect of the program's assessment has depended heavily on more qualitative efforts: surveys, focus groups, observations, and artifact collection. It also includes less formal data collection. Evaluators should recognize the value of "serendipity": useful data that may simply appear in the forms of e-mails, student testimonials, faculty anecdotes, and collegial conversations. Although these data elements may not be quantifiable and may not ultimately appear in any formal report, they can still be useful in validating other assessment information or in identifying potential problems, enrollment trends, shifts in the institutional environment, and they may provide some impetus for further exploration and assessment. As well, such informal elements of a larger assessment plan are not only consistent with but necessary to the "constant reconnaissance" approach.

Summative Assessment Protocols

Summative evaluation protocols have been useful in determining whether the FIG program is achieving its mission to improve student achievement and retention. This evaluation process has depended largely on quantitative institutional data. The protocol begins by comparing the demographic profiles of FIG and non-FIG student cohorts, then compares academic achievement of these groups as measured by cumulative GPAs, retention rates, and so forth. Specifically, the following data are collected and analyzed as part of the evaluation process:

- ACT scores
- High school class rank
- High school GPA
- Cumulative GPAs of freshmen (FIG and non-FIG) at the end of the fall semester of the FIG experience
- Cumulative GPAs of FIG and non-FIG students by ACT scores
- Gender (percent of males/females compared with cohort profile)
- Ethnicity (by percent, compared with cohort profile)
- Retention rates
- Graduation rates of FIG and non-FIG students, including graduation rates of targeted minority students

Although formative assessment can utilize many of the same quantitative data points that have been effective in our summative evaluations, the data we have collected to shape (rather than measure the effectiveness of) our program have included many qualitative variables. Qualitative protocols are of particular value when considering the direction of a program as no institutional data point such as a GPA can indicate a student's satisfaction with the program or a faculty member's preference for it to be managed in a certain way. Each program utilizing this kind of assessment requires unique questions tuned to the specifics of its particular model, and will reveal findings specific to that model. In addition, the same protocol of questions and approaches can, and will, reveal different results and different implications for practice.

By using surveys and focus groups, the formative assessments of FIGs have sought student stakeholder input in a number of areas related to recruiting students, transition issues, general satisfaction, and recommendations for future improvements. One specific area of exploration, for example, has been in marketing FIGs: How did students learn about FIGs? Which "marketing" strategies are most effective? How did students make their decisions to enroll in FIGs? What FIGs experiences were most memorable? Did FIG participation ease the transition to university life? If so, how? Were the courses in the

FIG appropriate? Did students understand the curricular connections? What, if any, influence will the FIG have on a student's future course enrollment or choice of major? And of course, are there any recommendations for improvements in FIGs, including topics, courses, program structure, and so forth?

Faculty, another important stakeholder group, have been similarly surveyed and invited to participate in focus groups; they also have had frequent informal opportunities to provide information and recommendations. Besides being asked for their observations regarding the effect of the FIG experience on their students, they have been asked about their own motivations for teaching the small FIGs seminar courses, how this experience may or may not have influenced their pedagogy, how teaching in FIGs may or may not have helped them achieve personal and professional goals, and how the program's administrators might make improvements and provide more support for faculty.

For each of these stakeholder groups, it has been necessary to ask a range of questions, and to ask them often, to capture a more complete range of answers and perceptions, as well as any change that has occurred in each population over time. Our experience over the decade with this program is that subtle shifts occur in these answers as new generations (of students, in particular) enroll in FIGs. Those shifts necessitate adjustments in administration of the program that would not be otherwise discovered. A simple example occurred early in the history of this program. Originally, FIG enrollments were tied to residence halls: specific FIGs were linked to specific halls, and only students who would be living in those halls could enroll in those FIGs. In response to formal and informal input from students, faculty, academic advisors, and residence hall staff, this restriction was eliminated.

Summative and formative approaches are necessary to paint the most accurate portrayal possible of a program, and are in many ways complementary. Each approach can work with a wide range of data, but each favors certain sources. When assessing educational environments as complex as the linked course experience of a FIG, a diversity of approaches are necessary to fully develop an understanding that can be used to make decisions that will affect the program as a whole.

Measuring Basic Success

One of the first, and most basic, assessments we have undertaken to gauge the program's success has been to compare the average first-semester GPAs of our FIG cohort to that of the general student population. In this comparison GPA becomes the dependent variable that may or may not be affected by the independent variable, in this case, FIG participation. In other words, does participating in a FIG have a detrimental, neutral, or beneficial effect on students' GPAs? Fortunately for the longevity of the program, and ultimately to the benefit of participating students, the results of this particular measure have consistently indicated that FIG participation has a genuine benefit to students' GPAs. As shown in Figure 12.2, we have plotted the GPAs of FIG and non-FIG cohorts of the last ten years.

As the graph indicates, FIG students have earned higher GPAs in their first semester than non-FIG students every year during the ten-year history of the program. Although this particular assessment measure is not nuanced enough to parse the reasons for the effect, it is a useful measure to indicate general success, and—in the experience of the UW FIG program—has helped to secure continued support for both operation and expansion.

Comparing Populations

Notwithstanding the encouraging results gained by comparing our most basic populations of FIG and non-FIG cohorts, our assessment plan has also

FIGURE 12.2.
First-Semester GPAs: FIGs and Non-FIGS

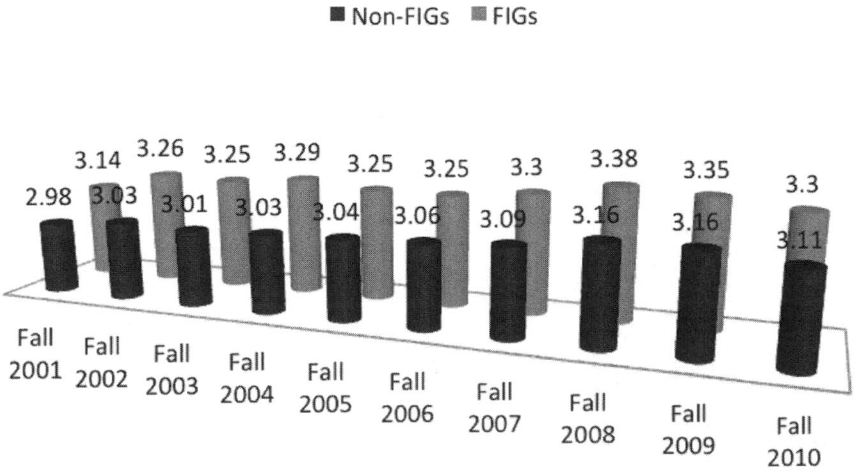

■ Non-FIGs   ■ FIGs

included attempts to answer more nuanced questions about our students and their success. For instance, is the GPA effect the same for all of the diverse populations who attend our university? If students enrolling in FIGs earn higher GPAs, might that effect simply be because higher achieving students are self-selecting into this program? Does participating in a linked course program like FIGs show equal benefit for all students, or does it only benefit certain populations?

Straightforward comparison of various student populations along a number of different variables is a basic assessment function, but by gathering more detailed demographic information on our students we are able to gain a more subtle view of their learning outcomes, and the success of the program. We solicited demographic data from the University's data warehouse, and found that—year after year—the demographic profiles of FIG and non-FIG students at UW-Madison have been quite consistent.

FIG students tend to have slightly lower composite ACT scores; fewer graduated in the top 10 percent of their high school class; more are first-generation college students. In addition, targeted minority students (African American, Native American, Hispanic, and Southeast Asian) represent a far larger percentage of FIG participants than the freshman class as a whole. As shown in Table 12.1, the most recent cohort in fall 2010 was fairly representative.

By most standard measures—more first-generation students, higher proportion of targeted minority students, lower ACT scores, lower levels of high school preparation—FIG cohorts would seem to be less prepared and more "at risk" than their non-FIG peers, and they should therefore perform at a lower level by traditional success measures (GPA, retention). Despite the fact that their academic profiles, on average, continue to indicate that they come to UW-Madison less prepared than their non-FIG peers, FIG students continue to outperform their peers each year in terms of cumulative GPA at the

TABLE 12.1
Comparison of FIG and Freshman Cohorts

	Fall 2010 FIG Cohort	*Fall 2010 Freshman Cohort*
Composite ACT	27	28.3
Graduated in Top 10%	52%	56%
Female/Male	66% female/34% male	53% female/47% male
Targeted Ethnic Minority	20%	9%
First-Generation	26%	19%

end of the first semester. We have also found, by combining data on GPA and ACT scores, we can further focus on the FIG effect for specific groups of students. We explore this aspect of our assessment approach in the next section.

Targeted Groups

Campus leaders, like many at similar institutions that enroll relatively small proportions of minority students, have been conscious of a significant "achievement gap" between the performance levels of minority students compared with those of majority students. Addressing that achievement gap has been part of the mission of FIGs, and by designing assessments that focus on these students, we have been able to demonstrate that the program has been effective in this regard. In fall 2010, the average GPA of targeted minority students enrolled in FIGs was 3.14, compared with 2.75 earned by peers who were not enrolled in FIGs. Again, by collecting these data each year, we can demonstrate that these results are consistent with previous cohorts over the history of the FIGs program (Figure 12.3).

Working under the assumption that ACT scores have some predictive value in determining student success in college, the campus admissions office continues to use ACT scores as one way of determining admissibility; indeed, recent studies indicate that although high school GPAs do have predictive value, composite ACT scores are more reliable in predicting first-year college

FIGURE 12.3
First-Semester GPA of Minority Students: FIGs and Non-FIGs

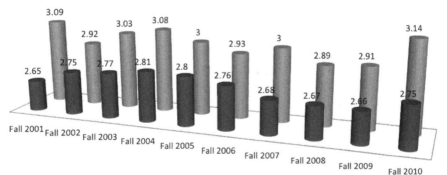

■ Non-FIGs   ■ FIGs

GPAs of 3.0 or higher (Noble & Sawyer, 2004). Students with lower composite ACT scores are generally less likely to achieve college GPAs of 3.0 or higher. This tends to be true of UW-Madison freshmen, as demonstrated by data from fall 2010. Just 50 percent of non-FIG freshmen admitted with average composite ACT scores in the mid-range (23–25) earned first-semester GPAs of 3.0 or better compared with 75 percent of FIGs students. As shown in Figure 12.4, these results are consistent as one looks at all levels of ACT scores and have been consistent throughout the history of the program as well.

Targeted minority students with these average ACT scores showed even greater differences except for those targeted FIG students with the lowest ACT scores, below 20 (Figure 12.5). Of students in that ACT category, just 30 percent of FIG students earned a first-semester GPA of 3.0 or better, compared with 33 percent of targeted non-FIG students. However, for those students with ACT scores in the 20–22 range, 55 percent of targeted students enrolled in FIGs earned a first-semester GPA of 3.0 or better, compared with 28 percent of targeted students not enrolled in FIGs. Even for those targeted students admitted with higher ACT scores in the 26–28 range, FIG students performed better, with 67 percent earning a first-semester GPA of 3.0 or higher compared with 53 percent of non-FIG targeted students. Of targeted

FIGURE 12.4
Fall 2010: First-Year Students With 3.0 GPA or Higher

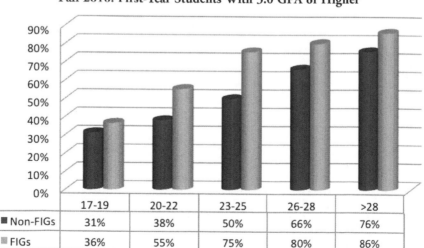

	17-19	20-22	23-25	26-28	>28
■ Non-FIGs	31%	38%	50%	66%	76%
▨ FIGs	36%	55%	75%	80%	86%

FIGURE 12.5
Fall 2011: Targeted Minority Students With GPA of 3.0 or Higher

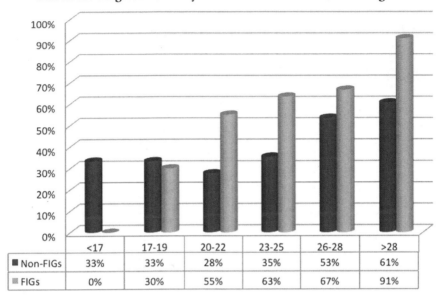

	<17	17-19	20-22	23-25	26-28	>28
■ Non-FIGs	33%	33%	28%	35%	53%	61%
■ FIGs	0%	30%	55%	63%	67%	91%

students with ACT scores higher that 28, 91 percent earned a GPA of 3.0 or higher, compared with 61 percent of non-FIG students.

Grade Distributions

Another way to measure students' academic success, as well as the effect of their linked course experience, is to look at grade distributions (Figures 12.6 and 12.7). Looking more closely at where the grades that make up the higher average GPAs fall within the grade point spectrum can indicate which students are gaining the most from the FIG experience. A full 80 percent of the fall 2010 FIG cohort earned a GPA of 3.0 or higher, whereas only 2 percent earned GPAs less than 2.0. In contrast, just 66 percent of the non-FIG cohort had earned GPAs of 3.0 or higher, and 6 percent had earned GPAs of less than 2.0. This is another measure that indicates that participation in the FIG linked course experience has a positive effect on student performance.

Long-Term Effects

At the end of seven semesters, the GPAs of students who had participated in FIGs are still higher than the GPAs of their non-FIG peers (Figure 12.8 and

FIGURE 12.6.
Fall 2010 Grade Distribution: FIG Students

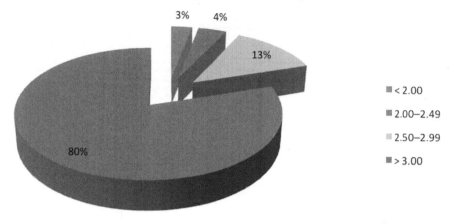

FIGURE 12.7
Fall 2010 Grade Distribution: Non-FIG Students

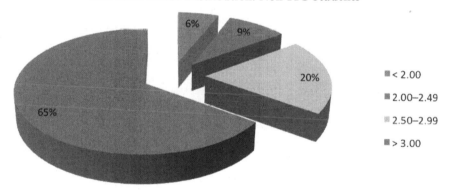

Figure 12.9). Seen in total context, these differences are significant. Considering that at their matriculation FIG students generally have lower ACT scores, lower high school GPAs, and lower high school class rank, it would be expected that their level of achievement might be to be less than that of their non-FIG peers who, on average, have higher ACT scores and better records of high school achievement. After seven semesters, 83 percent of FIG students had cumulative GPAs of 3.0 or higher, compared with 75 percent of non-FIG students. Of targeted minority FIG students, 50 percent maintained a cumulative GPA of 3.0 or higher, compared with 45 percent of targeted minority students who had not been enrolled in FIGs.

FIGURE 12.8
Cumulative GPA After Seven Semesters: All FIG Students

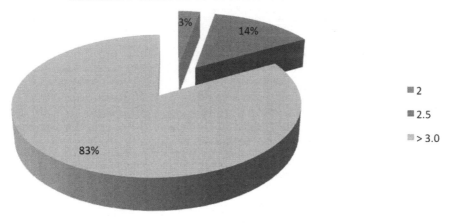

FIGURE 12.9
Cumulative GPA After Seven Semesters: All Non-FIG Students

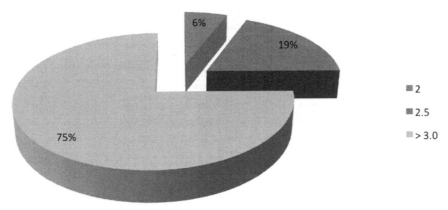

Into the Black Box

Until now, the assessment approaches we have discussed have shown that the FIG experience has a marked benefit on student achievement when measured along several quantitative variables. Indeed, this kind of quantitative analysis, using readily available institutional data, can simply and clearly provide bountiful data for the purposes of summative assessment: It is clear that students participating in FIGs have higher levels of academic achieve-ment and that the program works. To gain some understanding of just what it is about students' experience that generates these outcomes depends on qualitative assessment approaches. Although quantitative data are important in building a skeleton of assessment, qualitative data help flesh it out and give it a face and a voice. Primary stakeholders provide that voice and are the key sources of information for this level of assessment. Students enrolled in FIGs and the faculty who teach the primary FIG seminars are particularly important stakeholders, and we collect information about their levels of sat-isfaction, their experiences, and their recommendations for improvement in a number of different ways.

In-Class Surveys

All students in FIGs are asked to complete a satisfaction survey at the end of the semester. FIGs faculty are asked to administer the survey during their classes in an effort to reach as many FIG students as possible. The survey asks students to rank aspects of the program and their experiences on a Likert scale; they also have the opportunity to respond to open-ended questions regarding their FIG experiences. Having both quantitative and qualitative measures provides a richer picture of students' responses.

Though we maintain a core set of satisfaction-related questions on this survey, we have in recent years included additional, specially targeted ques-tions that address more specific concerns or student populations. We have kept the core questions relatively stable throughout the history of the pro-gram to provide a "longitudinal" measure of the program.

Online Surveys

Each spring, graduating seniors who took a FIG as freshmen are surveyed via a web-based instrument. In addition, volunteers from this cohort are asked to participate in focus groups, again led by independent facilitators, in an effort to gain more insight into the students' experiences. As the program has grown older, we have been able to compile more data about students who are completing or have completed their college experience, and we hope to eventually follow students into graduate school or careers. Results from surveys of faculty have helped administrators understand faculty motivations for participating in the program—information that has been helpful in recruiting more of their colleagues as FIG instructors—as well as improve lines of communication with faculty and enhance orientation efforts directed at faculty working with FIGs.

Focus Groups

Toward the end of the fall semester, we partner with independent facilitators who are trained and supervised by staff from the campus Office of Quality Improvement to conduct focus groups of current FIG students for the purpose of gathering information regarding their impression of the program, its goals, their courses and professors, and their transition to university life. Faculty have also participated in focus groups. The primary purpose behind having multiple focus groups is to flesh out and help confirm survey findings. Focus group facilitators are able to ask probing questions that describe participants' experiences and attitudes in ways that are more nuanced than Likert scale survey questions. The focus groups allow FIG program planners to learn of any student and faculty concerns and to be able to make recommendations for the improvement of the program.

Other Initiatives

The approaches listed previously make up the core qualitative methods we use every year to continue our assessment of the program, and are effectively an institutionalized aspect of the program's operation. On occasion, we also pursue additional inquiry initiatives that target specific aspects of the program, specific populations, or delve more deeply into hypothetical ways to improve program administration to the benefit of students. To pursue these initiatives, we may utilize the methods and instruments discussed previously or include any of a variety of additional approaches including classroom and extracurricular activity observation, faculty interviews, collection of student-produced artifacts for analysis, as well as the constant reconnaissance methods of informal assessment discussed earlier.

We endeavor to gather students' qualitative impressions in the variety of ways listed previously for a number of important reasons. First, each instrument has specific strengths, biases, and logistical challenges to deploy. For example, although a survey is relatively cheap to duplicate and distribute widely, it cannot be used efficiently to question students in depth. Using a range of instruments allows us to ask a range of questions—and keeps us from being limited in our inquiry. Second, gathering information from different angles is useful to validate data. A pattern that emerges in a survey can be easily confirmed or challenged in a focus group or interview. Multiple instruments provide a soft "member check" in the process. Finally, related to the first two points, each instrument has strengths and weaknesses, biases and blind spots. Some of these characteristics are predictable and others are hidden. By employing a varied approach, we can insulate ourselves against undesirable or unpredictable effects inherent to our methods and ensure that our results are sound.

General Survey Results

Surveys of students have yielded useful and positive results. Students have very consistently reported that being part of a FIG eases their transition to university life and that they make close friends more easily. They comment on how their FIGs influence their ensuing course enrollments: In the spring 2010 survey of graduating seniors who had enrolled in FIGs during their first semester, 89 percent reported that their FIGs included courses they never would have considered taking otherwise, and 80 percent reported that after their FIG semesters they subsequently enrolled in courses that were related to their FIGs:

> My FIG definitely had a strong influence on what I studied afterwards. I continued to take Yoruba language classes for three more semesters, and the culture classes eventually led me to major in anthropology.

> My FIG inspired me to take more courses that weren't in my major. I wanted to experiment with other disciplines so I wouldn't be limited by my major.

In a survey administered to FIGs students at the end of the fall 2010 FIG semester, students indicated that helping them make the academic transition to UW-Madison was one of the greatest achievements of the program: 80 percent agreed or strongly agreed that FIGs aided in the academic transition. Students also appreciate the academic aspect of FIGs: 85.2 percent indicated that they "felt intellectually challenged by [their] FIG classes." Most students (84 percent) agreed or strongly agreed that they "would recommend FIGs to incoming freshmen."

Students and faculty alike frequently comment on how different their FIG experiences have been compared with their experiences in other class-room settings. Faculty have repeatedly stated that "FIG students are not like regular students." In addition they comment that their FIG students rarely if ever miss classes, that they are enthusiastic contributors in class discussions, and that they often perform better on exams and class assignments than other students. Faculty have also remarked that their FIG students often outperform their upper-class and, in some cases, even graduate students on some critical thinking tasks.

Some faculty have been able to collaborate with the instructors teaching the courses linked to their FIGs, and for these individuals, the opportunity for interdisciplinary teaching has been described as "unmatchable" and "the most memorable part of the experience." Faculty have also reported that FIGs give them opportunities to develop new courses or to revise old ones, to involve students in off-campus research and community service projects, and to develop grant-funded projects for themselves and their graduate students. Some FIGs have also become feeder pathways into a number of majors and certificate programs (e.g., gender and women's studies, African languages and literature, Japanese, and educational policy studies). Faculty in African languages and literature and Japanese have also seen significant growth in their study abroad programs as a direct result of collaborations with FIGs. According to one FIGs professor from the Japanese department,

> The FIG has turned out to be a great feeder program for the Japanese language floor in the International Learning Community, which itself is a great feeder for our study abroad programs. The combination of these three is strengthening the Japanese program as a whole and we're seeing higher numbers in our upper-level courses and more majors.

Although the main emphasis of the program is to assist first-year students to make the transition to campus and develop strong learning communities, one of the unanticipated consequences uncovered by our assessment efforts is a shift in how faculty connected with the program view their students. In their responses to survey and focus group questions, faculty frequently comment that teaching their FIG classes has helped them to understand how the needs of freshmen differ from those of upper-level students, and that teaching FIGs has helped them to better understand how students in general learn. As a result, pedagogical change is another unanticipated effect of the FIG linked course model that we have been able to measure through our assessments. In fact, most faculty responding to our most recent fall survey indicated that they had made significant changes in the way they teach, not only in their small FIGs seminars but also in their larger lecture classes. They commented that they had developed more Socratic, discussion-based pedagogies; had engaged students in case-based learning and in research; and had developed more out-of-class learning experiences like field trips and service learning.

Over the years, most FIG faculty have commented—in focus groups, via e-mail, in conversation, at orientation meetings, in interviews, or in surveys—that they see students differently, that they have made changes in their approaches to teaching, and that they have developed new collaborations with faculty peers and with campus resources.

A Three-Legged Stool

Over ten years spent assessing various aspects of the FIGs program, we have learned much (including those things listed previously) about our participants, but student responses on surveys, in focus groups, and in interviews have always hewn quite closely to three major categories that we have dubbed the "three-legged stool" of FIGs success. In order of importance, freshmen and seniors have consistently reported that they valued these three elements of their FIGs experiences the most: the strong sense of community that they felt, the faculty connections that were created, and the integrated curriculum that led to greater appreciation and understanding of how disciplines are interrelated.

A Transitional Community

Taking courses and studying together tend to create solid bonds of community, and students find this to be the most valuable part of their experience. This kind of open-ended questioning provides a wealth of information about what students value about their FIGs experiences. Our first question, for example, asks, "What did you like most about your FIG experience?" In their responses to this open-ended query, students frequently comment on the social, "community-building" aspect of participating in a FIG. The following statement is fairly typical:

> The FIG experience was a highly valuable experience in helping me form a community at UW-Madison, because of the fact that our FIG was a community in itself. The twenty students in my FIG were all committed

to the same goals as I, and throughout the semester we organized multiple review sessions that helped our overall success throughout the semester.

Students also frequently refer to their "FIGs families": "We formed a family within my FIG." "The students in my FIG were like my brothers and sisters." The opportunity to create solid bonds, make friends, and form study groups consistently comes to the top of the list each year as students reflect on what they appreciate most about their FIGs experiences.

Unfortunately, not every student has had this community-building experience, possibly because of the "chemistry" among members or because students' expectations were not met. Occasionally, a student would make a comment like this one: "Honestly, my FIG in particular did not evoke the sense of community that I had been looking forward to." Fortunately, this sentiment is rare.

Faculty Connection

Students also comment on the strong connections they developed with faculty, and on the opportunities to discuss delicate topics within a safe environment:

> Our FIG professor taught my classmates and me that we must teach each other and we must also teach him as well. He always found a way to make us think deeper about the readings, discussions, debates. . . . There are a couple of valuable morals I learned from the FIG and that is: don't be afraid to speak your mind, respect others, volunteer, and explore the world.

In describing the connection created by the professor who taught the FIG seminar, one student said, "I liked my main FIG class the most. The experience was straight out of a movie: life changing, emotional, and engaging."

In surveys and focus groups, students indicate that their learning is enhanced when the faculty teaching their various FIG classes collaborate. At the same time, they indicate that even more collaboration would be helpful; students suggest that the faculty of the three courses in each FIG should meet regularly to plan and coordinate class assignments and out-of-class activities.

Students report that they appreciate out-of-class experiences—workshops, guest speakers, films, exam-review sessions, meals, and so on—that are part of their FIGs. In response to the open-ended questions asking for any "highlights" of their FIGs experience, students frequently refer to movie nights, study groups, field trips, evening lectures, and other events of that sort. In some cases, the FIG faculty have organized these events; sometimes social events or study groups have been organized by the students themselves without any faculty assistance or participation. In focus groups, students have recommended strongly that FIG faculty be involved in helping students make initial contacts with each other and help organize out-of-class events and gatherings, such as study groups.

Faculty, too, often comment on the bonds that are created between them and their FIG students, connections they apparently crave but are unable to develop in their large-enrollment lectures. "It was satisfying to have a personal relationship with first-semester students" is a comment that frequently appears on faculty surveys. Although teaching a seminar to first-year students may require some extra effort, faculty typically enjoy the results:

> Was it worth the work? Absolutely. It was that much fun. It allowed me to interact intensely with students and figure out how they were thinking. I had not interacted with freshmen before, and it was kind of exhilarating. You get forced to look at your field in different ways.

In an unsolicited testimonial, one faculty member wrote about having lunch with one of her FIG students and his parents when they visited campus:

> I had lunch with one of my FIG student's parents and his mother said, "You have changed my son's life because all he talks about now is [your FIG class]." I can never thank this university or college enough for introducing the FIG program because of the way it is changing the lives of our undergraduates and even us, the professors who encounter them in our FIG courses.

An Integrated Curriculum

It is no surprise that developing a strong sense of community should rise to the top in terms of what FIG students value most. Pascarella and Terenzini (1991) report that informal peer interactions are especially strong influences on change during the college years, not only in psychosocial development but also in other areas, including academic and social self-concept and educational aspirations and attainment. And the fact that they next value their connections with faculty should also come as no surprise. There is extensive evidence that student–faculty relationships have a strong, positive effect on student persistence and learning and are critical to student success. (Astin, 1993; Pascarella & Terenzini, 1991). Yet the fact that FIG students have continually cited the "integrative learning" aspect of their FIGs as so important has been a pleasant surprise. Although our FIG model was developed to stress interdisciplinary approaches to learning, it was unexpected that eighteen-year-old freshmen would "get it." Student comments on surveys, in focus groups, and in unsolicited testimonials, however, do demonstrate that they not only "get it" but they truly value this aspect of their FIG experiences; seniors have frequently commented that they have tried to re-create the "integrative learning" aspect of FIGs on their own when enrolling in courses in subsequent semesters.

This focus on integration distinguishes the FIG program at UW-Madison from similar efforts at other universities: The professor teaching the core class in a FIG makes a concerted effort to integrate or synthesize material from the two linking classes. Because developing opportunities for "integrated learning" is a major part of the mission of FIGs, our surveys have included questions relevant to that mission. Responding to the statement, "I understood some connections between and among the different disciplines and courses in my FIG," 91.2 percent of students responded with "agree" or "strongly agree." To probe further, we also asked students to respond to the statement, "I applied what I learned in one course to another course in my FIG"; 89 percent responded with "agree" or "strongly agree," and these responses to open-ended survey questions have been remarkably consistent over the years.

We have also found that similar themes emerge in response to focus group questions in which students have frequently commented on "the amazing overlap and correlation" when professors were able to integrate course content among the linked classes. The majority of students have noted that this was an important aspect of their FIG experience. One student remarked, "I feel as though I've been given a pair of glasses that allow me to see the world in ways that other students don't because I see how my courses are connected." Other students have expressed similar sentiments:

> The integration of class material has helped me to understand the classes I was taking in multiple perspectives. It helped me to not only think about my class within that class but also relate it to the other courses I was taking and look at the different concepts that were presented from a different perspective.

I loved that the classes were so nicely intertwined. It was easy to flow from one to another. It was easy to take what we learned from one lecture or discussion and use it for another class. The FIG made it possible to make connections and argue sides because there were multiple views on the main subject they all had in common. The information I learned from one class could be used in a paper for another class.

Faculty comment on how important the interdisciplinary aspect of the program is to the development of critical thinking in their students. One professor, describing the integration of course material and service learning, wrote, "These freshmen barely looked old enough to tie their shoelaces! What happened in the next fourteen weeks 'blew my mind.' Why? Because it was a profound learning experience for all concerned." Another faculty member, in describing the experiences of the students enrolled in his FIG, wrote,

Many students are surprised to learn that they can study history in seven or eight different academic departments, literature in twenty or so, because in their high schools, history was simply a component of the social sciences department, while literature meant English. While these facts seems obvious and self-evident to most faculty members, they're real eye openers to the students, who begin to see the world in much larger terms, but also in disciplinary terms.

Another faculty member wrote about her experience teaching a FIG seminar and the way it had a positive effect, not only on her students, but on her as well:

The FIG program is a fabulous way to make interdisciplinary connections for other faculty and students. I gained new perspectives on my work, new colleagues and friends, and renewed commitment to help students synthesize their learning.

Occasionally, students complain that that some of the "linking classes" did not seem to be good fits. Indeed, as program administrators looked into these complaints, it was discovered that in at least one FIG, which had been taught successfully for seven years with the same course combination, a new instructor had been assigned to a linking class and had redesigned and redirected the course so that it no longer fit the theme or topic of the FIG. Without deliberate, qualitative inquiry of this nature, findings such as this would be impossible to obtain, and future students' experiences would suffer accordingly. The FIG was taught again in fall 2011, but the errant course was replaced with another. The course syllabus that was submitted to FIGs indicates that this substitution will be a better match for this particular FIG, but further assessment will check to be sure.

Integrated Learning: Delving Deeper

Although these three components have been consistently cited by both students and faculty as the most important aspects of the UW FIG experience, integrated learning has proven to be the most difficult to assess. This difficulty is a result of a number of factors. For instance, integrated learning is not simply a one-way equation, but consists simultaneously of both pedagogical approaches and learning approaches; integrated learning is a combination of curriculum and activities and the manner in which the two are intertwined. Integrated learning is not limited to the moment but is a composite effect achieved over a (potentially) extended time frame, and therefore cannot be captured in a single measurable variable. For these reasons and others, an effective description—or definitional statement—that accurately describes integrated learning as well as its process in clean and quantifiable language akin to GPAs plotted on a graph has been elusive.

To take on the specific problem of assessing the complex set of conditions that give rise to an integrated learning enterprise, we decided to embark on a focused inquiry into integrated learning in FIGs. We hope that our efforts help to provide a starting point for future in-depth assessment of integrated learning in FIGs while also providing a new language, methodological approach, and theoretical framework for assessments of all manners of integrated learning opportunity. Considering the large number of FIGs across a wide range of disciplines, the diversity of the students involved, and with the varied approaches (pedagogical, research, and personal) of each participating faculty member, our task was from the outset an ambitious endeavor.

In keeping with our assessment approach, we conducted in-depth, open-ended faculty interviews that focused on their personal and pedagogical understandings of integrated learning. We pressed each faculty member specifically on how he or she instantiated these understandings in the curriculum, how they were reflected in (both explicit and implicit) learning goals, and how the goals were communicated to students. We then followed with discussion about how each professor sought to assess or measure students' progress toward the goals he or she had set out.

Concurrent with these interviews, we also conducted a metaanalysis of half of our FIG syllabi to gain understanding of one of the main communication approaches that professors use to guide their students' experiences. The syllabi provided a focal point concerning learning goals and the priorities given to various components of each course as well as a basic comparison between FIGs. It also broadened our net; logistically we were able to analyze many more syllabi than we were able to interview faculty.

To provide a complementary viewpoint, and to involve all of our FIG stakeholders, we also conducted a significant amount of open-ended surveying of students participating in FIGs. We queried students broadly about their understanding of integrated learning, the goals of their courses, classroom assessment practices, and their perceptions of the effect of integration on their success throughout their semester. We surveyed students in the very first week of the semester (when students had been freshly introduced to their FIG courses and campus) and again in the second-to-last week of the semester to capture any change in understanding or perception that students may have experienced over the course of their semester's experience.

Finally, we also engaged in a fair amount of standard "reconnaissance" in the form of classroom observations, attending extracurricular activities, corresponding with students in informal assessment settings, and collecting student-produced classroom artifacts that came in many forms: essays, reflections, evaluations, and performances as well as various other unique assignments.

Staying consistent with our overall assessment principles, we engaged all of our stakeholders in a "doable" assessment procedure that sought to interrogate one of the program's core purposes or intended outcomes (to provide integrated learning experiences), and were ultimately able to uncover very useful information. For example, we found that faculty who approached the integration of course content explicitly and intentionally were more successful in communicating the connections across the courses in their FIGs. As well, we found that faculty who utilize pedagogy that includes the modeling of integrative thinking and analysis are similarly more successful developing connections in their curricula. Using this information we have begun working closely with faculty to provide pedagogical guidelines that, if employed, will improve students' experiences.

These findings, although uncovered in pursuit of a summative understanding of integrated learning, actually point to ways we can improve the FIGs program for both students and faculty in a predominantly formative manner. Applying the lessons we have learned in this round of inquiry not only improves the opportunity for our next participants but also completes the assessment circle while laying the groundwork for the next round evaluating our recommended changes.

Using Assessment for Change: Sharing Results

There is no doubt that linked course experiences like FIGs, by their very nature, pull together and rely on more campus resources than traditional stand-alone courses—and this kind of collaboration can be rare. In fact, it can take significant effort to combat resistance to change, to break down bureaucratic barriers, and to challenge the "traditional way of doing things" for partnerships between campus entities to work smoothly. Although there are multiple ways to garner such cooperation, one we suggest is to widely share assessment results. By building on the demonstrable benefits of linking courses and highlighting the success stories to shift the narrative from "change" to "opportunity," assessment results can be used to their fullest potential.

Using early assessment results in FIGs, we have been able to take a number of noteworthy steps forward with regard to developing partnerships across campus. These efforts have expanded the program's reach in important ways, including:

- Expanding FIGs beyond the College of Letters and Science into a campuswide program
- Creating collaborations among faculty and campus colleagues (Writing Center, Writing Fellows program, librarians, residence life staff, etc.)
- Developing partnerships with programs that support targeted minority students
- Developing FIGs to meet requirements of specific majors
- Partnering with the Honors Program to develop "Honors" FIGs

Beyond simply expanding the program, we have used assessment to improve faculty members' experiences teaching and designing a FIG. Following are some initiatives along this theme:

- Enhancing faculty orientation, creating informal faculty discussion group

- Streamlining process for faculty to propose FIGs
- Creating new initiative: peer mentors and educators

Finally, our assessments have helped us to recognize that students often need additional assistance in the logistical aspects of finding FIGs, enrolling for them properly, and making sure that there is adequate information available on the specific credits and requirements that each FIG fulfills. To this end, assessment has helped us to do the following:

- Work with the registrar's office to streamline timetable process, footnote FIGs classes, and provide credit information for each linked course.
- Enhance our web presence to provide in-depth information about FIG offerings and linked courses.

Neither this collaboration and cooperation, nor the partnerships necessary to their existence, would have been possible without deliberate efforts to share assessment results widely. Through such vehicles as our annual reports, summary pages, website, campus meetings, campus administration summits, and simply word-of-mouth, we have made sharing information about our program a cornerstone of its administration. As a result, we have been able to make enormous strides toward enhancing and expanding the reach of the program across campus, while showing that the changes we have been making are well supported and legitimate.

For example, our results have encouraged academic departments from across campus to see that participating in FIGs benefits course enrollments by increasing the number of students exposed to, and eventually pursuing, those majors. As a bottom-line outcome of assessment, most departments could not be happier than to be given a mechanism by which they can boost enrollments and retention.

Assessments and Future Directions: Cycle of Assessment

One irony inherent to continual programmatic assessment is that evaluation results often lead to, or create, new questions while simultaneously answering old ones. Pursuit of these new questions can then lead to new assessment projects that themselves exhibit the same essential quirk. We call this the *cycle of assessment.*

For example, although our data indicate that participating in FIGs can have a significant positive effect on the academic performance and retention of minority students, we are led to ask *What are the specific aspects of this experience that lead to these results? Can such aspects of the program be enhanced, and if so, how? Are there elements of the FIG experience that could be replicated by other support programs on campus? How can we continue to shrink the achievement gap between minority and majority students?* In fact, these additional questions, informed by our previous efforts, are central to a new assessment undertaking we are exploring.

Our assessment results have also unveiled data concerning students' choices of majors, suggesting that there is a relationship between the topic or theme of the FIG a student has chosen and his or her eventual major. Some further questions that are then indicated include *To what does the FIG experience help some students choose their majors? What aspects of the FIG experience, such as thematic course content or connecting with faculty mentor, might influence students' decisions regarding choices of majors?* Answers to these newly identified questions would be informative to administrators of the FIGs program as well as academic departments across campus.

As a result of our experiences assessing these unique environments, we have come to think of assessment as a recursive cycle that provides continual opportunity for additional inquiry. Fortunately, in education—with new students each term, new faculty ready to participate, and new and evolving curricular offerings each year—this cyclical characteristic can be seen as a great strength of the process, not an obstacle to summative knowledge.

Conclusion

Assessment can be a daunting proposition, and the assessment of linked course experiences can seem even more challenging. With a solid set of tools from which to pull and an underlying philosophy to guide the process, however, it can become not an obstacle but an opportunity. Indeed, as budgets tighten, and accountability continues to grow in importance, assessment may become not just an opportunity, but a necessity.

Throughout this chapter we have endeavored to provide an outline of useful assessment strategies, illustrated by examples from UW-Madison's FIG program. As such, this chapter is the story of just one program's "adventures in assessment." From the very beginning, regular program evaluation has been a fundamental part of how we "do business." We have attempted to frame assessment not as a chore or difficulty but as a mindset with requisite philosophical underpinnings that can help to improve practice around serving students. By following the techniques we have included in this chapter, practitioners can develop a culture of assessment with their colleagues to better understand their own programs by asking intelligent questions, measure success and effectiveness, identify areas for improvement, and discover new questions to ask. Furthermore, the key philosophical principles we have outlined—focusing on the mission, engaging in constant reconnaissance, and sharing results widely—will help administrators to develop relationships across campus, from students, faculty, department chairs, and deans, all the way up to the chancellor. This has been the case in our experience.

At its most narrowly defined, assessment is little more than a measurement of variables, or a way to discover relationships between seemingly unrelated domains. We welcome practitioners in higher education to follow and engage our broader definition of *assessment* and utilize the techniques and principles we have laid out. Doing so will help to develop that culture of assessment and harness the power of regular program evaluation. It will transform that narrow definition into an opportunity to serve students with an eye toward improving their experiences on campus. And ultimately, it is students' experiences that are the golden variable by which we should measure our success, and the fundamental reason why we do our work.

References

Astin, A. W. (1993). *What matters in college: Four critical years revisited.* San Francisco: Jossey-Bass

Noble, J., & Sawyer, R. (2004). *Predicting different levels of academic success in college using high school GPA and ACT composite score.* Retrieved from http://www.act.org/research/reserachers/reports/pdf/ACT_RR2002–4.pdf

Pascarella, E. T., & Terenzini, P. T. (1991). *How college affects students.* San Francisco: Jossey-Bass.

EDITORS AND CONTRIBUTORS

Editors

Margot Soven is a professor of English at La Salle University and the director of the Core Curriculum. Her essays and reviews have appeared in journals such as *College Composition and Communication, Journal of the Council of Writing Program Administrators, Journal of Teaching Writing, Biology Teacher, Hispania, Journal of Teaching Social Work, Performance Improvement Quarterly*, and *Freshman English News*. She is the author of *What the Writing Tutor Needs to Know: Teaching Writing in Middle and Secondary Schools* and *Write to Learn: A Guide to Writing Across the Curriculum*. She has coedited (with Susan McLeod) *Writing Across the Curriculum: A Guide to Developing Programs, WAC for the New Millennium* (with McLeod, Miraglia, & Thaiss), *Writings From the Workplace* (with Carolyn Boirasky), and *Composing a Community: A History of Writing Across the Curriculum* (with Susan McLeod). She is coediting (with Susan McLeod) a series of books on writing program administration.

Dolores Lehr is currently the web editor at La Salle University and an adjunct lecturer at Pennsylvania State University–Abington. Formerly an assistant professor of English at La Salle, she served for five years as the coordinator of the Freshman Writing Program and for thirteen years taught numerous courses in rhetoric, composition, electronic publishing, technical writing, and professional communication. She has presented her research on writing at conferences held by the College English Association, Conference on College Composition and Communication, Association for Business Communication, and the Society for Technical Communication. She is a contributor to Dona Young's *Foundations of Business Communications: An Integrative Approach* and the author of *Technical and Professional Communication: Integrating Text and Visuals*.

Siskanna Naynaha is the composition coordinator at Lane Community College in Eugene, Oregon. She teaches courses in African American literature, Latina/o literature, and across the writing sequence. In addition to her work in assessment, learning communities, and integrating pedagogies of social justice, she also serves on the Pacific Northwest Two-Year College English Association Executive Committee and the Oregon Writing and English Advisory Committee, and is an active member of the Council of Writing Program Administrators. Her work appears in Lane Community College's *CC Moment* and *On Language and Value: Political Economies of Rhetoric and Composition*, coedited with Wendy Olson and Victor Villanueva, forthcoming.

Wendy Olson is assistant professor of English and director of composition at Washington State University–Vancouver, where she also oversees writing assessment. She teaches graduate and undergraduate courses in composition, rhetoric, and literacy studies, and serves as affiliate faculty for American studies and the Center for Social and Economic Justice. Her work has appeared in *Rhizomes, Composition Studies,* and *Open Words: Access and English Studies.* Coedited with Siskanna Naynaha and Victor Villanueva, the collection *On Language and Value: Political Economies of Rhetoric and Composition* is forthcoming. She is currently working on a monograph that examines basic writing programs in two-year colleges.

Contributors

Betsy Barefoot serves as vice president and senior scholar for the John N. Gardner Institute. Dr. Barefoot holds PhDs in education from the College of William and Mary. In her work at the Institute, Dr. Barefoot is directly involved in the development of instruments and strategies to evaluate and improve the first college year experience. Dr. Barefoot has conducted numerous workshop and seminars on the first year experience. She has authored and coauthored many publications including *Achieving and Sustaining Institutional Excellence for the First Year College* (2005), and *Challenging and Supporting the First Year Student: A Handbook for the First Year of College* (2005). She also edited the winter 2008 volume of *New Directions for Higher Education.*

Bethany Blankenship is associate professor of English at the University of Montana Western. She teaches composition and British literature. Her research interests include composition pedagogy and the scholarship of teaching and learning. Her most recent article, "Producing the Canterbury Tales," can be found in the Modern Language Association's second edition of *Approaches to Teaching The Canterbury Tales.*

Irene Clark is professor of English, director of composition, and director of the master's option in rhetoric and composition at California State University–Northridge. Her most recent books are *Concepts in Composition: Theory and Practice in the Teaching of Writing* (2002), *Writing the Successful Thesis and Dissertation: Entering the Conversation* (2007), *Writing in the Center: Teaching in a Writing Center Setting*, 4th edition (2009), and *College Argument: Understanding the Genre* (2010). She is currently working on a new book titled *Genres of Academic Writing: Theoretical Insights, Pedagogical Opportunities, New Directions*.

Lynn Dunlap has a PhD in English, University of Washington. She taught composition and literature at Skagit Valley College since 1979 and has designed and taught learning communities since 1986. From 1995 to 2006, she coordinated the Mount Vernon Campus General Education program. She has presented sessions about learning communities at regional and national conferences, evaluated learning community programs, and facilitated faculty retreats and workshops at colleges across the United States. Dunlap regularly serves as a resource faculty member for the annual National Summer Institute on Learning Communities, Washington Center for Improving the Quality of Undergraduate Education. In addition to several articles about learning communities, she coauthored with Julia Fogarty *Learning Communities in Community Colleges*, part of the monograph series published by the National Learning Communities Project.

Scott E. Gaier is associate professor and coordinator of academic enrichment at Taylor University. He teaches reading and study skills courses to underprepared students and also teaches a graduate course on facilitating student learning. His research interests include how students learn, deep learning, and attribution theory. Dr. Gaier earned his PhD in educational studies from Purdue University in 2003. While at Purdue, Dr. Gaier was the corecipient of the Department of Educational Studies graduate teaching award. Most recently, Dr. Gaier received the 2011 Dr. Joe Burnworth Teaching Award at Taylor University. The Burnworth Teaching Award recognizes faculty in their first five years of teaching at Taylor who exhibit promise and have made noteworthy contributions to the academic and community life of the institution.

Alex Kappus is a second-year graduate student in the College Student Affairs Administration MEd program at the University of Georgia. Alex holds an assistantship in the Department of University Housing as a graduate resident for a first-year residence hall of 1,000 students. This residence hall is also home to the UGA Learning Communities initiative. Last year, Alex worked as the academic initiatives graduate resident for University Housing and worked to maintain, create, and expand partnerships with various offices on campus.

Brandi Kutil is an instructor in the First-Year Learning Communities Program at Texas A&M University-Corpus Christi. Since 2005, she has taught first-year seminar classes in the science learning communities for freshmen majoring in biology, chemistry, and biomedical sciences. She earned her PhD in genetics from Texas A&M University–College Station and continues to research molecular evolution in invasive, endangered, and threatened species.

Jeffrey LaMonica is an assistant professor of history at Delaware County Community College in Pennsylvania. He is a PhD candidate at Temple University, where his dissertation deals with the U.S. army in the First World War. He teaches courses on world civilizations, the American Civil War and Reconstruction, and the World Wars. He has been teaching interdisciplinary linked courses for more than ten years.

Bruce A. Leauby is associate professor of accounting, School of Business, at La Salle University in Philadelphia, Pennsylvania. He has extensive presentation and publication experience in the accounting and tax disciplines but enjoys researching and writing about pedagogical issues related to accounting education.

Geoffrey Mamerow is a doctoral student who studies higher education in the Educational Leadership and Policy Analysis department at University of Wisconsin–Madison. He also works for the campus's FIGs program as a project assistant and assessment researcher.

Maggie C. Parker received both her bachelors of science in psychology and a masters in public administration, specializing in higher education, from the University of Georgia. She worked in the Office of the Vice President for Instruction with the UGA Learning Communities for three years as the primary administrative support person for the initiative. Her current position at UGA, as an assessment specialist in the Office of Academic Planning, focuses on general education assessment and learning outcomes assessment.

Maureen Pettitt has a PhD in education from Claremont Graduate University in California. In 1993 she left a tenured faculty position at California State University–Los Angeles, after a decade of teaching aviation management there, to work on a multiyear, $3 million W. K. Kellogg Foundation grant for Western Michigan University's aviation program. Dr. Pettitt was also chief scientist for human factors at the Federal Aviation Administration. She is the director of institutional research at Skagit Valley College in Mount Vernon. She has published extensively on topics ranging from airline crew resource management to learning community curriculum design and assessment.

Mary C. Robertson has a PhD in English literature, is director of the Sheeky Writing Center and Supplemental Instruction at La Salle University. She has given conference presentations related to learning support, the teaching of writing, and writing centers. She is also interested in environmental and ecological issues. She is coauthoring two ecological papers. As Writing Center director, she has been actively involved in La Salle University's Writing Across the Curriculum program.

Michael Roszkowski is currently the director of Institutional Research and assistant provost for Evaluation Services at La Salle University. Previously, Dr. Roszkowski worked at The American College, where he served as an associate professor of psychology and director of marketing research. He worked as an evaluation specialist at The Woodhaven Center, a residential facility for developmentally disabled individuals run by Temple University. Dr. Roszkowski has been on the Board of Editors for the *Journal of Genetic Psychology* since 1984. He is also on the advisory board for *Behavioral and Experimental Economics Abstracts* and serves on the Scientific Review Committee of the Delaware Valley Science Fairs, Inc. He holds a BS in psychology from St. Joseph's University, MEd (with certification) in school psychology, and a PhD in educational psychology from Temple University.

Greg Smith is an assistant dean in the College of Letters and Science at University of Wisconsin–Madison. For most of his career, he has taught first-year students and coordinated academic support programs at both two- and four-year institutions. Currently his primary responsibility is directing the First-Year Interest Groups program at UW-Madison.